CW01618698

The Ultimate MUSHROOM BOOK

The Ultimate MUSHROOM BOOK

The complete guide to identifying, picking and using mushrooms – a photographic A–Z of types and 100 original recipes

Peter Jordan & Steven Wheeler

Consultant: Geoffrey Kibby

HERMES HOUSE

DISCLAIMER

The publishers and authors cannot accept responsibility for any identification of any mushroom made by the users of this guide. Although many species are edible for many people, some species cause allergic reactions or illness to some people: these are totally unpredictable. Therefore, the publishers and authors cannot take responsibility for any effects resulting from eating any wild mushroom.

This edition published by Hermes House in 2001

Hermes House is an imprint of
Anness Publishing Limited, Hermes House
88–89 Blackfriars Road, London SE1 8HA

A CIP catalogue record for this book is available from the British Library.

Publisher: Joanna Lorenz
Project Editor: Claire Nicholson
Indexer: Alex Corrin
Designer: Michael Morey
Illustrator: Adam Abel
Photography for field guide Peter Henley
Photography for cookbook James Duncan
Production Controller: Don Campaniello

Also Published as The Practical Mushroom Encyclopedia

Typeset by MC Typeset Ltd

Printed and bound in China

1 3 5 7 9 10 8 6 4 2

CONTENTS

Introduction

Foreword

I was introduced to wild mushrooms by my grandfather who was a farmer in Norfolk, England. From the age of four I would go out in the fields with him to collect not only what he described as field mushrooms, but also some weird and wonderful looking toadstools which I thought were poisonous – they certainly looked menacing to a child. However, he taught me one very good lesson: so long as you can identify absolutely accurately what you are picking you will be safe. From these early beginnings developed a lifetime's interest in wild mushrooms.

The excitement of walking along a woodland path in the autumn, and finding in front of you two or three perfectly formed ceps is wonderful. During fifty years as a mushroom hunter, I have graduated from the relatively common horse and field mushrooms to the more exotic chanterelles and ceps. I am still excited when I find the first morels of the spring, or the year's first patch of chanterelles hidden in the leaf litter; of course, the more elusive the mushroom, like the horn of plenty or the winter chanterelle, the greater the excitement. Imagine the ultimate triumph of finding your first truffle – of beating the pigs and squirrels to them! But, as well as providing excitement and good eating, mushrooms can be dangerous; correct identification is the key to successful mushroom collecting.

The fruits, nuts and mushrooms of autumn are obvious and most are easy to spot. But have you ever realized that the winter, spring and summer can be as productive – at least as far as mushrooms are concerned? Mushrooms are one of the few wild treasures available nearly all the year round. Even on a crisp winter's day you can find a bouquet of silver-grey oyster mushrooms or the wonderful velvet shank growing out of a tree stump and it is so much more satisfying to pick them like this than from a supermarket shelf. Because, of course, the excitement of finding the mushrooms is closely followed by the satisfaction of cooking them within hours if not minutes of their harvest.

Identifying mushrooms, utterly essential though it is, can be frustrating if you have to wade through hundreds of illustrations, many of which look the same. This book is designed to make that task easier. It illustrates the best of the edible mushrooms, and so will help you pick your way wisely through the year's mushrooms, alerting you not only to a season's treasures, but also to the poisonous lookalikes and really deadly fungi that all too often grow alongside innocent and delicious mushrooms. The section that deals with the poisonous species will help identification and give the faint-hearted confidence to take their finds back to the kitchen. But do follow the advice given in this guide carefully. If clear identification is not possible from this book, consult others – the bibliography lists some of the best. And remember that the best advice of all is: if in doubt do not collect a mushroom and never, ever, eat anything you cannot identify with certainty.

Peter Jordan

What are mushrooms?

The terms mushrooms, toadstools and fungi (singular fungus) are often used loosely and interchangeably. However, this can be misleading.

The fungi are a very large group of organisms and include moulds, yeasts, mushrooms and toadstools. None of these organisms contain the green pigment chlorophyll, so they cannot make their own food by the process known as photosynthesis. So, although you may encounter some mushrooms with a distinctly greenish tinge, none are green in the way that a tree or a flowering plant is.

Mushrooms are usually defined as the edible, spore-producing bodies of some fungi. In contrast, the term toadstool is commonly applied to the spore-producing bodies of those fungi that are not only inedible but may also be highly dangerous. From this you will realize that while the terms fungus and fungi have a very precise scientific meaning, mushroom and toadstool do not. In this book mushroom is used whether, or not, the fruit body of that particular fungus is edible. It is used to cover a large number of different types of fungi such as mushrooms, boletes, bracket fungi, puff balls and cap fungi.

Ascomycetes

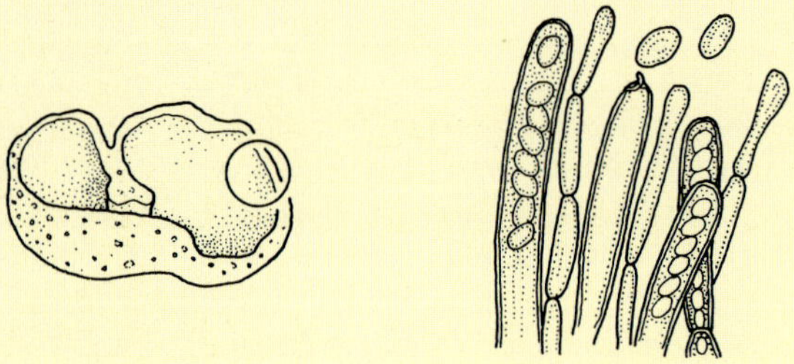

The cup fungi circle shows details of the spore-bearing surface.

Basidiomycetes

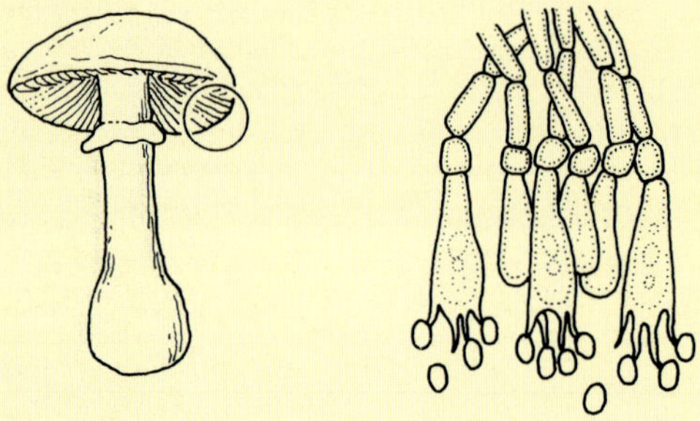

The gilled mushroom circle shows the enlargement of the gill edge.

Tuber aestivum, *the summer truffle, an example of an ascomycete fungus.*

The fungi in this book divide into two main groups: the Ascomycetes and the Basidiomycetes. The Ascomycetes produce spores that are spread by the wind. Among this group are many of the cup fungi, including the common morel and *Gyromitra esculenta*. Because the wind spreads the spore of many of these mushrooms, it is worth remembering when you find some morels, for example, to check downwind and you will almost certainly find some more.

The second group, and by far the largest as far as the collector is concerned, is the Basidiomycetes, which includes the large and well-known Agaric and Boletus families. These two families, in fact, form sub-divisions within the group.

A mushroom of the Agaric type is illustrated here with the various parts clearly identified. This is a gilled mushroom and sometimes grows from an egg-shaped volval bag. Care must be taken when dealing with any mushroom that grows from a volval bag, because this is how the *Amanitas*, the most deadly of all mushroom species, grow.

Parts of the Agaric-type fungi

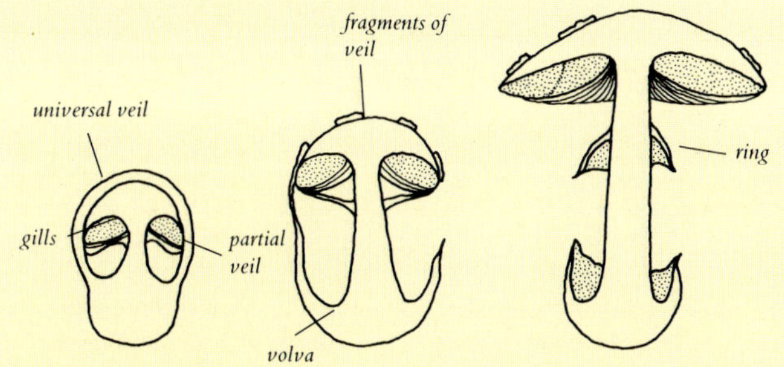

The universal veil encloses the whole mushroom and the partial veil covers the gills. As the mushroom grows the universal veil ruptures to leave a volva and fragments on the cap, and the partial veil ruptures to leave a ring on the stem.

Parts of the Boletus-type fungi

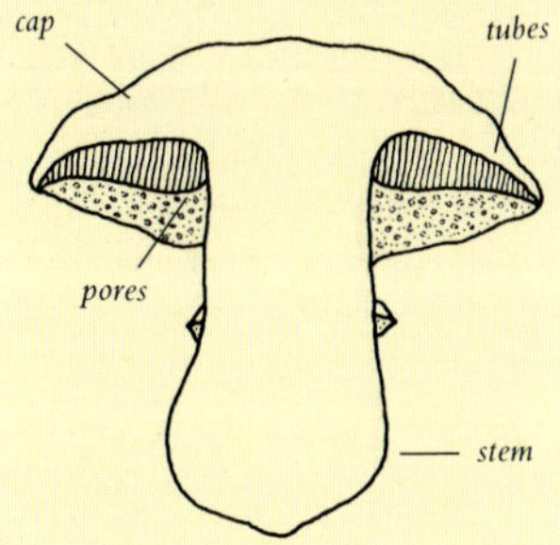

A second sub-division is the Boletes. Instead of having gills, mushrooms in this group have tubes and pores which vary widely in colour. Boletes, like Agarics, are fleshy and decay readily. This separates them from the Polypores. It is important to note their colour because this can be a clear indicator of the mushrooms you have found. The cep is the best-known member of this group.

A third group of fungi illustrated in this book is Aphyllophorales. This group includes the polypores and chanterelles and a number of other mushrooms that have irregular shapes. A number of fungi fall into this group, for example, the hedgehog fungus, which, instead of gills, has tiny spines from which it gets its name. Another member of the group is the cauliflower fungus. It may look odd, but it is a wonderful find from a culinary point of view. Other unusual types are the beefsteak fungus and the sulphur polypore or chicken of the woods. Both are excellent for cooking as well as being quite spectacular when you encounter them in the wild.

Examples of the two types of fungi which form sub-divisions of the Basidiomycetes. The horse mushroom (above) and the cep (right).

Cauliflower fungus is an example of the third major group of fungi, the Aphyllophorates.

The different parts of mushrooms

When collecting wild mushrooms it is important to consider carefully what it is that you are collecting. The mushroom itself can be divided into various parts. From both the collecting and culinary points of view the cap or fruit body is the most important part. The shape, size and colour of the cap can show tremendous variation within a species, which is one of the reasons why mushrooms are so difficult to identify accurately. It is also important to note whether the cap has gills or pores, what the colours of these are and whether they are crowded or open.

Stems can also vary considerbly and they, too, can often be an important indicator of precisely which mushroom you have discovered. Does the stem have a veil or not? The base of the stem is a vital means of identification, particularly if you have any doubts about the specimens you have found. If you are not sure what it is, carefully dig out the mushroom so that you can see the base of the stem. If there is any sign of a volval bag have nothing more to do with the mushroom. Incidentally, whatever the mushroom that you are digging up proves to be, do be careful not to do too much damage to the mycelial threads that connect it to the rest of the underground part of the fungus.

The colour of the mushroom's flesh is another important means of identification. Not only should you look at the whole mushroom, you should also cut it through in cross-section. Some important details, such as whether the stem is hollow, can of course, only be seen in cross-section. In some species the stems change colour quite dramatically when they are cut. Take note of any such changes, because they can be a reliable identification feature in certain types of mushroom.

Spore prints are also a good means of identifying mushrooms and are very easy to do. Take a cap or fruit body of a mature specimen of a mushroom and place it on black or white paper on top of a container, so that air can circulate around it. Leave in a warm place for up to three days so the mushroom sheds all its spores and you will have a very clear spore print. If you do not know what colour the spore will be, put down a piece of black paper and overlay part of it with white paper. Then place the cap so that it is half on the black paper and half on the white.

Examples of different shapes of stems

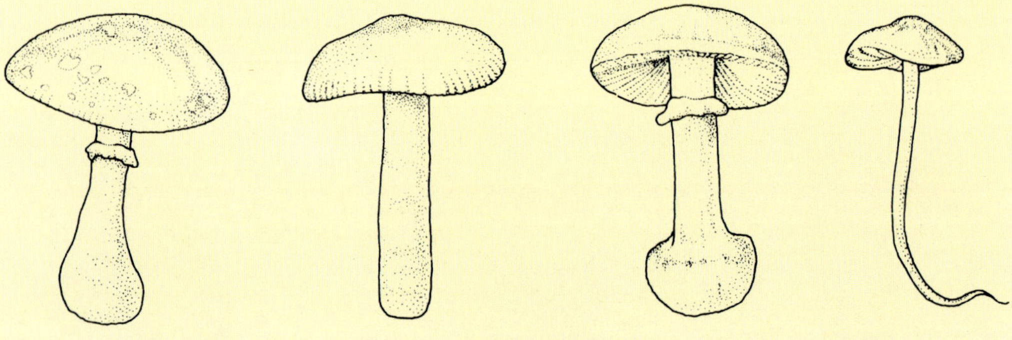

LEFT *To take a spore print you will need a mature specimen, white, or black and white paper and a container to place it on.*

LEFT BELOW *Leave the mushroom in a warm place for a few days.*

LEFT BOTTOM *Do not use just black paper because it will not show up if the spore print is a dark colour.*

BELOW *Taking a spore print is a very reliable way of making an accurate identification.*

Where to collect mushrooms

Always take care when you are out mushroom collecting that you do not trespass. Always get the permission of the landowner before you go on to any land that is not open to the public. When you are mushroom collecting be careful of the surrounding countryside and its animals, otherwise not only will you soon get a bad reputation, but you will give other collectors a similar reputation whether they deserve it or not.

Most people limit their mushroom hunting to meadows, but these have suffered from being over enriched with nitrates, which have denuded many previously good mushroom-hunting territories. If you want to find meadowland mushrooms it is best to examine those meadows and marshes that have been treated with natural organic fertilizers and not nitrates. But why restrict yourself to meadowland species when eighty per cent of fungi grow in association with trees? Woods, forests and copses are the places where you should really be looking for mushrooms, but only, of course, once you have established you will not be trespassing.

Established woods and forests containing a wide variety of species provide the very best places for mushroom collecting and it is in such areas that the vast majority of species are to be found. Many of these fungi have a symbiotic relationship with trees and their roots, with some fungi growing only with a particular species of tree, while other fungi can be found in association with a number of different trees. For example, many boletes grow only with one type of tree such as the species of *Suillus* which only grow with conifers, or the species of *Leccinum* which are very specific: *Leccinum versipelle* grows with birch and *L. aurantiacum* with aspen. Chanterelles on the other hand can effectively grow with birch, pine, oaks or even beech trees.

Soil type is also important. Although many trees grow on a variety of soils, you will find that some fungi will only grow with a particular tree on a particular soil, rather than across the whole range of soils on which the tree grows. For example the bay boletus grows under beech trees or under conifers on acid soils, and the panther cap grows under beech trees on chalk.

ABOVE *The early morning is prime mushroom hunting time.*

OPPOSITE *Do not restrict your mushroom hunting to meadows and woodlands: marshes and heathland can be surprisingly productive too.*

LEFT *Many mushrooms grow in rings, some of which reach several metres wide.*

When to collect mushrooms

Most people associate mushrooms with the autumn, but, in fact, they grow throughout the year.

The spring brings morels and the St George's mushroom *Calocybe gambosa*. The fairy ring champignon, *Marasmius oreades*, also appears quite early in the year. The first of the summer mushrooms is usually the field mushroom, *Agaricus campestris*. Another mushroom to appear fairly early in summer is the chicken of the woods, *Laetiporus sulphureus*, indeed it often catches collectors unawares with its early appearance. When, or indeed if, there is a spell of hot weather, there is usually little to be found, but these conditions are, nevertheless, important, because they help the mushrooms' underground mycelial threads to mature before the autumn's great burst of growth. If the weather is mild, the autumn can extend into early winter. The first touches of frost may herald the coming of winter, but they can often bring exciting finds of both the field blewit, *Lepista saeva*, and the wood blewit, *Lepista nuda*. Both these species will continue until the weather turns quite frosty.

When winter takes hold, most people give up and just look forward to the next mushroom season. But don't be fooled: on mild winter days go out searching and you will be surprised at what you find. Oyster mushrooms, *Pleurotus ostreatus*, will continue to grow almost right through the winter, together with the Jew's ear, *Auricularia auricula-judaea*, and the velvet shank, *Flammulina velutipes*. Finding these can make a cold winter walk tremendously exciting, and shows that even in the depth of winter you can enjoy a dish with ingredients freshly picked from fields and woods.

The mushroom collector's year never ends and even when you're not actually hunting, always be on the look-out for new spots. Use winter walks to examine pastures and woodlands that you have not been to before, to see if they give any clues as to what they are likely to produce when spring comes again.

It may seem surprising, but time of day is most important to the mushroom collector. This is because mushrooms grow almost exclusively

during the hours of darkness. As a result, the best specimens are picked when they are fresh in the early morning before the rising temperature of the day has brought out the flies to lay their eggs, so giving rise to maggot infestation, or the animals of the woods and fields have had their pickings of the overnight growth, which can be quite amazing in its quantity.

It is also worth revisiting a place you have picked after two or three days, because the mushrooms will usually have regrown. Ceps are known to regrow to a weight of ¾ kilo (1¾ lb) within two or three days of the first growth having been picked – an enormous rate of growth by any standard.

It is useful to keep a diary of what you find, when and where you found it, and what the climatic conditions were, as this will give you a key to subsequent seasons and help you develop a knowledge and understanding of your local area. Noting climatic conditions is also interesting as well as useful. Good fungal growth needs periods of damp, but also periods of dry and cold, as the mycelial threads seem to benefit from a degree of stratification which, in turn, gives rise to better fruiting, and thus to better collecting.

OPPOSITE ABOVE *Chicken of the woods grows from late spring to early autumn.*

OPPOSITE BELOW *Oyster mushrooms continue to grow through the winter.*

ABOVE *The poisonous* Clitocybe rivulosa *appears in summer and autumn.*

LEFT *Wood Blewits.*

How to collect mushrooms

Very little equipment is needed for mushroom collecting. Tough outdoor clothes and a strong pair of boots are essential and you should make sure that your jacket or anorak has a pocket large enough to carry a small field guide. It is not an exaggeration: some mushrooms are just too dangerous to take home. You may find a wide-brimmed hat useful to wear in the autumn, as the days shorten and the sun is low. It is easier to spot those interesting little humps and bumps that could well prove to be an exciting find if you are not having to shade your eyes with your hand all the time.

One or two baskets are, of course, essential. They should be light, easy to carry and not too open in weave. A sharp knife and brush are also important, the knife to cut the mushroom's stem through cleanly and the brush to remove obvious dirt and debris such as pine needles and leaf litter. Cleaning your specimens as you pick them will mean there is less to do when you get home. Several polythene bags or disposable gloves are also essential items to take

OPPOSITE *Results of a successful morning's mushroom collecting.*

RIGHT *A selection of hand-made baskets.*

with you. You can put these over your hands when handling any specimens about which you are doubtful. Don't forget to throw them away after you have used them. A packet of tissues or a cloth will also be useful as your hands can get quite dirty. You will also need them to clean your knife, as you should clean it each time you use it.

The final item of equipment is a good strong stick or thumb-stick. You can use it to part bracken and undergrowth to see if any mushrooms are hidden there. It will be handy to turn over any specimens you may not wish to touch, as well as being useful as a tool to dig out specimens so that you can check if they have volval bags or not.

When you find a specimen that you want to collect, it is best to cut through its stem rather than dig it up. While it is possible to use the stems of mushrooms such as ceps and chanterelles, there is a danger of disturbing the mycelial threads if the entire mushroom is removed from the ground. The only possible exception to this rule is if you are confronted by what you think may be a poisonous mushroom. Then dig it up with your stick, being careful not to damage it. If there is anything that looks even remotely like a volval bag at the base of the stem, leave the whole specimen very well alone.

Having cut through the mushroom's stem, wipe or brush clean the mushroom before putting it in your basket. As the basket starts to fill up, a layer of bracken fronds will prevent the bottom mushrooms from becoming damaged.

BELOW *A good knife is an essential part of any mushroom collector's equipment. Two of the knives double up as a brush as well.*

Storing mushrooms

There are certain times of the year when mushrooms grow in great profusion. It is important, therefore, to find ways to preserve this abundance for those times when few mushrooms grow. Preserving food is as old as time itself and long before refrigerators, salting and drying were used as methods of preservation. There are many different ways to store mushrooms and some species are more suited to a certain type of preservation than others. Information as to the most suitable method for each species is given in the relevant entry.

Whatever method of storage you are going to use, it is important to select the very best of the mushrooms you have collected. Do be careful to make sure that they are completely free of maggots and other insects because there is nothing worse when reconstituting dried mushrooms to find you have maggots floating on the top of the water in which they are being reconstituted. Also make sure there are no twigs, leaves or other debris among them.

Drying preserves the flavour and colour quite well, although unfortunately it often destroys the shape of the mushroom. There are several methods of drying. In warmer climates, slicing the mushrooms and laying them on muslin trays in the sun can be quite sufficient. In cooler, less sunny regions, mushrooms can be dried on open trays in a warmstore, airing cupboard and on window ledges. It is important to remember that the mushrooms must be dried thoroughly, which may take several days and while drying is in progress an intense mushroomy smell will pervade wherever you are drying them.

In recent years, fruit dryers and drying machines have become available. Some can take up to ten trays and are capable of drying a large quantity of wild mushrooms very effectively over several hours. The advantage of this is that it prevents the whole house smelling of mushrooms for days afterwards, and you can also be totally confident that your dried mushrooms are completely free of moisture. With this accelerated form of drying it is possible to dry even shaggy ink caps, so long as you use very young specimens. Ordinary drying methods are much too slow and they would collapse into an inky mess and probably ruin any other mushrooms you were drying with them.

Another effective way of drying mushrooms is to thread them with a needle and cotton and hang them up in strings in the kitchen. It is important to remember, however, that mushrooms such as morels could well have creepy-crawlies hiding inside so partially dry them somewhere before hanging them in your kitchen. This will prevent any wildlife dropping into your food. When the mushrooms are dry, carefully lay them on a sheet and pick the individual specimens over before placing them in airtight containers for storage. Don't waste any powder that may remain on the sheet, it can be stored separately and used to flavour soups and stews.

Dried mushrooms can be used straight in soups and stews, but for other dishes it is best to reconstitute them in lukewarm water for around twenty minutes. Do not use boiling water as this will impair the final flavour. The water in which they have been reconstituted can be used as stock or to make gravy, but, before you do so, pour it through a sieve to remove any extraneous matter or grit that might have been contained within the mushrooms.

An alternative to drying, is freezing. Perhaps surprisingly, this is not a very good method of preserving mushrooms. For best results, make up the mushroom dishes and then freeze the finished dish or make up mushroom butter. To do this, slice

RIGHT *Mushrooms that have been dried and preserved for later use.*

OPPOSITE FAR LEFT AND MIDDLE *It is essential to brush and wipe clean mushrooms before they are dried or stored.*

OPPOSITE NEAR RIGHT *A mushroom drier.*

your mushrooms, add them to melted butter and freeze the result. Preserved like this you have the mushrooms and the butter for use with sauces, to flavour various dishes and to add to your meat or fish dishes as a topping.

Salting is one of the oldest methods of preserving food. It works extremely well for mushrooms. The most important thing to remember is to have clean, fresh mushrooms. The quantities required are one part salt to three parts mushrooms. It is important to layer the mushrooms and salt alternately, and make sure the final layer of mushrooms is completely covered with salt. Use containers that the salt will not corrode. Although a sterilized jar is best, you could also use polythene ice-cream containers. When preserving mushrooms in this way you will eventually have a lot of seasoned juice and you will not need to use salt in any dish you make using salted mushrooms.

Mushrooms can be pickled in either oil or good vinegar. It is most important when using this method to clean the mushrooms well and then blanch them. If you are pickling them with vinegar, remember that the better the vinegar, the better the results will be, so it is not worth putting good mushrooms in inferior vinegar. The same applies if you are pickling mushrooms in oil. It is also a good idea to put peppercorns and half a dozen cloves of garlic into each jar, together with two or three bay leaves. Make sure the containers you use have a good seal, and when they are filled, seal tightly.

Once the seals have been broken, use the contents fairly quickly. And it is a good idea to keep the container in the fridge while you are doing so. Even when you have finished the mushrooms, the oil or vinegar in which they have been stored will make a wonderful dressing. If you preserve mushrooms by pickling, you must remember to sterilize everything you use. You can do this by immersing all your utensils in boiling water, or by using a sterilizing solution. Boiling water is probably best as there is always a danger that the sterilizing solution might affect the taste of the mushrooms. Remember, too, to keep a watchful eye on your pickled mushrooms for any sign of mouldiness. If there is, discard the top few mushrooms and use the rest fairly quickly.

Edible Mushrooms

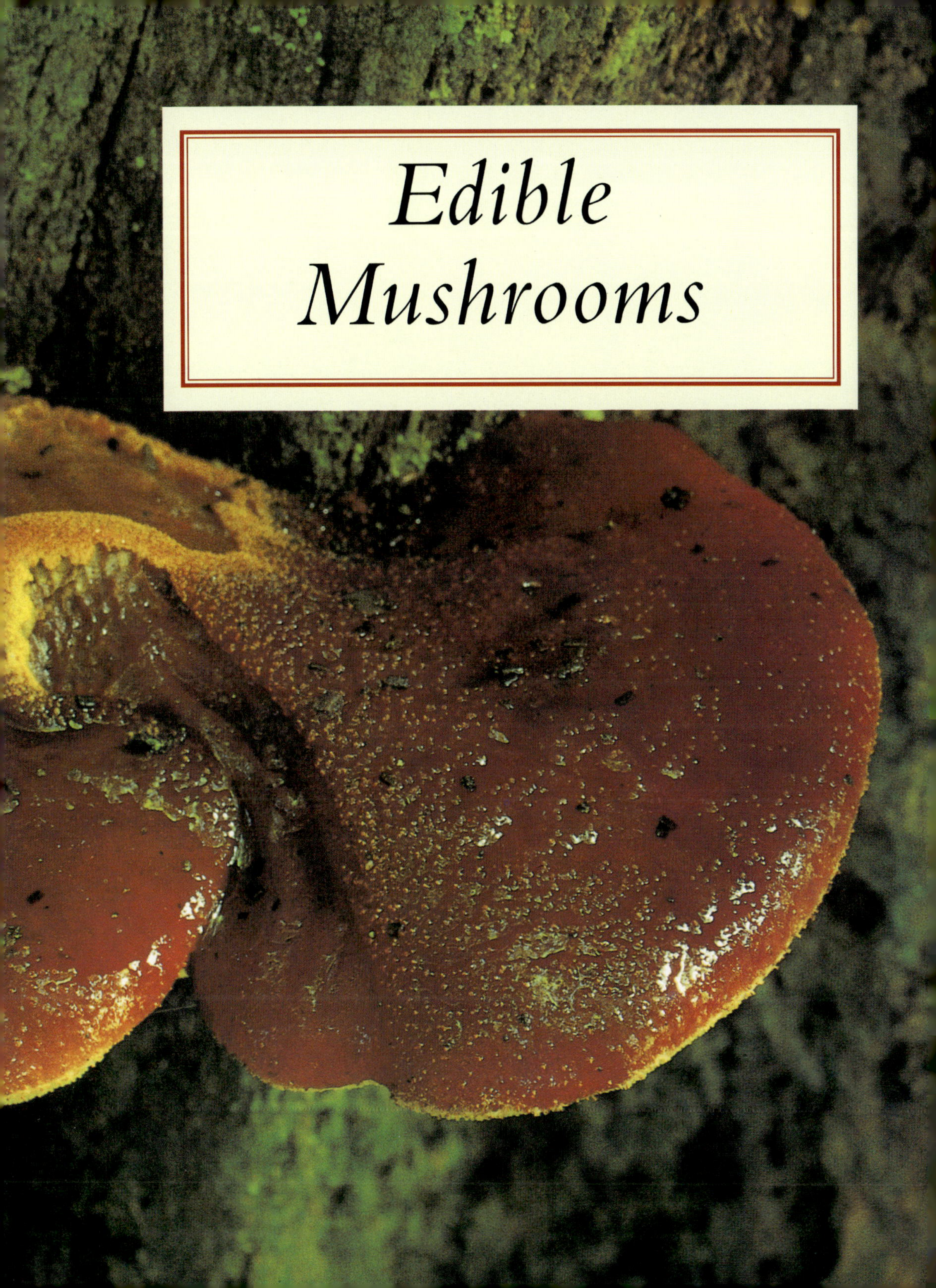

INTRODUCTION

This section illustrates and describes the best of the edible mushrooms that grow in our fields and woods. There are in fact over a thousand edible species and but only a small proportion of these are prized for their flavour and texture, and although personal taste will vary many consider the finest to include the cep *Boletus edulis*, bay boletus *Boletus badius*, morels *Morchella elata* and *esculenta*, chanterelle *Cantherellus cibarius* and chicken of the woods *Laetiporus sulphureus*. To enable identification each entry has a description of the mushroom in question, information on its habitat and season of growth, as well as hints on storage and cooking preparation for when you return home.

As you learn about mushrooms you will become more respectful of the rules of identification. No mushroom looks exactly like another, and sometimes the differences are great within the same species. Many species have poisonous lookalikes, which are also mentioned here. Take particular care with such mushrooms. It is also essential that you never pick immature specimens, because only with mature specimens can you be sure of an accurate identification.

Mushrooms are quite rich and even edible ones can cause stomach upsets. Some people seem more prone to these than others, so be careful if you are serving a mushroom dish to guests.

Although some mushrooms can be eaten raw, others must be cooked first. Among this group are honey fungus *Armillaria mellea*, wood blewit *Lepista nuda*, field blewit *Lepista saeva*, and the morels *Morchella elata* and *esculenta*. These all contain a small amount of poison which is removed by cooking.

One of the best ways to learn about mushrooms is to go on a foray led by an expert. Not only will you have the chance to question the expert about the location, type and size of the various mushrooms that you find, but, at the end of the foray, you will have a chance to examine what everybody else has found and have them identified by the expert. In this way you will have an opportunity to see far more species than you would if you had just gone out collecting on your own.

Forays are run by many organizations, including mycological societies, local naturalists trusts and local experts who organize them on an ad-hoc basis. Details of forays can usually be found in your local library and they may also be advertised in the local paper.

Enjoy your mushroom collecting, but don't take any risks with mushrooms you cannot identify.

PREVIOUS PAGE *Beefsteak fungus,* Fistulina hepatica. *Although these mushrooms are usually found at the base of tree trunks they can grow high up on the branches.*

LEFT *Field blewit,* Lepista saeva.

OPPOSITE *Amethyst's deceiver,* Laccaria amethystea, *is a tasty mushroom that has a long season from late summer to early winter.*

Agaricus arvensis

HORSE MUSHROOM

This is one of the larger varieties of mushroom. It is quite meaty in texture and has a very distinctive aniseed smell. Horse mushrooms are best picked when they are young because not only are they soon attacked by maggots, but also the flesh becomes dark brown with age and will turn any cooked dish muddy brown in colour.

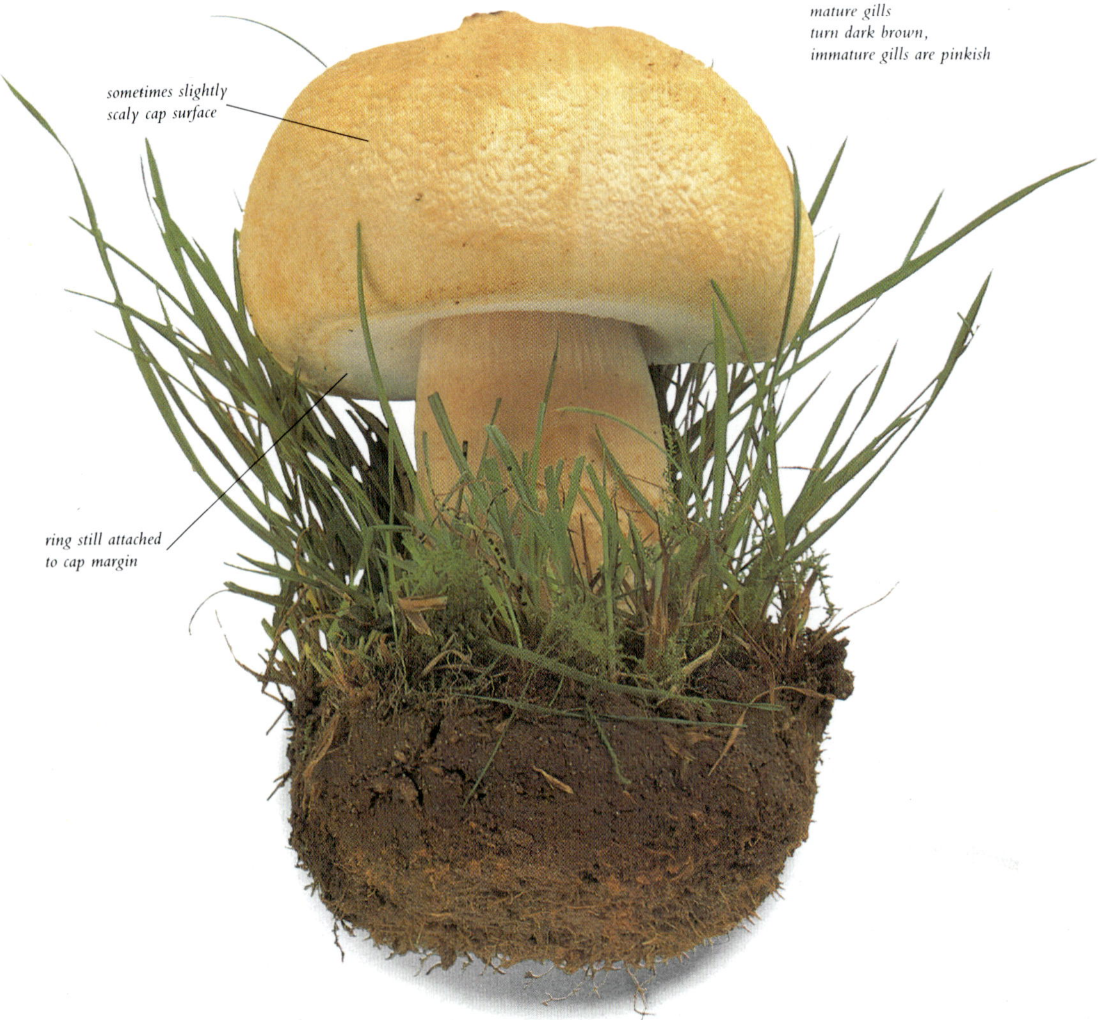

These mushrooms tend to come up in the same fields year after year, so having once found a good growth keep watching in future years.

The horse mushroom often has yellowish markings on the cap. When you find one like this, check it particularly carefully to ensure that it is not, in fact, the yellow stainer, *Agaricus xanthodermus*, which will make you very ill if you eat it. This mushroom is dealt with in detail in the section on poisonous mushrooms so you can compare the two. Unlike the yellow stainer, the horse mushroom does not colour when pressed or cut; the yellow colouring of the cap is its natural colour.

IDENTIFICATION

The cap can be from 10–25 cm (4–9¾ in) across. It is domed at first, but eventually expands to a fully convex shape. It is white but yellows with age. The stem is 8–10 cm (3–4 in) and has a large double ring. It may become hollow with age. The gills, which are white at first, turn a delicate pink and eventually dark brown in mature specimens. The flesh is thick and white but darkens with age and can become a little woolly lower down the stem. It has a distinct smell of aniseed. The spore print is dark brown.

HABITAT AND SEASON

Horse mushrooms favour grassland and pasture, particularly, as the name suggests, that where cattle or horses have grazed. Chalk meadows are often good places to look. The season is from midsummer to quite late autumn and they often grow in quite large rings.

STORAGE

These mushrooms dry well, but it is important to check thoroughly that they are maggot free. Slice and then dry either with open driers or with an electric drier.

PREPARATION AND COOKING HINTS

These mushrooms make wonderful meals, provided, of course, that they are not infested with maggots. Remember, too, if you are using older specimens when the flesh has turned dark brown, that they will change the colour of your dish.

ABOVE *The yellow stainer.*

ABOVE LEFT *The horse mushroom prefers open meadows and woodland edges.*

BELOW *The mature cap may turn brassy yellow with age or when wet.*

Agaricus augustus
The Prince

The prince is a good mushroom to find, not only does it look attractive, it also has a lovely flavour and makes excellent eating. These mushrooms tend to grow in deciduous and coniferous woodland, and in clumps rather than rings.

IDENTIFICATION
The cap is 10–25 cm (4–9¾ in) across. Button-shaped at first, it opens to a convex form and is often irregular in shape. It is light brown in colour and has clearly marked rings of brown fibrous scales joining in the centre. The stem is 10–20 cm (4–7¾ in), off-white with small scales and a large floppy ring. The gills are off-white at first, turning dark brown with age. The flesh is thick, white and smells mushroomy. The spore print is brown.

HABITAT AND SEASON
The prince grows mainly in coniferous and deciduous woods, often in clumps. The season is late summer to late autumn.

STORAGE
As these mushrooms grow fairly large, make sure you have good specimens before slicing and drying them in the usual way. This is a good mushroom to store for winter use as it has an intensity of flavour which will enhance any mushroom dish.

PREPARATION AND COOKING HINTS
A nice mushroom that needs very little preparation. The stem tends to be quite fibrous, so is best discarded. The cap does not need peeling, just wipe lightly with a damp cloth before slicing. The prince makes an extremely good addition to omelettes, but is also nice on its own.

ABOVE *The prince is usually found at the edges of woods, clearings or pathsides, rarely very far from trees.*

Agaricus bisporus

Agaricus bisporus smells and tastes very similar to the field mushroom. It is believed to be the species from which most of the cultivated varieties come. It can grow in quite large quantities and is mostly found on wasteground and compost heaps. It is quite common.

IDENTIFICATION

The cap is 5–10 cm (2–4 in) across, button-shaped before opening almost flat. It is whitish to mid-brown in colour with flaky scales. The stem is 3–5 cm (1¼–2 in) and white, with a distinct ring below the cap. It has pink gills which become darker with age. The flesh is white, bruising slightly reddish and it has a distinct mushroomy smell. The spore print is brown.

ABOVE AND BELOW Agaricus bisporus *is the species that cultivated varieties come from. The button, cup and flat mushrooms, that are widely available, are the different stages of growth of this mushroom.*

HABITAT AND SEASON

It grows on compost heaps, in garden waste and beside roads, occasionally on the edges of hedges and small plantations, but very rarely in grass. The season is quite early in the spring through to late autumn.

STORAGE

This mushroom tends to be quite small and dries well, either whole or cut. It is full of flavour.

PREPARATION AND COOKING HINTS

Because this mushroom often grows on compost heaps or in rough ground, it is best to wipe the cap very thoroughly, cutting off the bottom of the stem and slicing through.

Agaricus campestris

FIELD MUSHROOM

The field mushroom is probably the best known of all wild mushrooms. Years ago fields were often carpeted with these small white mushrooms, but due to changes in farming technology and the greater use of herbicides, pesticides and, particularly, nitrates, many of the wonderful pastures where field mushrooms grew have disappeared. If you are lucky enough to have some old meadows and pasture near you, keep an eye open for a wonderful feast that can come at any time from quite early in the summer through to autumn. These mushrooms are best picked early in the morning, not only to beat other mushroom collectors, but also to ensure that they have not yet been attacked by maggots.

IDENTIFICATION

The cap is 3–12 cm (1¼–4¾ in) across. It retains its dome shape for some time before opening out fully. It is silky white, ageing to light brown. The stem is 3–10 cm (1¼–4 in),

LEFT *An example of a typical cultivated edible* Agaricus *species.*

RIGHT *Note that the gills are not attached to the stem, this is common to all* Agaricus.

BELOW Agaricus campestris *varies widely in nature and scaly forms are known as shown here.*

white, tapering to the base, and has a thin ring which is often torn away. Even in unopened field mushrooms the gills are deep pink, an excellent identification feature. The white flesh bruises slightly pink. It has a pleasant smell. The spore print is brown.

HABITAT AND SEASON

Field mushrooms grow in mature pasture and often favour chalky soils. They can grow any time from early summer through to late autumn.

STORAGE

An excellent mushroom for storing dried as it retains its flavour extremely well. The smaller specimens can be threaded on string and dried whole, but larger ones should be sliced.

PREPARATION AND COOKING HINTS

These do not need peeling, a wipe with a damp cloth is sufficient, but do check them carefully to make sure there is no maggot infestation. The best way to do this is to trim the stem carefully and slice through the centre – any maggots will then be easy to see. The older specimens are best used for ketchup, sauces and stews, as these give a quite intense, dark brown colour to the dish. Young specimens can be used as you like. They are delicious for breakfast with bacon and eggs.

Agaricus macrosporus

This is quite a common autumn mushroom. It grows in rings and is extremely good to eat. Some care over identification is necessary, because it can look like the poisonous yellow stainer. However, the shape of the cap and, in particular, the smell are reliable aids to ensuring you have the right mushroom.

IDENTIFICATION

The domed cap is 8–10 (3–4 in) across. It is off-white with light brown scales. The scaly stem is 5–10 cm (2–4 in) long, off-white and quite thick, with a slightly pointed base. The gills are pale pink at first, turning darker brown with age. The flesh is white and has a fairly distinct smell of almonds. The spore print is brown.

HABITAT AND SEASON

Grows in rings in mature pastures that have not been treated with chemicals. The season is from late summer to autumn.

RIGHT *Often very large, the white cap may develop fine scales on the surface, as here.*

STORAGE

This mushroom is very good to eat. It is best dried for storage, but specimens can be quite large so it is important to slice them first.

PREPARATION AND COOKING HINTS

Clean the stem carefully and brush the cap: peeling is usually unnecessary. Check your specimens carefully, especially the larger ones, which may have become maggot infested.

Agaricus silvaticus

This is a mushroom of mainly coniferous woodland, which grows in the same places year after year. It is also extremely good to eat.

IDENTIFICATION

The cap is 5–10 cm (2–4 in) across, convex and covered with brown scales which give it an overall broken pattern. The stem is 5–8 cm (2–3 in), whitish, but striated with brown markings; it has a brown ring. The gills are pale cream at first but turn quite red with age. The flesh is white and stains bright red when cut at the base or lengthways. It has very little smell. The spore print is brown.

HABITAT AND SEASON

The usual habitat is coniferous woods and the season is from early summer to late autumn.

STORAGE

This mushroom has quite an intense flavour. It is best dried, but as it is often large, it should be sliced first.

PREPARATION AND COOKING HINTS

Because this mushroom grows mainly in coniferous woods, the top will need brushing and any pine needles removing. Cut off the lower portion of the stem and slice. It will give a wonderful flavour to your dishes. It is also good on its own, lightly fried with a little butter and basil, and served on toast.

Agaricus silvicola

Wood Mushroom

The wood mushroom has many similarities to the larger horse mushroom but, as the name suggests, it grows almost exclusively in woodland. Take care, however, not to confuse it with either the yellow stainer, *Agaricus xanthodermus*, or some of the deadly *Amanitas*. Check identifying features carefully. It does not grow out of a volval bag, so there will be no sign of one, and if you turn the mushroom over or cut it you will quite clearly see the identification features. If in any doubt, leave it alone.

IDENTIFICATION

The cap is between 5–10 cm (2–4 in) across, domed at first before opening out to be almost flat. It is a creamy yellow which darkens with age. The stem is 5–8 cm (2–3 in), quite thin and with a clearly marked ring. The gills are mid-pink before turning dark brown. The flesh is white and has a distinct aniseed smell. The spore print is dark brown.

HABITAT AND SEASON

The wood mushroom is quite common in coniferous and deciduous woods. Its season is the autumn.

STORAGE

These mushrooms do not store well, so use and enjoy them as soon as possible after you have picked them.

PREPARATION AND COOKING HINTS

The young specimens are particularly tasty. Try coating the caps of young mushrooms in seasoned flour, dipping them in a batter made with beer or lager and then deep frying them: delicious.

ABOVE *Always a graceful slender mushroom, the wood mushroom grows exclusively inside woodlands.*

Aleuria aurantia

ORANGE PEEL FUNGUS

This wonderfully bright fungus has a nice taste and texture. It is a useful addition to all wild mushroom dishes.

IDENTIFICATION

The cap is small, just under 0.5–5 cm (¼–2 in) across; it is cup-shaped and becomes quite wavy at the edges. The inner surface is bright orange in colour. The underside is much lighter and almost velvety to the touch.

HABITAT AND SEASON

The orange peel fungus grows in fairly large clumps on almost bare earth in light grassland, along roads and in lawns. It is quite common and the season is from autumn through to early winter.

STORAGE

Drying is the best method of storage.

PREPARATION AND COOKING HINTS

Apart from cleaning it carefully, the orange peel fungus needs very little doing to it. It is fairly tough, so can be lightly rinsed in water, then sliced thinly and added to your wild mushroom dishes, to which it will add both flavour and colour.

ABOVE RIGHT *Often growing in large clusters, the orange peel fungus prefers disturbed soils along paths and trackways.*

RIGHT *The inner surface (the hymenium) contains the spore-producing cells which are called asci.*

Armillaria mellea

Honey Fungus or Boot-lace Fungus

The honey fungus (*Armillaria mellea* and closely related species) is the dreaded enemy of the gardener. This mushroom grows from black cords known as rhizomorphs which can travel enormous distances. They kill the host tree and infect large areas of woodlands. It is, without doubt, the most dangerous of all the tree parasites, causing intensive rot and a very untimely death. If you find honey fungus growing in your garden take specialist advice fast. However, honey fungus is extremely good to eat and grows in very large quantities during the autumn.

IDENTIFICATION

The cap can range from 2–20 cm (¾–7¾ in) across and is also variable in shape and colour. It starts by being convex, then flattens and is centrally depressed. The colour varies from almost honey to dark brown. The stem is 5–15 cm (2–6 in) and can vary quite considerably in width, sometimes being quite tuberous and at

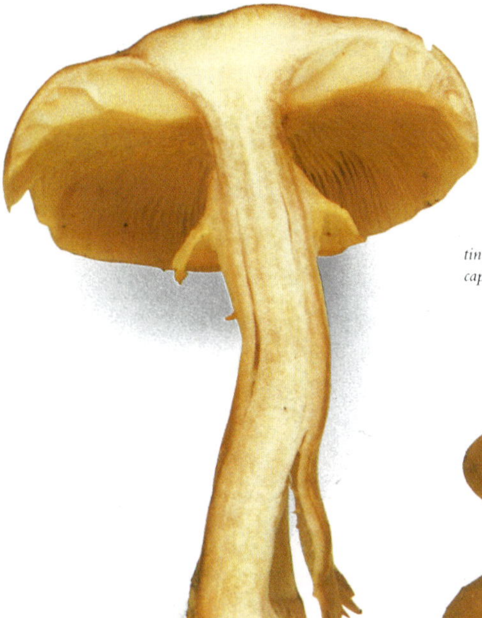

tiny scales at cap centre

yellow-white, cottony ring

stem bases fused together

others very slender. The ring is always clearly visible. The gills vary from off-white to dark brown. The flesh is white with a smell that is quite strong and sweet. The spore print is off-white. It is now thought that there are five or six different forms of honey fungus in Europe. They usually grow in large clumps, either on dead tree trunks, tree stumps or living trees.

HABITAT AND SEASON

Honey fungus is fairly widespread in deciduous and coniferous woods, infecting living trees as well as dead trunks and stumps. The season is from early summer to early winter and they can appear several times at the same place during a season.

ABOVE *The scales of the cap vary considerably, ranging from almost smooth as seen here to quite coarse.*

BELOW *When old, the gills can be quite brownish but the spores are pale cream.*

STORAGE

Drying tends to toughen this mushroom, so it is best to make up dishes first and then freeze them.

PREPARATION AND COOKING HINTS

Only the caps are edible – the stalks are very tough. Boil the caps for two or three minutes in lightly salted water, which must then be discarded as the mushroom may contain a mild toxin. Then cook as you wish. After the initial cooking the caps are particularly good sautéed lightly with onion, garlic and basil, thickened with a little cream and served with pasta.

Auricularia auricula-judae (syn. *Hirneola auricula-judae*)

JEW'S EAR OR TREE EAR

A common fungus with a very long growing season. It has some lookalikes, so take care with identification.

IDENTIFICATION

The fruit body is 2–7 cm (¾–2¾ in) across with a jelly-like texture and an ear-shaped appearance. In dry weather it becomes hard. It is tan-brown with small greyish hairs on the inner surface.

HABITAT AND SEASON

Grows on a wide variety of trees and is particularly common on elder trees: it gets its name from Judas Iscariot who was said to have been hanged on an elder tree. It has an extremely long growing season and therefore can be collected throughout the year.

STORAGE

Best dried. In fact if they are picked during dry weather when they are hard, they can be stored straight away. Before using, reconstitute by putting in lukewarm water.

PREPARATION AND COOKING HINTS

Wash thoroughly with several changes of water. As they have quite a gelatinous texture it is important to cook them well. A very nice way to serve them is to make a sauce with onions, garlic, basil and finely sliced Jew's ears, thickening it with a little cream, and using it to fill small vol-au-vent cases or to spread on croûtons.

LEFT *If in doubt of your identification of this species, try stretching it between your fingers, it should be elastic and rubbery rather than brittle.*

BELOW *The colour can vary greatly. These specimens are very young and fresh and so are quite pale: they may be quite purple-brown with age.*

Boletus badius

BAY BOLETUS

ABOVE *Bay boletus found under conifers (left) are usually darker, smoother and more maroon-bay in colour than those found in deciduous woods(right).*

Bay boletus does not become infested with maggots as much as some of the other boletus, but it is still best to pick only clean specimens. The flavour is excellent.

IDENTIFICATION

The cap is 4–18 cm (1½–7 in) across, it is usually pale to mid-brown, although lighter specimens may be found. It has a polished appearance, and feels tacky when wet. The stem is 4.5–12.5 cm (1¾–5 in) and similar in colour to the cap. The pores are light yellow, but stain blue if pressed or cut, which is one of the principal identification features of the bay boletus. The white flesh has a faint mushroomy smell, and also stains blue when cut, but the stain soon fades. The spore print is light brown.

HABITAT AND SEASON

In all types of mixed woodland. The season is early summer to late autumn.

STORAGE

A very versatile mushroom. Small specimens may be stored in jars of extra virgin oil, or in wine or cider vinegar. Larger specimens, however, are best sliced and dried after the pores have been removed, because these will be quite wet and will not dry satisfactorily. These pores can be used in a mushroom ketchup or sauce if you are making one at the time.

PREPARATION AND COOKING HINTS

Bay boletus are best picked when they are dry. Wipe the caps of any wet specimens and let them dry before dealing with them. Thinly sliced, they are delicious eaten raw. However, fresh or dried, the bay boletus is very versatile and can be used in many soups, stews and wild mushroom dishes.

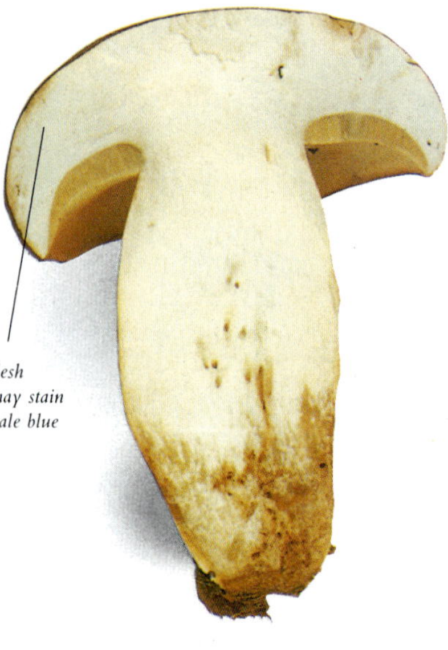

Boletus chrysenteron

RED-CRACKED BOLETUS

Although the flavour of this boletus is not as good as that of the bay boletus or the cep, young specimens are good in mixed mushroom dishes.

IDENTIFICATION

The cap is 4–10 cm (1½–4 in) across, snuff brown in colour, but cracks in the surface of the cap often reveal a slightly reddish hue below. However, the red markings on the stem are the real giveaway of this boletus. The stem is 4–8 cm (1½–3 in) with a distinct reddish tinge for most of its length. The pores are yellow and much more open than those of the bay boletus; they stain a light greenish colour. The flesh is cream to yellow and does not bruise on cutting. The spore print is light brown. The overall texture of this mushroom is much less dense than either the bay boletus or the cep.

HABITAT AND SEASON

Found in association with all broad-leaved trees. The season is throughout the autumn.

STORAGE

Dry this mushroom before adding it to your other dried mushrooms.

PREPARATION AND COOKING HINTS

Only pick young specimens, wipe or brush the cap to remove any loose particles of earth and slice thinly before cooking. However, because it can be a little mushy, it is best used in soups, stews and mixed dishes with other mushrooms and not on its own.

TOP *As the cap ages, particularly in colder weather, the entire surface may take on a reddish flush.*

Boletus edulis

CEP OR PENNY BUN

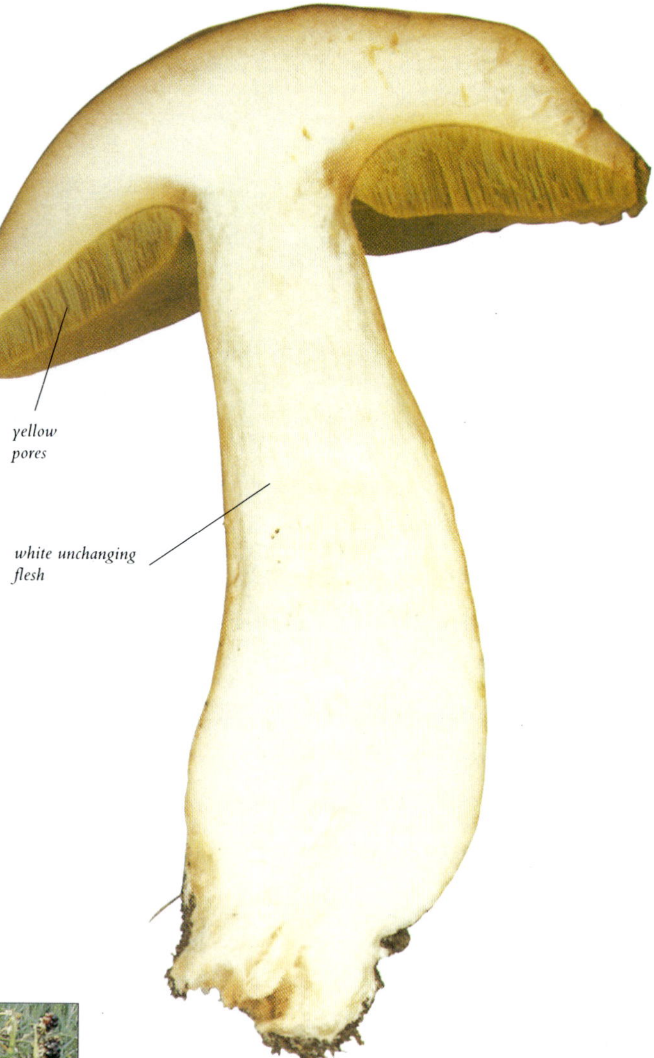

Mushroom hunters regard this mushroom as a great prize; it has a wonderful nutty flavour and is extremely versatile. It can also grow very big and weigh as much as 1 kg (2 lb 2 oz). It grows over a number of days and flies enter at the base of the stem and the maggots work their way up to the cap and tubes so it is important to pick only those in prime condition. When collecting large specimens cut the cap in half to make sure there is no maggot infestation before putting it in your basket.

IDENTIFICATION

The cap ranges from 6–30 cm (2½–11¾ in) across. Its light brown colour looks rather like freshly baked bread, hence the name 'Penny Bun'. The colour darkens as the cap opens, and it is at this stage that you should examine specimens for maggot infestation. In wet weather the cap can have a slightly sticky appearance, but in dry weather it has a nice velvety sheen. The stem varies from 3–23 cm (1¼–9 in). It is very bulbous and has a fine network, with markings that are more pronounced towards the cap. The pores are white at first, turning light yellow with age. The flesh is quite white and does not change as the mushroom ages. The spore print is light brown.

LEFT *Ceps are a great culinary delicacy and they are considered at their best for eating when they are small and tight.*

HABITAT AND SEASON

Coniferous, broad-leaved and mixed woodland; also beside grass pathways. It can also be found in association with heather, along with dwarf willows. The season is summer to late autumn and it is quite common.

RIGHT *A very variable species, some have swollen stems with much darker caps, particularly when found under conifers.*

STORAGE

Cut into thin slices this is probably the most important commercially dried mushroom in the world. Take your cue from this – drying is the best method of home storage. Small specimens can be kept in extra virgin olive oil, but it is really best to leave them so that they can grow on to more mature, and larger, specimens.

PREPARATION AND COOKING HINTS

Clean the caps well and cut in half to check for maggots before putting them in the basket. Brush the stem, cutting off the bottom or scraping it to remove any earth or fibres at the base. This is one of the most versatile mushrooms and it can be used in many cooked dishes.

Calocybe gambosa

ST GEORGE'S MUSHROOM

As its name suggests, St George's mushroom tends to appear around 23 April, St George's Day. It has a great variety of uses and is particularly welcome because it appears early in the year, at much the same time as the common morel. It frequently grows in rings which can be very large, although broken in places. The largest rings may be several hundred years old.

IDENTIFICATION

The cap is 5–15 cm (2–6 in) across with a slightly inrolled margin. Well rounded when young, large old specimens develop an irregular, wavy cap. It is white to cream in colour. The stem is 2–4 cm (¾–1½ in) and white. The gills are narrow and crowded. The flesh is white and soft. It has a mealy smell which is pleasant and strong. The spore print is white.

HABITAT AND SEASON

Tends to grow in rings in grassy locations and around wood edges with underlying chalk. The season is from the beginning of April and into May. For good growth St. George's mushroom relies on warmth and moisture so if the spring is cold it will not appear until the weather becomes warmer. Keep checking areas where you have seen it before.

RIGHT *The caps vary from white to a creamy yellow colour.*

BOTTOM *In these mature specimens note how the caps are irregular and wavy.*

STORAGE

St George's mushroom dries extremely well. It can also be stored in virgin olive oil or in vinegar.

PREPARATION AND COOKING HINTS

Brush the caps well because they can be quite gritty and dirty and there may be chalk particles on the underneath. When picking this mushroom always cut the stem to avoid damaging the mycelial rings. It goes particularly well with chicken and fish. Try St. George's chicken, an ordinary chicken casserole given extra zest by the addition of some of these tasty mushrooms.

Cantharellus cibarius

CHANTERELLE

The excitement of finding this mushroom is, for many, the highlight of the mushroom season – not only does it look beautiful, it tastes wonderful. Most collectors are secretive about their chanterelle patches because these mushrooms grow year after year, often in abundant quantities. It is, however, important to ensure you have found the true chanterelle and not simply the false chanterelle, *Hygrophoropsis aurantiaca.*

IDENTIFICATION

The cap is 2–12 cm (¾–4¾ in) across. Flat at first with a broken margin, it later becomes quite fluted with a central depression. The colour can range from very pale to deep yellow, fading a little with age. Occasionally specimens are almost orange. The stem is 3–8 cm (1¼–3 in), very solid and tapered towards the base. The yellow gills are blunt, narrow,

LEFT *The 'gills' run down the stem and are the same colour as the cap.*

irregular and run down the stem. The yellowish flesh has a lovely faint fragrance of apricots – another important identification feature. The spore print is pale cream colour.

HABITAT AND SEASON

In all kinds of woodland which have open mossy clearings. The season is early summer to late autumn.

STORAGE

All forms of storage can be recommended for the chanterelle. It is a particularly interesting one to store in spiced alcohol because of its very fragrant flavour, but it is equally good stored in extra virgin olive oil or vinegar, or else dried.

PREPARATION AND COOKING HINTS

It is important to clean chanterelles well when you pick them. Brush the caps, and wipe them with a damp cloth if necessary. Cut the stem to avoid any earth getting into your basket. The chanterelle has a good shelf-life: specimens can be kept fresh for some time either in a refrigerator or in a cool, airy place. They taste exquisite and are wonderfully versatile, whether on their own, in mixed mushroom dishes or with meat or fish dishes. They also give a wonderful colour to sauces and the overall appearance of a dish. Try mixing all different types of *Cantharellus*: this will combine the different flavours and textures and make a wonderfully colourful dish of wild mushrooms.

LEFT *Observe how the 'gills' of this species are very shallow, blunt and frequently forked, more like deep wrinkles or veins than true gills.*

Cantharellus infundibuliformis

WINTER CHANTERELLE

The winter chanterelle is so called because it usually appears much later than the ordinary chanterelle. It is quite an achievement to find these tiny little gems hidden under falling autumn leaves. But once you get your eye in you will find troops of them growing where before you had hardly seen anything. They tend to grow in the same place each year, so note where you find them.

IDENTIFICATION
The cap is 2–5 cm (¾–2 in) across, convex at first, soon becoming funnel-shaped with a fluted edge. It is dark brown on top, very much the same colour as the leaf litter under which it grows. The stem is 5–8 cm (2–3 in), yellow and hollow. The gills are narrow and quite irregular,

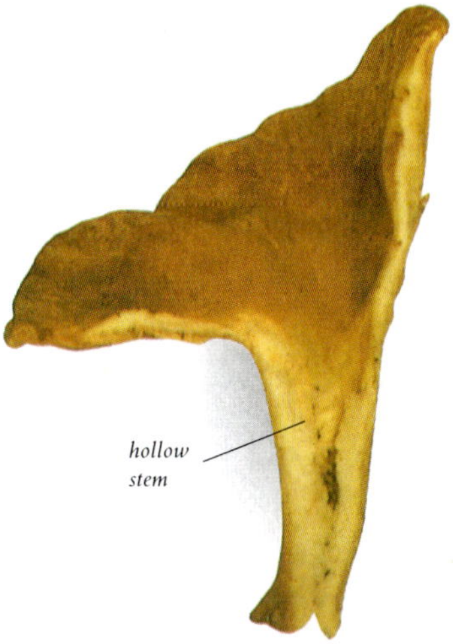

yellowish at first they are greyish lilac in older specimens. The flesh is yellowish and smells faintly sweet. The spore print is yellow.

HABITAT AND SEASON
Grows in large numbers in both deciduous and coniferous woods, preferring acid soil. The season is from late summer to late autumn.

STORAGE
Winter chanterelles dry extremely well, but can also be stored in extra virgin olive oil or wine vinegar.

PREPARATION AND COOKING HINTS
As these usually grow through leaf litter they are quite clean, so all they are likely to need is a dusting with your brush. And if you cut the stalks rather than pulling them up, you will avoid earth and other debris. They are very versatile in cooking, with an extremely nice, sweet flavour that goes especially well with fish.

ABOVE *A good tip for finding these mushrooms is to follow woodland streams and search on the mossy banks as this is one of their favourite habitats.*

ABOVE *When growing in fallen leaves winter chanterelles are very difficult to spot.*

Clitocybe odora

Aniseed Toadstool

The aniseed toadstool is most useful as a condiment. Take care when you identify it, because the verdigris agaric, *Stropharia aeruginosa*, looks rather similar, although it has a blunt knob at centre when open, and is always sticky and darkish-green in colour. As the name suggests, the aniseed toadstool has a very pungent aniseed smell.

IDENTIFICATION

The cap is 3–7 cm (1¼–2¾ in) across; button-shaped at first, it soon flattens and sometimes becomes wavy. The colour is a blue-green which darkens

RIGHT AND BELOW *This lookalike,* Stropharia aeruginosa, *has a sticky cap and a ring on the stem. It has no odour. The gills turn purple-brown when mature.*

BOTTOM *The colour may fade rapidly from that shown to almost white. These specimens are best avoided in case of confusion with the suspect* Clitocybe fragrans, *which is white and also smells of aniseed.*

with age. The stem is 3–6 cm (1¼–2½ in) and lightly striated. The gills, which are not very marked, are close and run down the stem. The flesh is pale and the smell is strongly of aniseed. The spore print is white.

HABITAT AND SEASON

In leaf litter along the edges of coniferous and deciduous woods. In the latter they are likely to be in association with beech or sweet chestnut. The season is from late summer to late autumn and they are relatively common.

STORAGE

Best dried and stored separately because of the intensity of its flavour.

PREPARATION AND COOKING HINTS

Best used as a flavouring: finely chop fresh specimens or powder dried ones.

Coprinus comatus

SHAGGY INK CAP OR LAWYER'S WIG

One of the most common mushrooms, they often come up in dense clusters on newly turned earth in meadows and gardens throughout the summer. Only the young specimens are edible and once picked they must be used quickly, otherwise they soon decay into a nasty inky mass. This is an easy mushroom to identify as it is very distinct, although care must be taken that the early stages of this and the magpie fungus, *Coprinus picaceus*, are not mistaken. However, the magpie fungus has something like a veil which the shaggy ink cap does not.

IDENTIFICATION

The cap is 5–12 cm (2–4¾ in) across; egg-shaped at first, it opens to a bell. White with a cream-coloured centre; it has large shaggy scales. The stem is 10–37 cm (4–14½ in) and white. The gills are white to start with, slowly changing to black from the edge inwards before becoming a mass of ink which, incidentally, makes good drawing ink. The flesh is white with a slight sweet smell. The spore print is brown-black.

BELOW *The very distinct narrow ring is not easily seen here, but as the cap expands it will be left behind on the stem.*

HABITAT AND SEASON
Widespread on grassy banks beside roads, on rubbish heaps, lawns and recently disturbed soil near building sites. The season is midsummer to late autumn. They are very common.

STORAGE
Best used fresh or dried in an electric drier. Do not attempt to air-dry them as they will turn into an inky mass.

PREPARATION AND COOKING HINTS
Although shaggy ink caps can be used dried; they are really best fresh, either on their own, or with the parasol mushroom, *Lepiota procera*, to make a wonderful soup. Use the two mushrooms, some onions and a little potato to thicken, sweated together and then liquidized. Simple and quite delicious.

ABOVE *This is the best stage to collect shaggy ink caps for cooking.*

LEFT *Magpie fungus,* Coprinus picaceus *can be confused with the shaggy ink cap in its early stages.*

Craterellus cornucopioides

HORN OF PLENTY OR TROMPETTE DES MORTS

Another wonderful mushroom of the *Cantharellus* family. Like the chanterelle and winter chanterelle, the horn of plenty appears in large groups in the same place year after year. These, however, are quite often covered by leaf litter and are difficult to spot because of their colour. Although the initial appearance is not inviting, the taste is excellent.

IDENTIFICATION
The cap is 2–9 cm (¾–3½ in) across; it is shaped like a tube or a trumpet and has an open flared mouth and is hollow. It becomes irregular with age and is thin and tough. In colour it ranges from mid-brown to black, though it fades with age. The gills are barely perceptible. The flesh is grey to black. The spore print is white.

HABITAT AND SEASON
Grows in large clusters among the leaf litter of deciduous woods. The season is from late summer to quite late autumn.

STORAGE
All forms of storage are appropriate for the horn of plenty, but it is probably best dried.

PREPARATION AND COOKING HINTS

Remember that these mushrooms are hollow. You will always need to brush them and, with larger specimens, it is best to slice them in half and remove any debris that has gone down the funnel-cap. The horn of plenty is very versatile in cooking, but goes particularly well with fish, its dark colour making a striking contrast with white fish.

BELOW *Like the winter chanterelle, this species is found in damp mossy banks alongside streams and in deep leaf litter.*

Fistulina hepatica

BEEFSTEAK FUNGUS

An important bracket fungus from a collector's point of view, not only is it interesting in colour and texture, it has a good flavour. Because the beefsteak fungus often grows fairly high up trees, you may well need to add a ladder to your collecting equipment.

IDENTIFICATION

The bracket can vary from 8–30 cm (3–11¾ in) across and is quite thick. It is usually in a single piece, although several may grow one above the other. Cut through, the beefsteak fungus really does look rather like a piece of meat. The colour of the bracket is an orange-red darkening with age, the pores are much lighter. The flesh is thick, succulent and mottled dark red; it has quite a pleasant smell. The spore print is brown.

HABITAT AND SEASON

Grows on chestnut or oak trees, usually, but not always, on the lower part of the trunk. Season is late summer to autumn, although it may appear earlier. Although this fungus causes rot inside a tree it does not kill it, but it makes the wood of infected trees much darker. Oak darkened in this way is in demand in the furniture

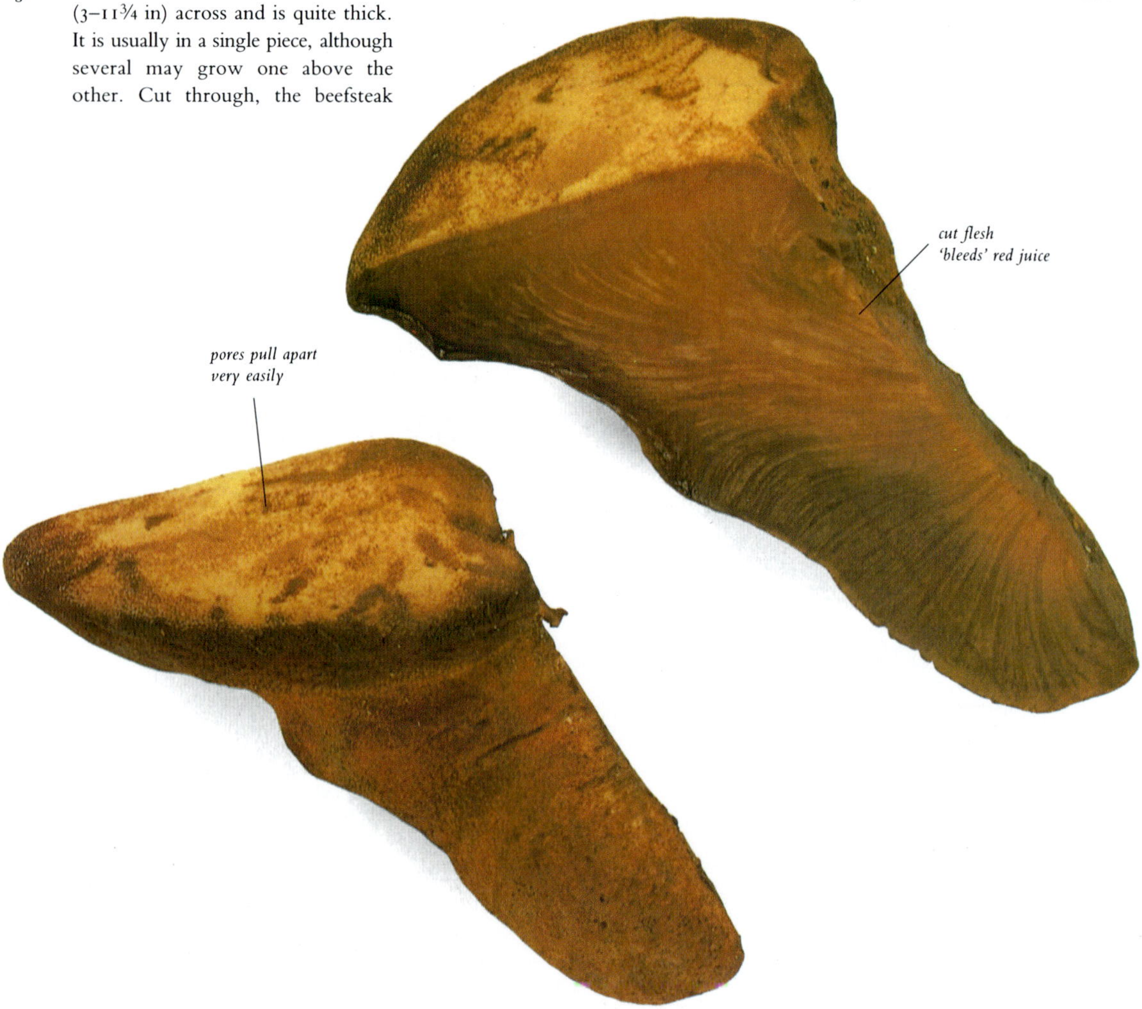

LEFT *Beefsteak fungi often grow very high up in trees. Another good clue to identifying this species is that the individual tubes separate from each other very easily, unlike all other bracket fungi.*

BELOW *The upper surface can be very moist and spongy when fresh.*

industry. Near Holt, in north Norfolk, England, there is a 980-year-old oak tree with beefsteak fungus growing up to a height of 12 m (40 ft) from the base, a little bit difficult from a picker's point of view, but nevertheless a wonderful sight.

STORAGE

Like other bracket fungi this will toughen if dried, so it is best to make dishes and then freeze them.

PREPARATION AND COOKING HINTS

Cut off any parts of the tree still attached to the fungus. Separate the various layers and wipe them with a damp cloth. The beefsteak fungus has a slightly metallic taste, so it is best to slice it into strips and soak these in milk for about two hours to remove the slight acidity and acrid flavour. Then it can be grilled as a piece of steak with a little onion, basil and garlic. Try it, too, on a charcoal grill or barbecue. It is also excellent added to soups and stews for extra flavour and colour.

Flammulina velutipes

VELVET SHANK

As the name implies, the velvet shank has a dark velvety stem. It normally grows during the winter months and can survive the frosts, indeed it may need a frost before starting to grow. It can be frozen solid, but still survive.

IDENTIFICATION

The cap is 3–10 cm (1¼–4 in) across and fairly flat. It is light orange in colour, paler at the edges and darker towards the centre. It is also quite smooth and shiny with a sticky surface. The stem is 1–3 cm (½–1¼ in), very tough and is, as the name suggests, velvety and dark in colour, particularly at the base. The flesh, which is yellow on the cap changing to dark brown on the stem, has little smell. The gills are pale yellow. The spore print is white.

HABITAT AND SEASON

The velvet shank often grows in very large clusters on dead or decaying wood, particularly in association with elm and oak, and also gorse roots. The season is long because they grow all through the winter months and so are useful when only a limited number of mushrooms is available.

STORAGE

The best method of storage is to dry and powder them.

PREPARATION AND COOKING HINTS

As they have a fairly tough texture they really are best dried. If using them fresh, cut off most of the stem, and slice the caps finely. Use to give a good flavour to soups and stews, but remember to cook them well.

LEFT *Difficult to confuse with anything else because of the unusual season of growth but note the absence of a ring on the stem. Poisonous lookalikes will have a ring or a veil.*

Grifola frondosa (syn. Polyporus frondosus)

HEN OF THE WOODS

BELOW AND BOTTOM *Look for small overlapping caps and flesh which does not turn brown when bruised.*

This is an unusual fungus which, like the cauliflower fungus, grows at the base of tree trunks and can be extremely large. Its many caps are joined together and a large specimen can provide a feast for many people. Good to eat and quite rare, so note where you find it as it will certainly grow there again.

IDENTIFICATION

The fruit body is 10–15 cm (4–6 in) across, and consists of a central section with many branch stems ending in individual caps. Each cap is 3–7 cm (1¼–2¾ in) across and has quite a wrinkled edge. The whole fruit body is greyish in colour turning brown with age. The stems are pale grey. The hen of the woods has tubes rather than gills. These are 2–3 mm (1/10 in) long and run down the stem. The flesh, which is white, has a slightly musty smell.

HABITAT AND SEASON

Grows at the base of the trunks of oaks or other deciduous trees. Occasionally it grows on tree stumps. The season of the hen of the woods is autumn to early winter.

STORAGE

The best method of storage is drying. Otherwise freeze dishes in which you have used this mushroom.

PREPARATION AND COOKING HINTS

It is important to clean the hen of the woods thoroughly as it has many nooks and crevices which harbour dirt. Due to its very tough texture it can be rinsed in cold water prior to cooking. It tastes good and goes well in a wide variety of wild mushroom dishes, but, because of its tough texture, make sure it is well cooked. Dried and then powdered, it can be added to soups and stews.

Hydnum repandum

Hedgehog Fungus

This little gem is often quite difficult to find on the woodland floor. Perseverance pays as it has great culinary value and is much sought after by collectors.

IDENTIFICATION

The cream-coloured caps are usually single and 2–15 cm (¾–6 in) across, flattening with a slight central depression and rolled rim. The stem is 3.5–7.5 cm (1¼–3 in) and quite bulbous. It is quite downy and is white, bruising slightly yellow when cut. In place of pores or veins, this mushroom has little spines, hence the name hedgehog fungus. The flesh is white with a very pleasant smell. The spore print is cream-coloured.

HABITAT AND SEASON

Grows in large numbers and under deciduous or coniferous trees, usually in quite damp situations such as along drainage ditches or where there are mossy patches. The season is late summer to late autumn.

STORAGE

These are best sliced and dried for winter use, although they can be kept in oil or vinegar.

PREPARATION AND COOKING HINTS

After cleaning, the smaller specimens can be cooked whole or else sliced. With larger specimens it is probably best to remove the spines, as although quite edible they look like small hairs and could spoil the appearance of the finished dish. This is a very versatile mushroom, going very well with both meat and fish dishes, but it is worth trying some on their own for their excellent flavour.

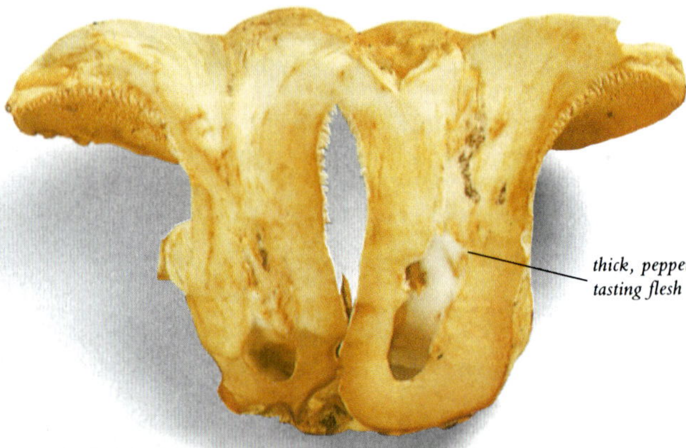

LEFT *The cap colour can vary from pinkish-buff to this rare white form.*

Hygrophorus nemoreus

BELOW *The different stages of development are clearly shown: with a bell shape at the beginning, the cap spreads with a very clear, round central area.*

Most *Hygrophorus* (250 species) have bright colours and often have a viscous or sticky cap. This species is an exception with a rather dull colour and a dry cap.

IDENTIFICATION

The diameter of the cap is between 8–12 cm (3–4¾ in). It is at first bell-shaped, then flattened, maintaining a darker umbo. The fibrillose-striate top is usually mat and dry. The colour is cream at first. The gills become pink or pale orange when older. The stem is whitish or pale brown like the cap but lighter. It is pointed at the end and often curved. Its surface is, on the whole, fibrous but shows around the top a floury-granular zone, that is to say granulose dots. The flesh is white and tender with a slight smell of flour.

HABITAT AND SEASON

Grows in deciduous woods in autumn.

STORAGE

Drying is a good way to store this species because of its soft and delicate flesh. To be sure the mushrooms do not contain any pests, it is advized to cut them longitudinally before cutting or slicing them. After that, thread the pieces onto a string or lay them on a tray.

PREPARATION

Clean your mushrooms "on site" and transport them carefully as they are very fragile.

The gills are well-spaced.

The base of the stem is pointed.

Laccaria amethystea

AMETHYST DECEIVER

The amethyst deceiver grows in large troops. It is colourful, edible and tasty, and so makes excellent additions to your cooking.

IDENTIFICATION

The cap is 1–5 cm (½–2 in) across. It is convex but flattens with age and develops a slight depression in the centre. Deep purplish-lilac in colour, it dries to an almost buff colour. The stem is 4–10 cm (1½–4 in), hollow and has slightly white fibres below the cap. The gills are a similar colour to the cap. The flesh is thin and tinged lilac. The smell is not distinctive. The spore print is white.

HABITAT AND SEASON

Grows in coniferous and deciduous woods, often with beech and chestnut. The season is late summer to early winter. It is very common.

STORAGE

Dries very well. It can also be stored in spiced alcohol to give a most unusual sauce to serve over ice-cream and desserts.

PREPARATION AND COOKING HINTS

As these grow quite densely and have wide open gills, they can be dirty, so it is important to clean them well before using. If you store them in spiced alcohol, blanch them first. It is important that if stored in alcohol these are kept in a refrigerator to prevent fermentation. They are also excellent fresh.

LEFT *When picked, amethyst deceivers are bright in colour but this will fade.*

Laccaria laccata

Deceiver

Like the amethyst deceiver, the deceiver grows in large troops.

IDENTIFICATION

The deceiver has a cap that can be slightly larger than the amethyst deceiver, but is also convex and flattening. It can open to look like a chanterelle. The colour is tawny to pale red and it dries to a paler colour. The stem is 5–10 cm (2–4 in), a similar colour to the cap, but often is twisted. The gills are well spread. The flesh is a pale reddish-brown and the smell is not distinctive. The spore print is white.

HABITAT AND SEASON

Grows in coniferous and deciduous woods. The season is late summer to early winter. They are very common.

STORAGE

The best method of storage is drying.

PREPARATION AND COOKING HINTS

Like the amethyst deceiver, it is important to clean it well before putting it in your basket. Follow the instructions on the opposite page for spicing in alcohol.

RIGHT, ABOVE AND BELOW *The deceiver is incredibly variable and it may take you many seasons to recognize the many variations.*

Lactarius deliciosus

SAFFRON MILK-CAP

A lovely, colourful mushroom to find. It grows very close to the ground and often on quite sandy soil, which can make cleaning difficult. It also has a hollow stem which can lead to problems with infestation. To avoid this problem just pick young fresh specimens, but make sure that they are mature enough for a positive identification, otherwise they can be confused with the woolly milk-cap, *Lactarius torminosus*, or *Lactarius pubescens*, both of which are poisonous.

ABOVE *As you can see, the cap becomes pale, almost silvery-white or dull greenish with age. Pick the fresher orange caps.*

IDENTIFICATION

The cap is 3–12 cm (1¼–4¾ in) across, convex with a depressed centre. It has concentric rings and, as the name suggests, is saffron in colour.

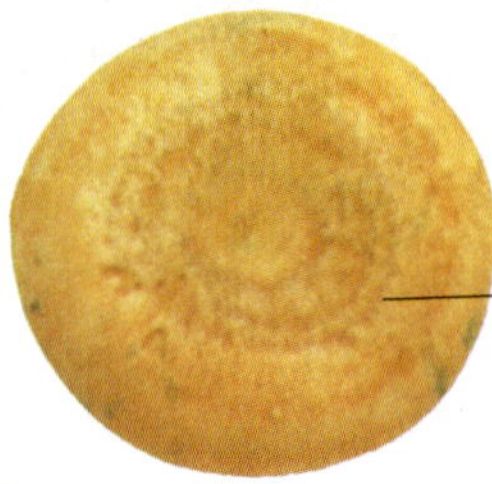

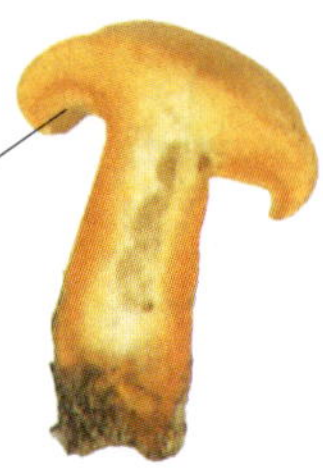

BELOW *In young specimens the margin is involuted.*

On cutting you will notice that it bleeds a saffron colour. It also has a clean, inrolled edge. This is an important means of identification, because neither the woolly milk-cap nor *Lactarius pubescens* have clean edges to the cap. The hollow stem is 3–6 cm (1¼–2½ in) pale, blotched with orange, and when bruised or broken, turns greenish. The closely spaced gills are saffron in colour. The flesh is pale. The saffron milk-cap is brighter in colour than either of its lookalikes, which is a useful aid to identification.

HABITAT AND SEASON

Always grows under pine or spruce trees, and can also be found beside paths on sandy heathland. The season is early summer to quite late autumn.

STORAGE

This stores extremely well, whether dried or in oil or vinegar.

PREPARATION AND COOKING HINTS

The sand and pine needles of this mushroom's habitat make cleaning important. Indeed, it may be necessary to wash your specimens immediately before cooking, but then dry them well before slicing and cooking them. The lovely crunchy texture and good flavour make this a much sought-after mushroom.

RIGHT *The cap margin is shaggy in these young specimens.*

Laetiporus sulphureus

SULPHUR POLYPORE OR CHICKEN OF THE WOODS

One of the more spectacular of all bracket fungi, this can grow in very large quantities and come quite early in the mushroom season. Its versatility makes it important from a culinary point of view, but only pick young specimens.

IDENTIFICATION

The bracket can range from 15–50 cm (6–19¾ in) across. Often the shape of a fan, it has a semi-circular growing habit and quite nice rounded edges. The colour is spectacular; lemon to orange-yellow, although it tends to darken with age. The brackets have an almost velvet-like appearance. It has yellow tubes. The flesh in young specimens is tender and exudes a yellow juice. The smell is quite pungent and a little acrid.

HABITAT AND SEASON

Grows on deciduous trees, particularly oak and sweet chestnut, but may also be found on yew, cherry and willow. The season is usually from late spring to early autumn, but if the winter has been mild it will often appear much earlier, so keep a look out for it.

STORAGE

Drying toughens this mushroom, so it is best used fresh and the finished dish frozen.

PREPARATION AND COOKING HINTS

Avoid the toughest specimens and only use young ones. Cleaning can be difficult but it is best to separate the individual layers, brushing lightly; bearing in mind that the dense texture makes it possible to wash it to remove any infestation or dirt. To remove the slight bitter taste blanch it for two to three minutes in boiling, salted water prior to cooking. The texture and flavour is of chicken, as the name suggests, and it is much prized by chefs. It is wonderful for vegetarian meals, making an excellent chicken of the woods risotto or chicken of the woods curry.

BELOW *The giant polypore,* Meripilus giganteus, *can reach 1½ m (4 ft) across. Its flesh stains black when bruised but it is edible when very young.*

BELOW LEFT AND BELOW *When young, the strange lumpy growths of* Laetiporus sulphureus *can look quite unlike the elegant brackets it will form with age.*

BOTTOM *This bracket lasts quite a while in the field and when old is soft, spongy and paler in colour. Pick the brightly coloured fruit bodies.*

Langermannia gigantea

GIANT PUFF-BALL

LEFT *Hedgerows and ditch banks are two of the favourite habitats of the giant puff-ball.*

The giant puff-ball can be truly spectacular. It is also versatile in the kitchen, but only pick specimens that are fresh and young and sound hollow when you tap the top of the mushroom. It is pointless picking this mushroom once the flesh has become discoloured. Check its age by cutting the specimen right through; the knife should not tear the flesh but pass crisply through it.

IDENTIFICATION

The fruit body can range from 5–80 cm (2–31½ in) across, although specimens of 120 cm (48 in) across have been recorded. When young it has a nice white appearance, although the outer wall may break away to expose the spore mass and become yellow. Avoid at this stage.

HABITAT AND SEASON

Grows in gardens, pastures, woodlands and a wide variety of other situations, such as along dyke banks. The season is any time from early summer to late autumn unless the weather is very dry, when it will not grow. There will usually be several in the same area and they grow in the same place year after year.

STORAGE

There is no satisfactory way of storing giant puff-balls, so it is best to make up the dishes and freeze them.

PREPARATION AND COOKING HINTS

Very little needs to be done to this mushroom. Wipe the specimens carefully with a damp cloth and, if you are not going to use them immediately, wrap in cling film and keep in the refrigerator for up to three days. The giant puff-ball goes extremely well in all wild mushroom dishes, soups and stews. It also makes a good breakfast sliced and fried with bacon or else dipped in beaten egg and breadcrumbs and lightly fried in bacon fat.

LEFT AND ABOVE *This shows another large edible species,* Lycoperdon excipuliforme, *which frequently grows in large clusters. It is common in woodlands.*

Leccinum scabrum

Brown Birch Bolete

Although the brown birch bolete is not as well favoured as the orange birch bolete, it is still quite useful in the kitchen. However, only pick young firm specimens as older ones tend to absorb a good deal of moisture and so have a very soft texture.

IDENTIFICATION

The cap is 5–12 cm (2–4¾ in) across and mid-brown in colour. It is dry, but can be slightly sticky in wet weather. The stem is 7–20 cm (2¾–7¾ in), white with brown to blackish flecked scales. The pores are brown. The flesh is white and the smell quite pleasant. The spore print is brown.

HABITAT AND SEASON

Grows under birch trees. The season is summer to late autumn.

STORAGE

Drying is the best method of storage. Cut it into sections and either air-dry or use an electric dryer.

PREPARATION AND COOKING HINTS

As this mushroom has quite a soft texture, it is best to use it in conjunction with other mushrooms in a mixed mushroom dish or in mushroom soups.

RIGHT *The brown birch bolete has recently been subdivided into a number of closely related species, all of which are edible.*

Leccinum versipelle

ORANGE BIRCH BOLETE

A bolete that is particularly good to eat. It can grow to a fairly large size and, as the name implies, is usually in close association with birch trees.

IDENTIFICATION

The cap is 6–25 cm (2½–9¾ in) across. It is a lovely orange colour and has a slightly fluffy appearance at first before becoming smooth or scaly depending on the weather conditions. It is usually dry. The stem can be up to 20 cm (7¾ in). It is white to greyish in colour and covered with brown to blackish scales. The stems of young specimens bruise a bright electric blue in patches. The pores are off-white to grey. The flesh is pale, becoming blackish with age. The smell is quite pleasant. When cut in cross-section this mushroom stains quite black on the inside, but you should not be put off by this as it is good to eat. The spore print is light brown.

HABITAT AND SEASON

Grows in association with birch and scrub. The season is midsummer to quite late autumn.

STORAGE

Because this mushroom can be quite large, it is best to slice it before drying, which is the best way of storing it.

PREPARATION AND COOKING HINTS

It should only be necessary to wipe the cap with a damp cloth and brush any loose dust particles from the stem. A versatile mushroom, it is much sought after by chefs.

ABOVE *The caps may expand to a much greater size in proportion to the stem than is shown here and the colour can fade to dull yellow buff.*

ABOVE *The cap may become quite felty and scaly with age, particularly at the centre.*

Lepista nuda (syn. *Tricholoma nudum*)
Wood Blewit

The wood blewit is useful because it appears late in the season. But beware – some people are allergic to it. Make sure you try only a little first and take care if you serve it to guests. It is also most important to remember it must be well cooked and never eaten raw.

IDENTIFICATION

The cap is 6–12 cm (2½–4¾ in) across. Convex at first, it eventually flattens and is sometimes quite convoluted. The cap starts by being quite blue but then turns an almost shiny tan. It dries a little paler. The stem is 5–9 cm (2–3½ in) and often has purple markings. The gills are crowded and very lilac, although they lose their colour with age they never turn brown. It is best to pick younger specimens that still retain the wonderful colour for they have the best flavour. The flesh is bluish and the smell is quite perfumed. The spore print is pale pink.

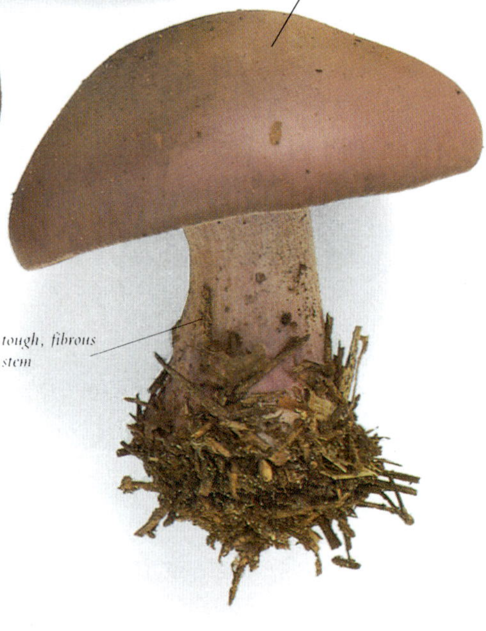

HABITAT AND SEASON

Grows in all mixed woodland, hedgerows and gardens and sometimes on open ground. The season is from autumn to early winter. It is quite common and often grows in large quantities.

STORAGE

Because the wood blewit must be cooked before it is eaten, it is best not to dry it. It does, however, keep extremely well if it is blanched and then put in wine vinegar, extra virgin olive oil or spiced alcohol. But, if kept in the alcohol, it must be stored in the refrigerator to stop fermentation. The colour and fragrance of this mushroom mean it can be used in both sweet and savoury dishes.

PREPARATION AND COOKING HINTS

Quite an easy mushroom to clean, gently wipe the top and cut the stem. It is good in all mushroom dishes, but as it has a very strong flavour it goes particularly well with strongly flavoured vegetables such as onions and leeks. Try a blewit bake by mixing onions, leeks and wood blewits in a béchamel sauce. Do not forget, however, that some people are allergic to it.

TOP *Note that the caps are smooth and not sticky. The gills remain violet, never turning rusty brown as do those of some lookalike species, such as* Cortinarius.

RIGHT *Although these specimens are under pines, the wood blewit is equally common in deciduous woods and gardens.*

Lepista saeva

FIELD BLEWIT OR BLUE LEG

The field blewit is most commonly found exactly where the name suggests. But, because they are low-growing, they are difficult to spot in long grass. Its other name, blue leg, comes from the brightly coloured stem. It is best picked young, to avoid infestation with maggots. Remember, like the wood blewit, this mushroom must be cooked before it is eaten and some people are allergic to it, so take care.

IDENTIFICATION

The cap is 6–12 cm (2½–4¾ in) across. Quite convex at first then flattening, it can be slightly depressed when fully opened out. The cap is a rather insignificant buff colour, but it has a nice shine. The stem, which is 3–6 cm (1¼–2½ in) is the most significant thing about the field blewit. It is often rather bulbous and has lilac markings. The gills are crowded and whitish. The flesh is quite thick and chunky and white to flesh-coloured. It has a perfumed smell very similar to that of the wood blewit. The spore print is pale pink.

HABITAT AND SEASON

Often grows in large numbers in rings in pastureland. The season is autumn through to the first frosts of winter, although it can stand some light frosts.

STORAGE

As this is another mushroom that must be cooked before it is eaten, it is best blanched and stored in wine vinegar or extra virgin olive oil. Store in spiced alcohol if you want to serve it as a dessert.

PREPARATION AND COOKING HINTS

Very similar to the wood blewit, the field blewit gives a really good flavour to stews if it is chopped up first.

ABOVE *Here, you can see clearly the complete lack of violet colour in the cap, compared to the wood blewit.*

Macrolepiota procera

Parasol Mushroom

BELOW *Usually found in fields, not in woodlands, where some related species grow.*

BELOW LEFT *Note the coarse brown scales on the cap, the white ring and bands of brown scales on the stem.*

The parasol mushroom can grow quite large and has a long growing season. They reappear in the same place year after year, and may well have several flushes of growth during the season. The name is appropriate for this mushroom does indeed look like a lady's parasol.

IDENTIFICATION

The cap, which is 10–25 cm (4–9¾ in) or more, starts by being very spherical, but soon flattens out though retaining a prominent centre. It is pale buff in colour and covered with symmetrical patterns of dark shaggy scales. The stem is 15–30 cm (6–11¾ in), white and has a large ring, the gills are white. The flesh is thin and white and has a fairly sweet, although not particularly distinctive, smell. The spore print is white. This mushroom is usually maggot-free and is best collected when dry as it soon absorbs moisture, becoming soggy and almost unusable.

HABITAT AND SEASON

In open woods and pastures, and along roadside hedges. The season is from early summer to late autumn.

STORAGE

This mushroom dries well. Discard the stems, which are tough, cut the cap into segments and dry. It reconstitutes well and makes an excellent addition to soups and stews.

PREPARATION AND COOKING HINTS

This mushroom is usually clean and maggot-free, so very little attention needs to be paid to cleaning. However, dust off any particles on the top, remove the stalk right into the cap and cut into segments. An excellent, if unusual, way of using it is to make up a batter with beer or lager instead of milk, dipping the pieces into the batter and then deep-frying them. Alternatively, you can dust the segments of cap in seasoned flour and shallow- or deep-fry. Cooked like this it makes a crisp starter to a meal or a good addition to a main course.

Macrolepiota rhacodes

Shaggy Parasol

The shaggy parasol is smaller than the parasol mushroom. Although it is edible it can cause stomach upsets, a point to remember when serving it to guests.

IDENTIFICATION

The cap is 5–12 cm (2–4¾ in) across; ovate at first, it expands to become almost flat. It gets its name from the cap's shaggy appearance. The markings are not as clear as those of the parasol, but it has quite a fibrous appearance. The stem is 10–15 cm (4–6 in), off-white with a pinky-brown tinge. The gills are white at first, becoming tinged with red as it ages. The white-tinged flesh bruises reddish-brown or pink. When cut it turns red. The smell is aromatic. The spore print is white.

HABITAT AND SEASON

Grows in woods and shrubberies of all kinds, often with conifers as well as under hedges and along roadside verges. The season is early summer to late autumn.

STORAGE

A mushroom that dries extremely well. Discard the stalk, cut the cap into sections and dry. Reconstituted, it is excellent in soups and stews or mixed wild mushroom dishes.

PREPARATION AND COOKING HINTS

Very similar to the parasol. The shaggy parasol has a clean cap which needs very little attention other than a light brushing. If using fresh specimens, discard the stalk and cut the cap into segments, then deep fry or add to mushroom dishes. The smaller caps are good for stuffing.

ABOVE *The form shown here is the typical woodland type with dull-brown colours. In gardens a larger white form with very bulbous stem base occurs.*

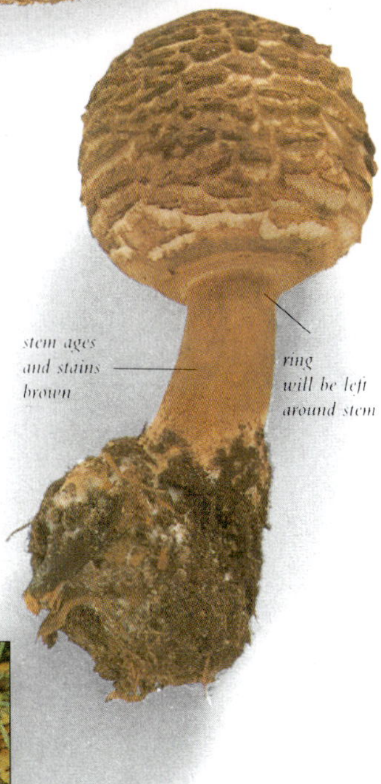

LEFT *The stems may be deep in the leaf litter so take care to observe the bulbous base which is a feature.*

Marasmius oreades

Fairy Ring Champignon or Fairy Ring Fungus

One of the first mushrooms to appear in spring, the fairy ring champignon tastes just as good as it looks. But beware, there is a poisonous lookalike, the *Clitocybe rivulosa*, that grows in a very similar way in very similar situations. It is most important to learn to identify these two. There is very little similarity once they are full grown, but it is important not to make any mistakes.

IDENTIFICATION

The cap is 2–5 cm (¾–2 in) across, convex at first, then flattening with quite a marked centre. Tan in colour, it dries to a fairly light buff. The stem is 2–10 cm (¾–4 in) and tough, so it is best when picking to remove the stem entirely. The gills are white to tan and quite distant. The flesh is thick. The spore print is white.

HABITAT AND SEASON

It forms rings in the shorter grass of old pastures or lawns. The season is from the spring to late autumn. It is very common. It is essential to be able to distinguish between this mushroom and *Clitocybe rivulosa*. The latter also grows in rings often very close, within a metre, to those of the fairy ring champignon. The colour and gills are quite different and *Clitocybe rivulosa* does not appear so early in the year, but it is important that you can identify them.

LEFT *This classic fairy ring is a few metres across, but they may reach over a hundred metres!*

STORAGE

These mushrooms are wonderful eaten fresh, but also dry very well. They can also be stored in spiced Cinzano, extra virgin olive oil or wine or cider vinegar after blanching.

PREPARATION AND COOKING HINTS

As long as you pick these mushrooms clean and cut off the stems when picking them from grass, the only problem you are likely to have is removing a few blades of grass. Occasionally a light dusting with a brush may be necessary, but washing definitely spoils the flavour. From a culinary point of view this is a versatile mushroom, going extremely well with meat and fish dishes as well as mixed mushroom dishes.

BELOW *Note how the grass is shorter where the mushrooms are growing because the nutrients have been absorbed by the fungi.*

Morchella elata

Black Morel

Another member of the highly edible morel family. This, like *Morchella esculenta*, grows in the early spring, so keep an eye open for it as soon as spring arrives.

IDENTIFICATION

Morchella elata is very similar to *M. esculenta* but much darker, often almost black with the ridges and pits aligned in vertical rows. The cap is often tall and pointed. The mushroom stands 5–15 cm (2–6 in) high.

HABITAT AND SEASON

Grows in gardens, wasteland, along roadsides and disused railway lines. Season is throughout the spring.

STORAGE

Like *M. esculenta*, the black morel is best dried.

PREPARATION AND COOKING HINTS

Clean thoroughly before cooking, slicing the fruit body in half to ensure it is free of woodlice and so on. Cook and serve as you would *M. esculenta* and, like that morel, it must be properly cooked before it is eaten.

BELOW LEFT AND RIGHT *Another similar morel is the common morel,* Morchella vulgaris. *Look closely at these two examples, their caps may be dark but they have completely irregular pits and ridges unlike the black morels.*

RIGHT *Often occuring in large numbers, the black morel may be found in both deciduous and coniferous woodlands as well as along tracks and in gardens.*

Morchella esculenta

The morels are among the most exciting springtime fungi. Careful examination of their habitat is necessary because they blend into their background so well. They usually grow singly; two or three can sometimes be found within a reasonably small area, but very rarely more. Excellent mushrooms from the culinary point of view, they must be cooked before eating – never, ever, eat them raw.

IDENTIFICATION

The fruit body is 5–20 cm (2–7¾ in) high. Although very convoluted, with a honeycomb effect, the overall shape is pointed. It is palish brown in colour and darkens to orange-yellow with age. Inside it is hollow. The flesh is white to cream.

HABITAT AND SEASON

Found among shrubs or in open woodland, on waste ground, along path edges and often along disused railway lines. The season is throughout the spring. Wind is very important in spreading the spore of this fungus so, if you find a good specimen, follow the direction of the prevailing wind and you will often find some more.

STORAGE

Best dried for storage. Because of all the nooks and crannies, this morel is often infested with woodlice and other wildlife, so specimens will need cleaning very thoroughly before drying and storing.

PREPARATION AND COOKING HINTS

The easiest way to clean this mushroom properly is to slice each one in half to make sure there is nothing hiding inside, rinse it in clear water and dry. One of the nicest ways to use fresh morels is to stuff the large fruit body. They also go well with meat dishes and provide a very rich sauce. Dried, the intensity of their flavour will enhance most dishes.

ABOVE *When young, the fruit body is often dull buff or brown in colour with blunt ridges.*

ABOVE *When mature, the colour changes to ochre or orange-yellow and the ridges become sharper.*

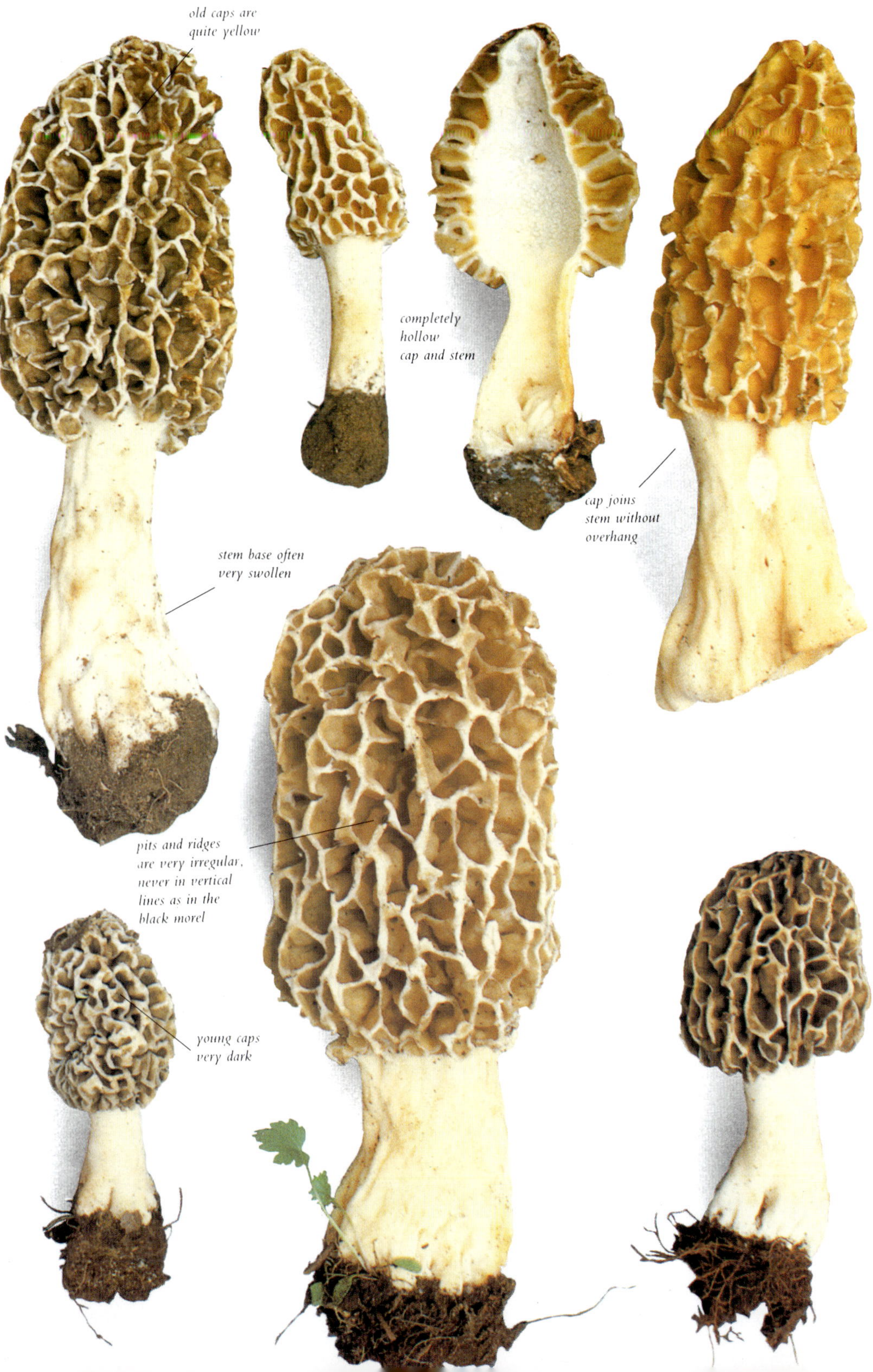
old caps are
quite yellow
completely
hollow
cap and stem
cap joins
stem without
overhang
stem base often
very swollen
pits and ridges
are very irregular,
never in vertical
lines as in the
black morel
young caps
very dark

Pleurotus cornucopiae

BELOW *The stems here are shorter than usual for they often reach 5–8 cm (2–3 in) in length. The way that the stems are fused together is quite characteristic.*

This member of the oyster mushroom family is fairly widely spread. It can be found on the same trees and at the same time as the oyster mushroom, so always have a good look for it before you leave the tree.

IDENTIFICATION

The cap is 5–12 (2–4¾ in) across and convex. It often makes quite a funnel-like shape, which frequently becomes fluted and split at the edges. Whitish in colour, almost a magnolia shade, it turns a fairly dark brown with age. The stem is 5–8 cm (2–3 in). Several fans may grow from the same stem, rather like flowers. The gills are quite deep and run down the stem; they are white to light tan in colour. The flesh is white and has a rather mealy smell. The spore print is lilac.

HABITAT AND SEASON

It grows in dense clusters on cut stumps of most deciduous trees, in particular elm, oak and beech. The season is spring to late autumn.

STORAGE

This mushroom air-dries well.

PREPARATION AND COOKING HINTS

If picked carefully, only a light wipe of the cap should be necessary. Discard most of the stalk as it will be quite tough, particularly where it was attached to the tree. The pleasant flavour makes it a good addition to all mushroom dishes.

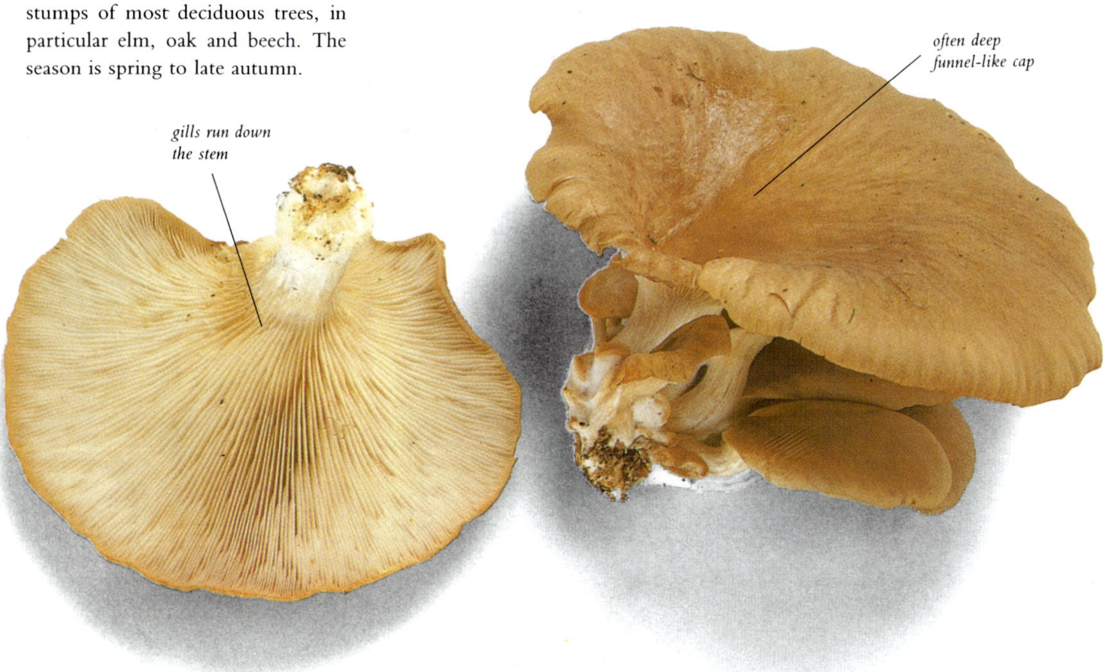

Pleurotus ostreatus

Oyster Mushroom

BELOW *This is the grey-brown late-autumn/winter form of* Pleurotus ostreatus. *In summer, the cream-coloured form,* P. pulmonarius, *is common.*

Now grown commercially on a fairly large scale and so quite familiar, it is still exciting to find a wild oyster mushroom. They grow on dead or decaying trees, often in large masses. They will grow in the same place in successive years, so remember where you picked them.

IDENTIFICATION

The cap is 6–12 cm (2½–4¾ in) across. It is shaped rather like a fan and larger specimens may have fluted edges. The colour can vary: usually a slate grey, they can sometimes have a slightly brown or bluish tinge. They have almost no stem. The gills run down the stem; pure white at first, they turn cream with age. The flesh is white with a pleasant smell. The spore print is lilac. Oyster mushrooms grow in groups, one on top of the other, and if carefully removed from the tree are usually very clean.

HABITAT AND SEASON

These occur in large clusters on standing trees or on the stumps of fallen trees. Most commonly found on beech trees, they will grow on other trees, especially elm. The season is all year round.

STORAGE

All methods of storage can be used for oyster mushrooms. If you separate the caps you can air-dry them very successfully.

PREPARATION AND COOKING HINTS

If picked carefully they are likely to be clean and a wipe with a damp cloth is probably all they need. The oyster mushroom's pleasant flavour means that it goes well with almost all meats and fish, making it extremely useful in the kitchen.

Russula cyanoxantha

Charcoal Burner

The charcoal burner is an excellent mushroom to eat. However, it is a member of a very large genus and identification within the group can be very difficult. Correct identification is essential because some are poisonous, in particular the beechwood sickener, *Russula mairei*, and the sickener, *Russula emetica*. As always, if in doubt leave it out.

IDENTIFICATION

The cap is 5–18 cm (2–7 in) across and slightly greasy. Convex at first, it opens out with a shallow depression in the centre. Occasionally a single colour but more often than not quite a mixed shade, ranging from purple to light green, frequently with a rather faded appearance. The stem is 5–10 cm (2–4 in) and white. The gills run down the stem and are whitish or pale cream in older specimens. A clear identification feature of the charcoal burner is that the gills do not break away if they are touched, they are quite clearly joined to the cap margin. This is in marked contrast to some *Russula* species. The flesh is white and the smell is pleasant. The spore print is white.

HABITAT AND SEASON

Usually to be found under broad-leaved trees, but can also grow in association with pine trees. The season is summer to late autumn and it can be very common.

STORAGE

Drying is a very good method of storing the charcoal burner.

PREPARATION AND COOKING HINTS

It is rare to find a perfect specimen, as woodland wildlife attack it from almost the moment it appears. As a result it will need careful cleaning. However, it is good to eat whether fresh or dried and will add an interesting taste and texture to your mushroom dishes as it retains quite a crunchy texture when cooked. But do remember to be careful with your identification of the charcoal burner and make sure it is not one of the poisonous *Russula* species.

RIGHT AND BELOW *The dull violet-purple cap shown here is typical, but beware, the cap can also be completely green. The best means of identification is to brush your fingers over the gills and they should be flexible and not crumbly as most other* Russulas *are.*

BELOW *A large and colourful group of mushrooms, all* Russula *species. The mushrooms in this family are some of the most difficult to identify accurately.*

Sparassis crispa

Cauliflower Fungus

The cauliflower fungus is quite unlike any other fungus you will find in the woods. When you find one you will understand why it got its name. It is quite unusual, but grows in the same place year after year, so make a note of where you find it. One large specimen can last for several days if stored carefully in a cool place with its base in water.

IDENTIFICATION

The cauliflower fungus has no cap in the ordinary sense of the word, instead the fruit body is built up of many layers that resemble a cauliflower or a brain. A short stem attaches it to the tree on which it grows. The fruit body ranges from 20–50 cm (7¾–19¾ in) in diameter. It ages from a pale yellow-white to brown. It has a sweet smell and a lovely nutty flavour.

HABITAT AND SEASON

It grows on the roots of pine trees, very close to the trunks. Be careful not to cut too deeply when picking this fungus so as not to destroy the main mycelial growth from the roots, then you will be able to come back for more in subsequent seasons.

Look out for *Sparassis vipes*, a subspecies of *S. crispa*. This lives on old oak stumps as well as pine trees and is slightly pinkish. Please do not pick this one, it is very rare and is best left where it is to protect a fragile species.

The cauliflower fungus grows from late summer to late autumn but is tender to frosts and so will be killed by the first hard frosts of winter.

STORAGE

This dries extremely well. Air-drying is probably best: hang your specimens up on strings in a light, airy place for several days. Very large specimens can be cut into sections so they will dry more quickly. As the fungi dry the wildlife in them will fall out, so do not attempt to dry them in

LEFT *Note the flattened crispy lobes. If they are pointed and branched you have probably mistakenly picked one of the* Ramaria *species which are often toxic.*

RIGHT *The fruit bodies are almost always at the base of a tree or stump, as seen here.*

your kitchen; an airy shed or outside storeroom would be best. Any hint of dampness will, of course, spoil the drying. It is very important to dry this mushroom thoroughly – be patient, it will be worth it.

PREPARATION AND COOKING HINTS

Pick only creamy white specimens, as this is when the fungus will be at its very best. Cleaning needs care as there are so many nooks and crannies in the cauliflower fungus and, as it grows so close to the ground pine needles can be a problem. If possible avoid cleaning in water. It is better to brush away any dust particles, cut into thin slices and clean each slice before cooking. If you do use water, remember to dry the fungus well on kitchen paper before cooking. One of the nicest ways to deal with this fungus is to cut it in thin slices, dip them in a batter made with beer rather than milk and deep-fry to make a wonderfully crisp nutty starter to a meal or accompaniment to a favourite dish. But it is equally good if sliced fresh and added to stews and casseroles.

Suillus luteus (syn. *Boletus luteus*)

SLIPPERY JACK, PINE BOLETE OR STICKY BUN

The slippery jack is quite common and a good find, although its open texture makes it prone to maggot infestation. Much prized by chefs, it is very versatile in the kitchen.

IDENTIFICATION

The cap is 5–15 cm (2–6 in) across; a nice mid-brown colour with a marked sheen. It tends to be very sticky when wet, so is best picked in dry conditions. The stem is 5–10 cm (2–4 in), pale yellow with a large, clearly visible ring. The pores are pale yellow. The flesh is white. It has no particularly distinctive smell. The spore print is light brown. Only pick mature fresh specimens.

HABITAT AND SEASON

Found in association with conifers, particularly Scots pine. The season is late summer to late autumn.

STORAGE

Because of its soft texture, this mushroom is best thinly sliced and dried for use in winter dishes.

BELOW *This and other* Suillus *species are only found growing under conifers.*

BOTTOM *Observe how the cap colours change from young to old. The purple-brown turns pale to orange-brown with age.*

PREPARATION AND COOKING HINTS

As the cap is slightly sticky in texture it is best peeled before use. Check carefully for maggot infestation. This mushroom exudes quite a lot of juice when cooking, so it is a good idea to sweat it out first on its own. Strain well and keep the resulting liquid to be used later for a sauce. Then add the mushrooms to other dishes. Slippery jack can be used in many ways. One nice one is to mix the sweated mushrooms with rashers of grilled or fried streaky bacon, add the strained juice, thicken with a little flour and serve it on toast.

Suillus variegatus

Another useful bolete to add to your collection, although it is not as good to eat as the cep or the bay boletus. Only pick young specimens. They are quite light in texture and therefore can become maggot-infested, so check specimens before collecting.

IDENTIFICATION
The cap is 5–12 cm (2–4¾ in) across and a rusty colour. It is sticky when wet. The stem is 5–9 cm (2–3½ in). The pores are quite clearly a snuff-brown colour. The flesh is very white. The spore print is light brown.

HABITAT AND SEASON
Found almost exclusively with conifers. The season is from late summer to late autumn.

STORAGE
Best dried.

BELOW *The rough, almost dry surface of the cap is seen well here.*

PREPARATION AND COOKING HINTS
A wipe of the cap is usually all that is necessary, but beware when slicing specimens to look out for maggot infestation. A good addition to mixed mushroom dishes.

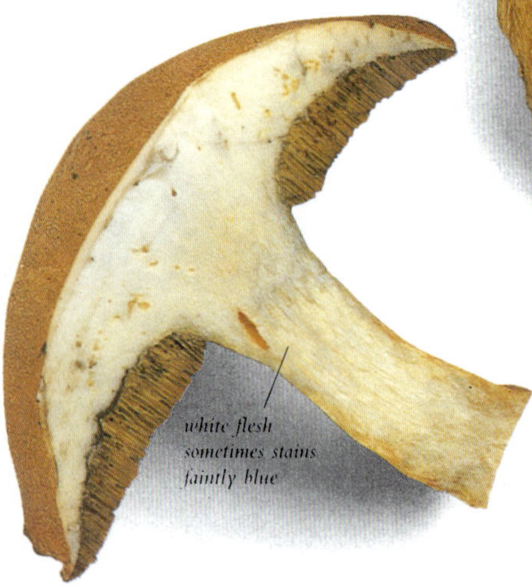

Tricholoma ponderosa

White Matsutake

BELOW *This large species has a single layered ring at the stem apex, some lookalike larger species will have double rings at the top.*

This is one of the larger mushrooms and is much favoured by the Japanese. It is excellent whether eaten fresh or dried.

IDENTIFICATION

The cap is 4–25 cm (1½–9¾ in) across, convex becoming flat, with a broken margin. It is slightly inrolled at first, but opens fully with age. It has a smooth surface which feels quite tacky when dry. It is pale white and can be streaked with light brown. The stem can be up to 15 cm (6 in); it is solid and is sheathed with a veil that runs from the cap to the base. It breaks in patches and can become pinkish-brown, and quite fibrous around the root. The gills are white, attached and crowded. The white flesh, which can stain light brown, has a slightly spicy smell. The spore print is white.

HABITAT AND SEASON

It is scattered in coastal areas in sandy soil and is usually found in conjunction with conifers. Not known to grow in Europe, it is common in North America. The season is late summer to mid-autumn.

STORAGE

Drying is the best method of storage. Whole mushrooms can be dried quite easily, using an electric dryer, by hanging them up or by placing them on drying racks. Dried ones can often be found in Japanese and Chinese supermarkets.

PREPARATION AND COOKING HINTS

Likely to be clean when you find it, it will need little more than washing. It adds an interesting flavour to wild mushroom dishes, but is quite strident, so be careful what you use it with and how much you use. As it has a large cap, it can also be used for stuffed mushroom dishes.

Tuber aestivum

SUMMER TRUFFLE

Although summer truffles grow far more extensively than most people realize, finding them is difficult for they grow beneath the surface of the soil. Animals love them, particularly squirrels and deer, so watching them might give you a clue as to where to look.

IDENTIFICATION

The fruit body is 2–10 cm (¾–4 in) across. It is irregular, though roughly globe-shaped, and covered in a host of tiny black warts. It is blackish-brown in colour. When cut through, it reveals a wonderfully marbled, reddish-brown interior. The smell is very distinctive and sweet and the taste is nutty.

HABITAT AND SEASON

The summer truffle favours calcareous soils and can be found in the ground near beech trees, and also, though less often, in association with sweet chestnuts and evergreen oaks. The season is from late summer to autumn.

spores are dispersed by burrowing animals and insects

STORAGE

One of the best ways of storing truffles is preserving them in olive oil. First of all clean the truffle carefully and shave off the skin which can be used in future recipes. Blanch the truffles very quickly before placing in oil in a completely air-tight container.

PREPARATION AND COOKING HINTS

As truffles have a very strong flavour they are best used in small amounts and even a tiny quantity can transform a dish. They are delicious served with egg and pasta dishes.

Tuber magnatum

The Piedmont or White Truffle

This must be the prize for all mushroom hunters. The most sought-after of the truffles, it is found in very limited areas, mostly in northern Italy, where the finest certainly grow. Unfortunately highly trained dogs or pigs are necessary to locate it.

IDENTIFICATION

The fruit body is generally 5–12 cm (2–4¾ in) across, although much larger, tennis-ball-sized specimens do occasionally occur. It is irregular in shape and yellowish-brown in colour. Indeed, in colour and size it is not unlike a new potato. The flesh is marbled and has a slightly reddish-brown tinge. The smell is highly distinctive and very sweet.

HABITAT AND SEASON

Just below the soil surface in mossy mixed woodlands. Its season is from late autumn through the winter to early spring. Due to its intense smell, it is found usually by dogs or pigs.

STORAGE

These truffles are best stored in closed containers and used fairly quickly after collecting. They have an intense flavour which can permeate foods, so use them to flavour eggs before cooking. Alternatively, put in a closed container with freshly made pasta and leave in the fridge overnight. This gives the pasta a most wonderful truffle scent. The best method of storage would definitely be in extra virgin olive oil. It will not only preserve the truffle but will flavour the oil and give it a wonderfully rich truffle taste. These are the most valued of the wild fungi and command extremely high prices. Excellent quality ones can be obtained from specialist importers and the truffle oil, the fresh truffles or the truffles in extra virgin oil are well worth buying.

PREPARATION AND COOKING HINTS

Very little needs doing to the truffle beyond a careful brushing. If they are to be used fresh, very finely sliced slivers, quickly cooked, are best for the intensity of the flavour. They can also be eaten raw.

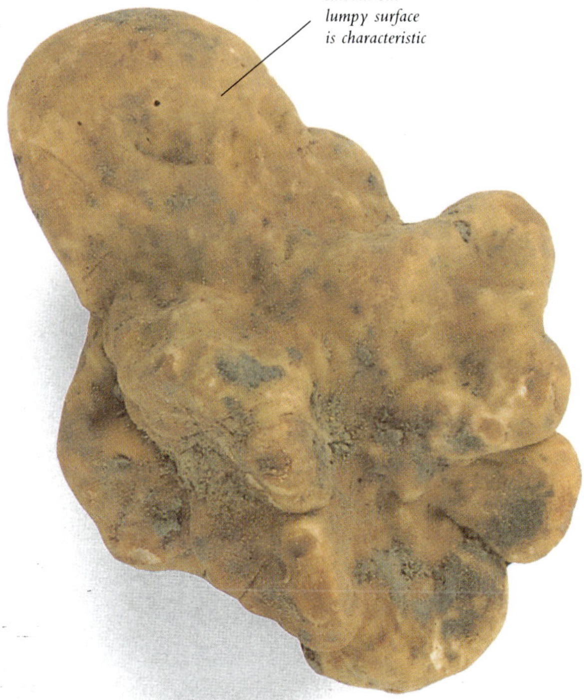

Poisonous Mushrooms

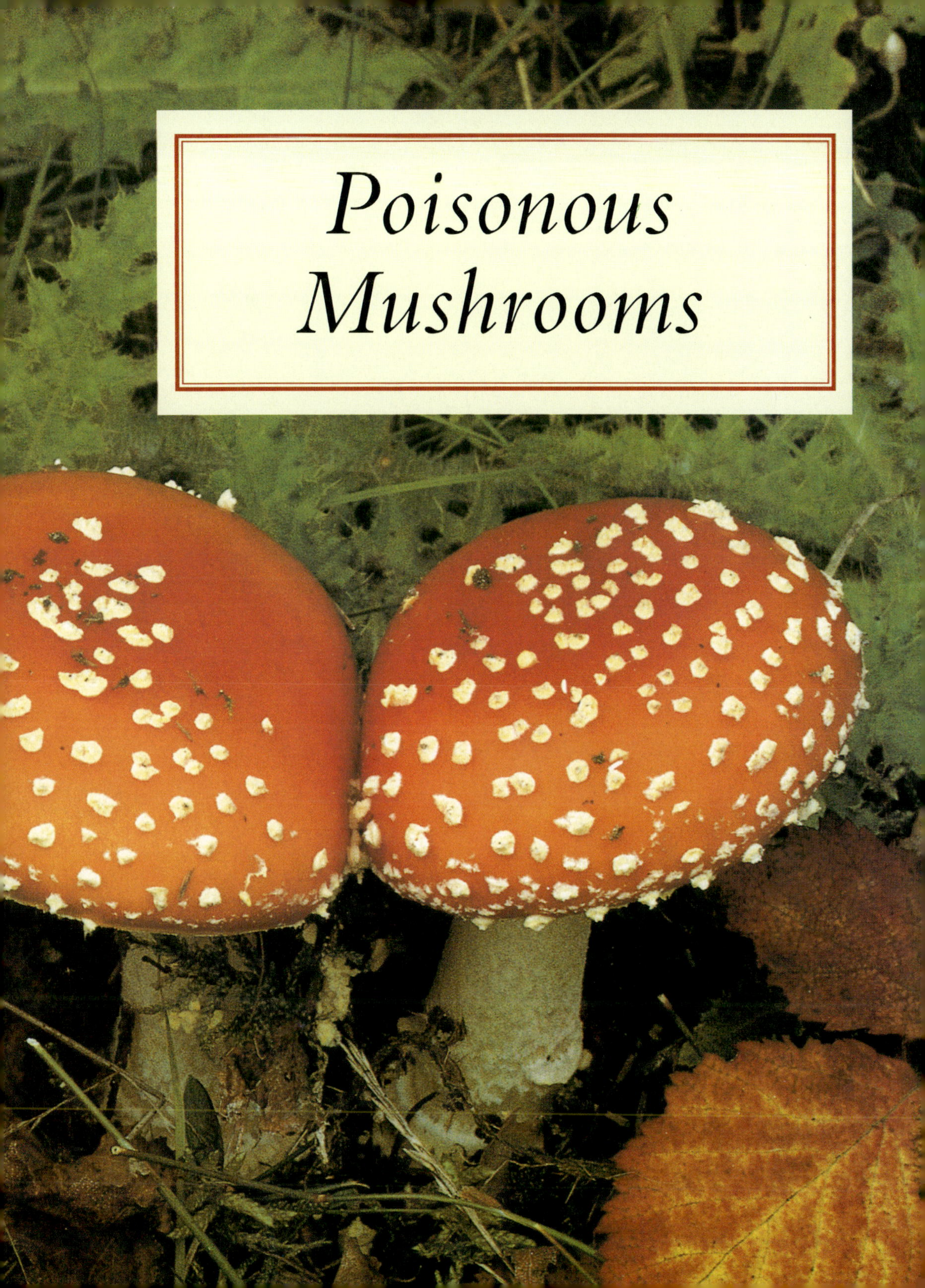

INTRODUCTION

Every year, in spite of repeated warnings, people die of mushroom poisoning. Such deaths emphasize the importance of identifying your mushrooms correctly. People often make the literally fatal mistake of assuming that if animals can eat a mushroom so can humans. Unfortunately this is untrue, for example, slugs eat death caps and other members of the genus *Amanita.* So do not be mistaken when you see signs of either bird or animal activity; it is probably safe for them but may not be for you. Be particularly careful if dealing with the *Amanitas*, remember that their spores are poisonous and that if eaten they will cause extensive damage to the liver and central nervous system. If you think you are dealing with an *Amanita*, dig out the whole specimen with a stick to examine the volval bag. It is a good idea to protect your hand with a glove.

Never, ever, put a poisonous mushroom or an unidentified one with others in your basket. If you require a specimen for identification, put it in a separate container, and always wash your hands after touching any unidentified mushrooms. If you pick a deadly *Amanita* for display, throw the mushroom and container immediately after use. A good way to transport and display such mushrooms is to put them in a plastic container on crumpled paper and to cover the whole box with clingfilm. People can then see the mushroom without having to touch it. There are many old wives' tales about how to identify edible and poisonous mushrooms. They are all false. Particularly dangerous is the saying that if you can peel it you can eat it. You can peel a death cap, which got its name for a very good reason! Other sayings refer to staining silver spoons black. Ignore them all, and take great care over identification so that you can be sure of living to enjoy your mushroom trophies.

Between the good edible mushrooms and the deadly poisonous ones, there is an enormous range of other mushrooms regarded as inedible or not worthwhile. These are not all included in this book. Should you require information about them, consult one of the guides listed at the end of this book.

Although most people can eat the edible mushrooms and fungi identified in this book, it is important to remember that eating large quantities of a very rich food can often cause upset stomachs and some people do have an adverse reaction to fungi. Among those that could cause problems are the wood blewit, *Lepista nuda*, and the field blewit, *Lepista saeva*. Should you ever become ill after eating mushrooms, it is important to see your doctor immediately. Mushroom poisoning can occur almost instantaneously or up to fourteen hours after eating the mushrooms, and at any time in between. It is imperative that you seek medical advice and, if possible, take a sample of the mushroom you have eaten. Correct identification of the poison could be life-saving, and there are many cases of *Amanita* poisoning being dealt with early enough to save the victim's life.

Another mushroom to beware of is the yellow stainer, *Agaricus xanthodermus*. A member of the genus *Agaricus*, it grows in similar situations to the ordinary field or horse mushroom and can be quite common in good mushroom years. Safety is the key for all collectors, so if you are not sure about a mushroom, leave it out of your basket.

PREVIOUS PAGE *A typical group of fly agarics,* Amanita muscaria, *showing how the red pigment fades at the edges with age or after rain.*

LEFT *The* Clitocybe rivulosa, *similar to the fairy champignon but highly toxic.*

OPPOSITE *The death cap,* Amanita phalloides. *The slight radial streaking on the cap can be seen well here.*

Agaricus xanthodermus

Yellow Stainer or Yellow-staining Mushroom

The yellow stainer accounts for approximately 50 per cent of the cases of mushroom poisoning among those who pick either field or horse mushrooms. It has an unpleasant smell and taste and must be avoided at all costs. Identification can be difficult and therefore take careful note of the identification features and illustrations. The symptoms of poisoning are sweating and flushing with unpleasant stomach cramps. Not everyone is affected by the yellow stainer, but it is not worth taking any risks – leave it well alone.

IDENTIFICATION
The cap is 5–15 cm (2–6 in) across. Convex and angular at first, it flattens out later with a dip in the centre.

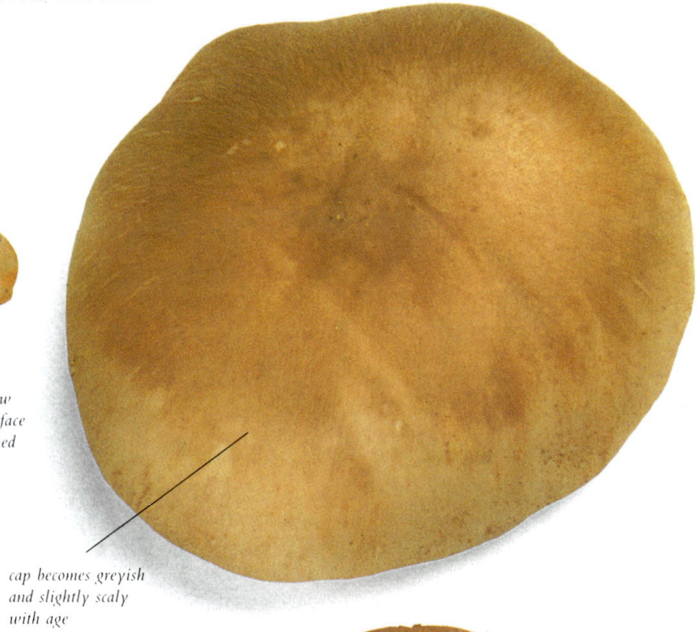

LEFT *Gardens, hedgerows and the edges of woodland are favourite habitats of this species.*

Very white when young, it darkens with age as it expands to a fairly large cap with greyish-brown scales. It bruises a very bright yellow as soon as it is touched or cut, making this a valuable identification feature. Although this mushroom has many similarities with other members of the agaric family, the bright yellow staining is the giveaway. The stem is 5–15 cm (2–6 in) and white, staining bright yellow at the base. The gills are flesh-coloured, darkening with age. The flesh is white. Smell is an important means of identifying this mushroom as it smells rather of carbolic. The spore print is purple-brown. Should you have picked a yellow stainer by mistake and put it in your pan it will quite often turn the rest of the contents a slimy sickly yellow. It will also give off an acrid smell in the kitchen that is very unpleasant.

HABITAT AND SEASON

It grows in woods, pastures and gardens. It has quite a long season, from summer to late autumn. It is quite common in certain areas.

Amanita citrina and *Amanita citrina* var. *alba*

FALSE DEATH CAP

There are two forms of the false death cap, *Amanita citrina* and *Amanita citrina* var. *alba*. Although neither are deadly poisonous, they are so easily confused with the death cap that it is best to leave them alone.

IDENTIFICATION

There are two distinct forms of this fungi: one with a pale greenish-yellow tinge to the cap (*A. citrina*) and the other with a pure white cap. (*A. citrina* var. *alba*). In both forms the cap is 4–10 cm (1½–4 in) across. It is usually covered with patches of the veil, which is one of the features that distinguishes it from the death cap which rarely has any veil remnants. The stem is 6–8 cm (2½–3 in). It has a large basal bag where the remnants of the veil can be seen and it has a clear ring around the stem. The gills are off-white at first, darkening with age. The flesh is white. The spore print is white.

HABITAT AND SEASON

Grows in deciduous or coniferous woods, especially beech woods, but can be found in a large variety of locations. The season is from summer to late autumn and it is quite common.

RIGHT *The false death cap grows in both coniferous and deciduous woodlands. A pure white form is common under beech. A potato-like smell is typical.*

BELOW *In this example, the prominent flat white patches of veil have washed off the cap leaving it quite smooth.*

Amanita muscaria

Fly Agaric

Without doubt this is everybody's idea of a toadstool or poisonous mushroom. The little flecks on the red cap which sometimes grows to 20 cm (7¾ in) across make it quite distinctive. Many fables of myth and magic are associated with this mushroom. One, which sounds like a myth but is not, is its use by the Sami people of Lapland to round up their reindeer herds. They take advantage of the reindeers' liking for the fly agaric and scatter dried ones for the reindeer to eat, which makes them more manageable. The toxins contained in *Amanita muscaria* attack the central nervous system producing intoxication, hallucination and a euphoria that is similar to drunkenness. The poison stays in the system for several months but the symptoms generally disappear in twelve hours, although it may take several days to fully recover.

The only mushroom you are likely to mistake for *A. muscaria* is *A. caesarea*. However, *A. caesarea* has a large volval bag whereas *A. muscaria* does not. In addition, when cut lengthways, *A. muscaria* is white whereas *A. caesarea* is yellow. Another pointer is that the cap of *A. caesarea* does not show flecks of the remnants of the volval bag. When the volval bag finally breaks, it leaves *A. caesarea* clean. *A. caesarea* grows in limited locations throughout Europe except the United Kingdom.

IDENTIFICATION

The cap of the fly agaric is 8–20 cm (3–7¾ in) across, cup-shaped at first, it then flattens right out. Although usually bright scarlet and covered with flecks of veil remnant, the colour may fade in wet weather, and a

BOTTOM *After heavy rain the flecks may wash off the cap and the red colour fade to orange.*

BELOW *One of the main distinctions between* Amanita muscaria *and* A. caesarea *is that* A. caesarea *has a large volval bag, similar to those shown in this picture of the* A. umbonata *but* A. muscaria *does not.*

few come up a fairly pale orange. The white stem is 8–18 cm (3–7 in). If you take a specimen right out of the ground you will see the rounded, swollen stem base. (The gills are white.) The smell is indistinct. These often occur in fairly large groups at all stages of development. The spore print is white.

HABITAT AND SEASON

The fly agaric is most often found with birch trees, although it can occur with a wide range of trees and in many locations. The season is late summer to late autumn and it is very common.

Amanita pantherina

PANTHER CAP

Less common than the fly agaric, the panther cap, *Amanita pantherina*, too, is severely toxic. The greatest danger with the panther cap is that it can be confused with the blusher, *Amanita rubescens*. Many people eat the blusher after first cooking it to remove the toxins and then using it normally. However, it requires a very expert eye to distinguish between young specimens of the blusher and the panther cap, so it is best to avoid both species for fear of making a mistake.

IDENTIFICATION

The cap is 5–10 cm (2–4 in) across, almost bronze in colour, and covered with small pure white remnants of veil. The margin also has remnants of the veil. The stem is 9–12.5 cm (3½–5 in), white with a ring. It has a very bulbous base and narrow ring, very

low down which forms a distinct free rim around the base. There are usually also one or two belted rings immediately above the bulb. The spore print is white.

HABITAT AND SEASON

The panther cap is very uncommon, growing with both coniferous and deciduous trees. The season is midsummer to late autumn.

ABOVE *Beech woods on limestone soils are the favourite habitat of the panther cap although it will grow under conifers as well.*

RIGHT *This picture illustrates the narrow hoop-like ring around the middle of the stem.*

Amanita phalloides

DEATH CAP

Each year the death cap accounts for most of the fatal poisonings caused by eating mushrooms. It looks fairly innocuous, smells pleasant and can be peeled. However, it is deadly and only one cap is needed to cause serious, possibly fatal, poisoning. The range of colours can be quite dramatic, making identification even more difficult. It can vary from a sickly green to dark brown to pale white, so great care must be taken over identification. If you go on a foray, make sure the foray leader finds one to point out to you. If it is dug out of the ground you will see the volval bag at the base very clearly. Take a good look and remember what you see, for a large specimen can kill several people.

IDENTIFICATION

The cap is 3–15 cm (1¼–6 in) across. It is quite round at first, flattening with age. It has a smooth, almost shiny surface. The colour is quite often greenish turning to a rather dirty brown, but beware, in wet weather the cap can become quite light. The stem is 5–12.5 cm (2–5 in) and white. The gills are free and quite crowded; white at first, mature specimens may have an almost flesh-coloured tinge. The flesh is white with a yellow tinge by the cap, and it smells quite sweet. The volval sac or bag is quite pronounced. The spore print is white.

HABITAT AND SEASON

Widespread in mixed deciduous woodland, particularly in association with oak. The season is early summer to quite late autumn.

The death cap deserves its name, it is the most deadly fungus known to

RIGHT *The caps often have a slightly radially streaked or fibrous appearance.*

mankind and years of research have not produced any antidote to the poison. Many have tried and some people have been saved by having their blood screened through charcoal, once the hospital had identified it as *Amanita* poisoning. The symptoms of poisoning take between 10 and 24 hours to become apparent, but during that time the poison has been attacking the liver and the kidneys. The first signs of poisoning are prolonged sickness and diarrhoea with severe abdominal pains; this is often followed by a period of apparent recovery when all seems well. However, death from liver and kidney failure will occur within a few days. There is a rare form of *A. phalloides* which is *A. phalloides* var. *alba*. Apart from being pure white throughout, which makes it look deceptively like an innocent mushroom, the features by which you will identify it are exactly the same and it is just as deadly.

ABOVE *The volva at the stem base may be completely hidden under the leaf litter, as seen here – beware!*

LEFT *Always carefully clear away around the stem base to expose the remains of a volva.*

Amanita virosa

Destroying Angel

Like many *Amanitas*, the destroying angel grows from a volval bag. It is deadly poisonous and well deserves its name, being white and fatal. The symptoms of the poison are the same as for *Amanita phalloides*.

IDENTIFICATION

The cap is 5–15 cm (2–6 in) across, bell-shaped at first, it becomes very irregular when open. It is pure white. The stem is 9–12 cm (3½–4¾ in) and grows from a fairly large volval bag that is not regular at the base, but can clearly be seen with the fungus growing from it. There is a white ring which is very fragile and often incomplete. The gills are pure white. The flesh is white and the smell is slightly sickly. The spore print is white.

HABITAT AND SEASON

Grows in mixed deciduous woodland and is happily not as common as the death cap. The season is usually midsummer to autumn. If you are on a foray, this is another mushroom that you should ask the foray leader to point out to you, for once seen you will be unlikely to forget it.

RIGHT *The cap of this species often has a distinct hump or blunt point at the centre.*

Clitocybe dealbata

BELOW *This shows the rather frosted appearance of the white caps and the slightly decurrent gills.*

Do not be fooled by this innocent-looking little mushroom, it is severely toxic. It often grows in just the places that many edible mushrooms grow.

IDENTIFICATION

The cap is 2–5 cm (¾–2 in) across, flat with a depression slightly inrolled and fluted round the edge. It is off-white in colour. The stem is 2–3 cm (¾–1¼ in) and whitish. The gills are quite crowded and run part way down the stem. They are almost cream in colour. The flesh is white and has a mealy smell. The spore print is white.

HABITAT AND SEASON

Grows in lawns, pasturelands and old meadows, often in troops or rings. It can be also be found in open woodland. The season is summer to late autumn and it is quite common.

Clitocybe rivulosa

BELOW *The* Clitocybe rivulosa *mushrooms are usually a silky greyish-white, as here.*

Another innocent-looking, but severely toxic mushroom that can easily be confused with the edible fairy ring champignon, *Marasmius oreades*. Both grow in rings, in similar situations and at much the same time of the year. Indeed it is not uncommon for rings of each species to grow within a few metres of each other. So take care. It would probably be a good idea to seek out live examples of both before you start picking the fairy ring champignon.

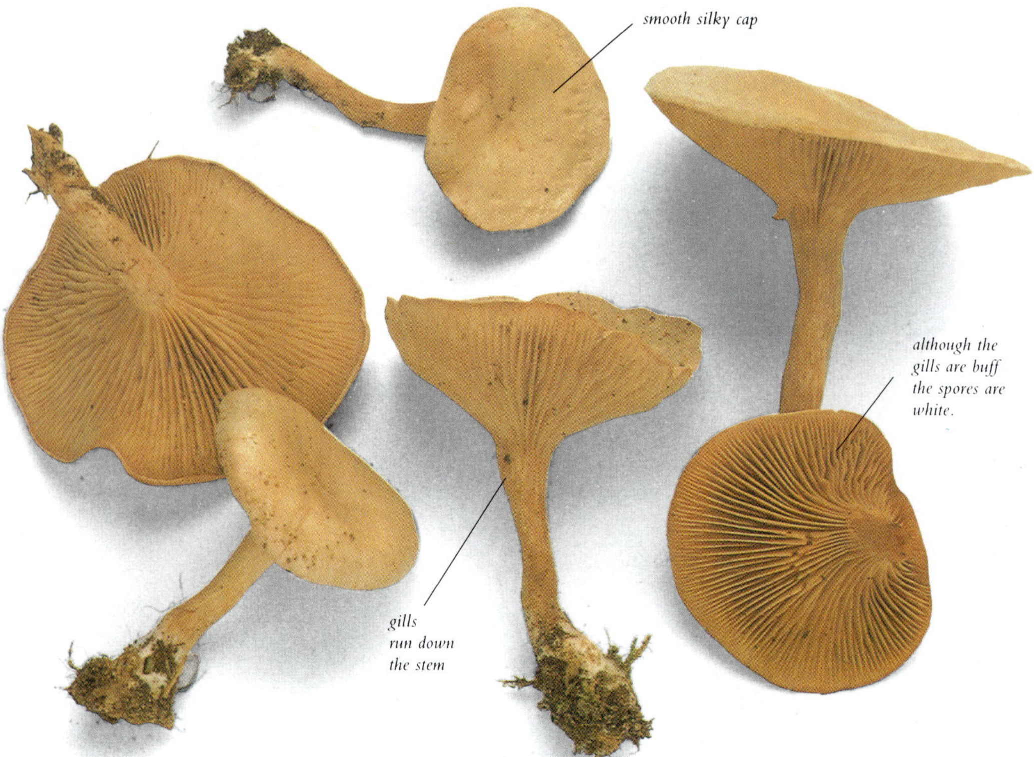

HABITAT AND SEASON

In troops or rings in sandy soil amongst grass, beside paths and roads. The season is late summer to late autumn and it is very common.

BELOW *These caps are rather waterlogged and so appear browner than normal. Usually they are a silky greyish-white.*

IDENTIFICATION

The cap is 2–5 cm (¾–2 in) across; cup-shaped at first, it soon flattens out with a small depression in the centre. The margin remains slightly rolled. It is grey and concentric rings are visible. The stem is 2–4 cm (¾–1½ in) and a similar colour to the cap. The crowded, grey gills run part way down the stem. The flesh is dirty white to grey. The closeness of the gills and the colour and shape of the cap are important ways to distinguish this mushroom from the fairy ring champignon. The spore print is white.

Coprinus atramentarius
COMMON INK CAP

The common ink cap is not poisonous in itself, but if eaten in conjunction with alcohol, it can cause alarming symptoms, such as nausea, palpitations and stomach cramps. For this reason it has been used over the years in attempts to cure alcoholics. The ink cap gets its name from the fact that it was used many years ago by monks to produce an exceptionally fine drawing ink, made by boiling the collapsed inky caps with a little water and a hint of cloves. The difference between the common ink cap and the shaggy ink cap is quite marked, but it is important that you recognize this one for it would be a catastrophe to make a mistake at a dinner party at which you were serving alcohol. Young specimens of the magpie fungus, *Coprinus picaceus*, could be confused with the common ink cap. Although not as common as this, it grows in fairly large quantities in the late summer to autumn. It is best avoided because although not poisonous it can cause nausea and vomiting in some people.

IDENTIFICATION
The cap is 2–4 cm (¾–1½ in) across, white and bell-shaped. Light grey to greyish-brown in colour, with veil remnants often attached to the cap. The stem is 7–17 cm (2¾–6¾ in) and white. The gills are crowded, white at first, they change from brown to a dark inky mass. The smell is not distinctive. The spore print is brown.

HABITAT AND SEASON
The common ink cap grows in tufts, often in association with buried wood. The season is from spring to late autumn and they are very common, often growing in large troops.

LEFT *This is one of the most common species in towns, gardens and woodlands everywhere, often associated with dead or buried wood.*

Galerina autumnalis

DEADLY GALERINA

This fungus is deadly poisonous and must be avoided. The poisoning is very similar to the effects of the *Amanita* family.

IDENTIFICATION

The cap is 2.5–7 cm (1–2¾ in) across. It is convex at first, becoming flat with a slight dome at the centre. It is a dark brown fading to a light buff with age, and when moist is quite sticky and shiny. The hollow stem is 2–10 cm (¾–4 in) and fairly bulbous at the base. There are slight brownish to blackish markings at the base of the stem, and the mycelial threads are clearly visible at the bottom. There is a veil that breaks fairly easily and is quite small. The gills are attached and quite close, yellowish in colour, becoming redder with age. The flesh is off-white. The deadly galerina has no distinct smell. The spore print is dull orange-brown.

HABITAT AND SEASON

The deadly galerina tends to live on well-decayed coniferous or deciduous wood, often in quite large troops. Its season is from late spring to autumn. The deadly galerina is not known in Europe, but quite common in North America. The very similar *G. marginata*, however, is quite common in Britain and is equally deadly.

ABOVE *Note the brownish-yellow gills which distinguish this from edible species such as the honey fungus.*

Hygrophoropsis aurantiaca
False Chanterelle

Although not poisonous in the way that agaric and amanita mushrooms are, the false chanterelle is known to cause gastro-intestinal problems.

IDENTIFICATION
The cap is 2–8 cm (3/4–3 in) across, flat at first with a slightly inrolled margin, it becomes more funnel-shaped with age. In large specimens the cap is more fluted and looks much more like a chanterelle. However, the false chanterelle's cap is orange rather than the yellow of the true chanterelle. The gills are dark orange, close and run down the stem. The spore print is white.

ABOVE AND RIGHT *The false chanterelle is very common under both pines and birch trees, and the cap becomes funnel-shaped with age.*

HABITAT AND SEASON
Grows in coniferous woodland and on heathland. It is very common and often grows in troops close to chanterelles. The season is from summer to late autumn.

Hypholoma fasciculare

Sulphur Tuft

This is a very common mushroom and grows all the year round, even in the winter. It is not deadly poisonous, but definitely should be avoided. It could be confused with other fungi, such as honey fungus *Armillaria mellea*, and brick cap, *Hypholoma sublateritium*, that are extremely good to eat, so take care with your identification.

IDENTIFICATION

The cap is 2–9 cm (¾–3½ in) across and is convex. The remains of the yellow veil often adhere to the margin. The cap itself is bright yellow with a dark orange centre. The stem is 4–10 cm (1½–4 in), curved and a similar colour to the cap. The gills start bright yellow, but turn dark sulphur-green then brown with age. The flesh is bright yellow, becoming brownish near the base of the stem. It has quite a mushroomy smell. The spore print is purple-black.

HABITAT AND SEASON

This occurs in dense clusters on the rotting timber and stumps of deciduous and coniferous trees. It grows throughout the year.

BELOW *One of the most common fungi everywhere on dead or dying wood, the sulphur tuft grows in large clumps.*

Inocybe patouillardii

Red-staining Inocybe

The red-staining inocybe is severely toxic and therefore must not be eaten. Many of the others in this family are poisonous, if not as deadly as this one, therefore it is best to avoid all the inocybes.

IDENTIFICATION

The cap is 3–10 cm (1¼–4 in) across, slightly conical and uneven. The margins are often cracked, giving the typical appearance of an inocybe. Cream-coloured, the cap has red-staining fibres. The stem is 3–10 cm (1¼–4 in), fairly thick and slightly bulbous at the base. The gills are quite pink at first, like those of a mushroom, and then darken to a light brown colour. The flesh is white and has no particular smell. The spore print is dull brown.

HABITAT AND SEASON

Grows along paths in mixed woodland on chalky soils, especially those with beech and, less often, chestnut. The season is spring to late autumn.

RIGHT *The white fibrous cap and stem, with blood red stains when bruised, are very distinctive. The red-staining inocybe likes open woodlands on chalky soils.*

Lactarius pubescens

BELOW *The cap should be pale pinkish-white, if the caps are deep pink you may have* Lactarius torminosus.

Lactarius pubescens is a member of the large milk cap family. It is important to be able to identify this mushroom for not only is it a strong emetic but it can be confused with the edible saffron milk cap (*Lactarius deliciosus*). The woolly edges of *Lactarius pubescens* are an important feature of identification.

IDENTIFICATION

The cap is 4–10 cm (1½–4 in) across, convex and slightly depressed with the margin markedly inrolled and woolly at the edge. It is often quite pale to rose pink; but this tends to fade in direct sunlight. The stem is 3–6 cm (1¼–2½ in) and a palish pink. The gills are crowded, light pink and tend to darken with age. They run down the stem. The flesh is quite thick and whitish, but can have a pinkish tinge. There is no particular smell. Equally common and shaggy is *L. torminosus*, a brighter pink and equally upsetting if eaten.

HABITAT AND SEASON

This mushroom tends to grow fairly widely but often near birch trees on fairly poor or sandy soil. The season is from late summer through to quite late autumn.

Paxillus involutus

Brown Roll-rim

ABOVE *A mature cap with margin unrolled.*

The brown roll-rim is a very common mushroom. It is also severely toxic. It can have a boletus-like shape, which makes matters worse, some boletus species being, of course, edible. The toxins have yet to be identified, but their effect is somewhat similar to leukaemia.

IDENTIFICATION

The cap size is 5–15 cm (2–6 in) across. It is quite flat when young, becoming convex and somewhat funnel-shaped with age. It gets its name from its clearly inrolled rim and mid- to red-brown colour. The cap is slippery when moist and shiny when dry. The stem is up to 7.5 cm (3 in) and similar in colour to the cap. The narrow, crowded gills are yellow turning brown to red-brown when bruised. The gills run down the stem. The spore print is sienna.

HABITAT AND SEASON

The brown roll-rim grows beside paths in broad-leaved woodland, especially with birch, and on quite acid heathland. It has a long growing season from summer to late autumn.

ABOVE *This is an immature cap with tightly rolled cap margin.*

Russula emetica

The Sickener

There are at least 150 different species of *Russula*, making it one of the largest groups of fungi. Some, such as the charcoal burner, are edible, but many are highly poisonous. The sickener and the very similar looking beechwood sickener, *Russula mairei*, did not get their names without good reason. It is really best to leave this family very well alone.

IDENTIFICATION
The cap is 3–10 cm (1¼–4 in) across and is quite cup-shaped, later flattening with a shallow central depression. The cap is a brightish red, but sometimes has faded white areas. When peeled, it shows red-coloured flesh underneath. The white stem is 4–9 cm (1½–3½ in). The gills are creamy, darkening slightly with age. The flesh is thin and fragile and can be quite sticky. It is white except under the cap. The smell is sweet and fruity. The spore print is whitish.

BELOW *The sickener is found under pines, especially in wet areas.*

HABITAT AND SEASON
Grows almost exclusively under pines. The season is summer to late autumn and it is very common. As its name suggests, the beechwood sickener, which has a similar season, grows almost exclusively under beech trees.

Cooking with Mushrooms

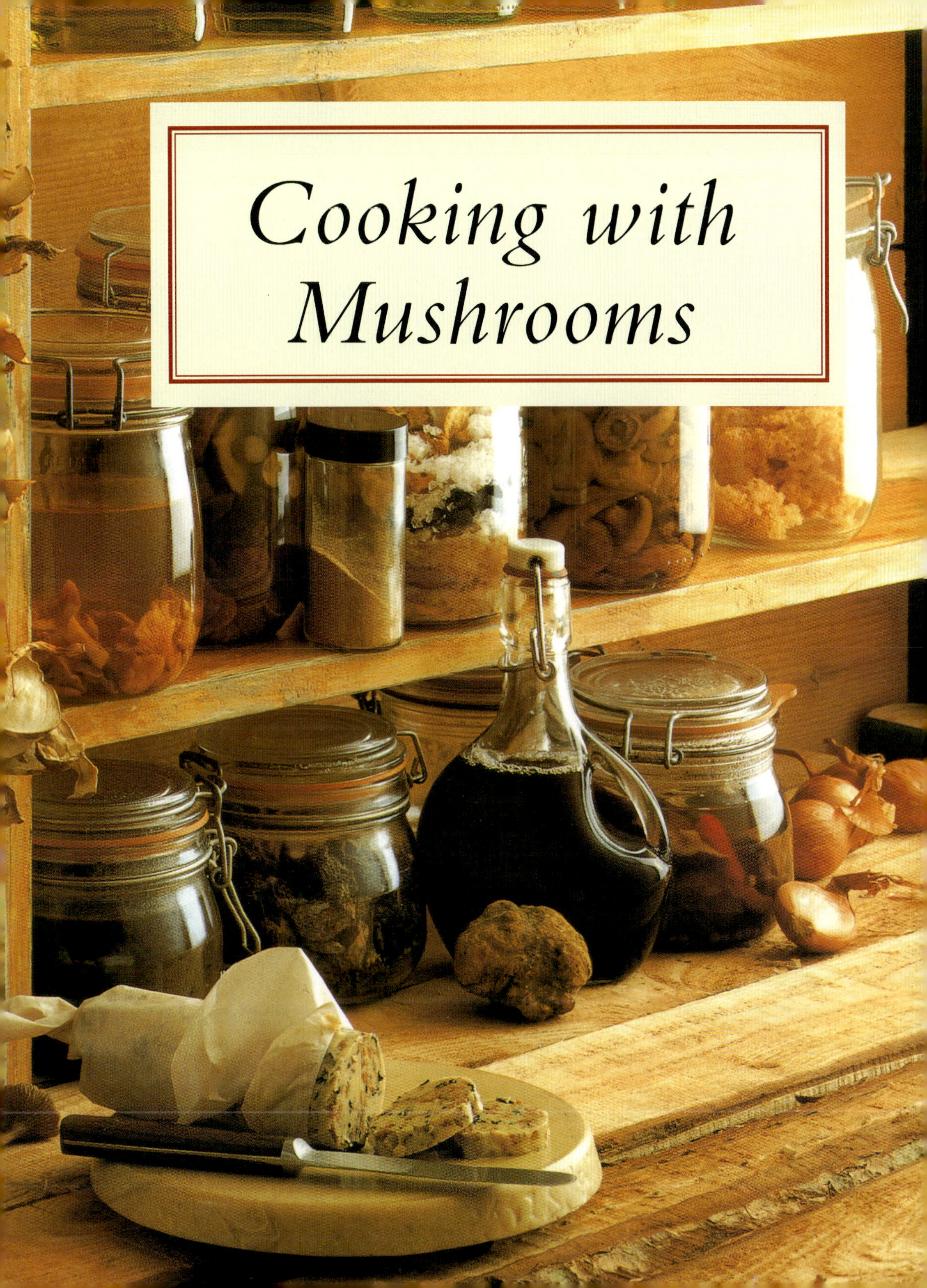

Introduction

From the cook's point of view, wild mushrooms are an irresistible source of flavour, texture and aroma. The recipes in this book explore the qualities of over thirty types of edible mushrooms and will show you how best to cook and enjoy them.

The passions associated with picking mushrooms are easily aroused when we realize how many good mushrooms there are growing freely in our woods and fields. Coupled with the excitement of picking mushrooms in the wild is the risk of handling poisonous varieties, such as the death cap *Amanita phalloides*, panther cap *Amanita pantherina*, yellow stainer *Agaricus xanthodermus* and destroying angel *Amanita virosa*. These often deadly poisonous mushrooms can easily be mistaken for the common and edible field mushroom *Agaricus campestris*. For your own safety, never touch a mushroom you cannot identify. When possible, accompany someone who knows which mushrooms are safe, and remember, if in doubt, don't touch them.

There are over a thousand varieties of mushroom known to be edible. The mushrooms which are best to eat are a question of taste, but it is generally agreed that the finest include the cep *Boletus edulis*, bay boletus *Boletus badius*, morel *Morchella esculenta*, chanterelle *Cantharellus cibarius* and chicken of the woods, *Laetiporus sulphureus*. These mushrooms fetch a high price at market and are sold mainly to the restaurant trade. Occasionally you may find them for sale in specialist food stores. Most precious of all is the fresh truffle which is found mainly in northern Italy and southern parts of France. Black and white truffles are found beneath the soil in mature woodland and are prized for their mysterious scent which, it is said, imitates the pheromone that cause pigs to mate.

The scent of wild mushrooms in damp woodland is enough to get most people on their knees scratching through the undergrowth. You may not be lucky enough to find a truffle, but there are many fine mushrooms to find and a home-cooked breakfast is a welcome return for the hungry mushroom picker. Even if you've only managed to find a few mushrooms, they will go a long way to flavour a plate of scrambled eggs. Parsley, thyme and fennel-scented chervil bring out their flavour as will a splash of sherry. Later in the day, wild mushrooms are ideal cooked in warming soups and broths. More delicate mushrooms are better suited to light broths.

Poultry and game taste good with mushroom flavours, either roasted, braised or sautéed. When cooking free-range chicken, try the delicate richness of the chanterelle, saffron milk-cap *Lactarius deliciosus*, hedgehog fungus *Hydnum repandum* and St George's mushroom *Calocybe gambosa*. Guinea fowl and pheasant carry the robust flavour of the fresh or dried cep, bay boletus, parasol mushroom and blewit. Wild duck mirrors the smoky richness of the morel and is good served with a glass of Madeira. Chicken of the woods has such a convincing taste, texture and appearance that it can be used as a substitute for chicken in chicken recipes.

Beef is a perfect match for the open field, horse and parasol mushroom. Cooked slowly with red wine, onions and a good stock, they are the making of a fine beef stew, rich and round with a luscious mushroom gravy. The delicate quality of lamb allies with the apricot sweetness of the chanterelle and saffron milk-cap. Pork belongs in a slow pot with a sauce of Jeruselem artichokes, horn of plenty *Craterellus cornucopiodes* and a purée of green olives.

The flavour of wild mushrooms is most effective with other wild foods. The sea is perhaps the most bountiful source of wild food, both fish and shellfish. Providing they are fresh (and in some cases alive), fish and shellfish are ideal ingredients to accompany a selection of wild mushrooms. When you have chosen the finest ingredients, simplicity is the best course of action, with particular care given to the preparation of sauces and garnishes. As a rule, if the fish has a delicate flavour, select a sweeter, subtle-tasting mushroom. Flat fish, such as sole, plaice and turbot suit closed field varieties with a little parsley, lemon and thyme. Stronger oily fish such as salmon, tuna and trout benefit from the assertive quality of the cep, bay boletus, shiitake, and blewit.

Wild mushrooms have been valued for centuries as an alternative to meat; a delight for those who know how and where to pick them. Meat has always been expensive at market and mushrooms have long been used make it go further. Presently, with eating habits veering away from meat for health reasons, vegetarians are discovering again the value of wild mushrooms for their first rate flavour, texture and goodness. Mushrooms contain essential minerals potassium, magnesium and iron. They are high in niacin and contain other B group vitamins. Mushrooms consist of 2–8% protein and contain around 35 calories per 100 g (4 oz). A section of this book has purely vegetarian recipes, while many recipes in the breakfast and starter sections will also appeal.

Good Edible Mushrooms

Amanita caesarea
Caesar's mushroom

Armillaria mellea
Honey fungus

Boletus edulis
Cep

Cantharellus cibarius
Chanterelle

Agaricus campestris and *bisporus*
Field mushroom

Boletus badius
Bay boletus

Calocybe gambosa
St George's mushroom

The assessment and value of edible mushrooms is open to opinion. Apart from the principle of putting delicate mushrooms with subtle foods and not putting mushrooms that stain black in creamy sauces, there are no rules to follow. Below is a brief and personal assessment of good edible mushrooms.

Agaricus campestris and *bisporus*
Field Mushroom
Open and closed field mushrooms provide a well-known flavour to everyday cooking. Take care when picking not to confuse this common mushroom with the poisonous yellow stainer *Agaricus xanthodermus*, destroying angel *Amanita virosa* and spring amanita *Amanita verna*.

Amanita caesarea
Caesar's Mushroom
The Caesar's mushroom is valued for its sweet chestnut quality. It has a russet orange to yellow glow. It is not found in Britain. Young specimens are best eaten raw in salads.

Armillaria mellea
Honey Fungus or Boot-lace Fungus
This fungus has a strong, often astringent, smell. It is edible only after blanching in water which must be discarded. However, after blanching, honey fungus softens and loses much of its appeal. It is an acquired taste.

Boletus badius
Bay Boletus
The bay boletus shares many qualities with the cep. Young specimens are particularly good and offer a lingering richness to be enjoyed raw in salads or cooked simply to respect their flavour.

Boletus edulis
Cep or Penny Bun
The cep is considered best when small and tight. Good specimens are heavy for their size and have an almost leafy, richness when eaten raw. Larger ceps are best cooked in butter with a few herbs. Another bolete which is popular and looks like the cep is *Boletus pruinatus*.

Calocybe gambosa
St George's Mushroom
The St George's mushroom has a rich meaty scent and a nutty flavour when cooked. They are good eaten raw or with a touch of garlic and a few chives in an olive oil dressing.

Cantharellus cibarius
Chanterelle
The intensely orange trumpet shape of the chanterelle has an appealing scent of dried apricots with a hint of

Coprinus comatus
Shaggy ink cap

Craterellus cornucopiodes
Horn of plenty

Hydnum repandum
Hedgehog fungus

Flammulina velutipes
Enokitake

Cantharellus infundibuliformis
Winter Chanterelle

Laccaria amethystea
Amethyst deceiver

Lactarius deliciosus
Saffron milk-cap

citrus. Chanterelle are best tossed in nut brown butter, although their colour and flavour remain true even after slow cooking. It is essential to avoid the false chanterelle *Hygrophoropsis aurantiaca* which can cause alarming hallucinations.

Cantharellus infundibuliformis
Winter Chanterelle
This mushroom has a rich mossy scent that combines well with other mushrooms. After trimming at the base, the winter chanterelle is best used whole.

Coprinus comatus
Shaggy Ink Cap or Lawyer's Wig
The shaggy ink cap has a delicate flavour not unlike the field mushroom. Pick young specimens that have yet to blacken and deteriorate around the fringe. Use in smooth soups and sauces. Do not use the common ink cap *Coprinus atramentarius*; this causes a violent reaction when consumed with alcohol.

Craterellus cornucopiodes
Horn of Plenty or Trompette des Morts
The horn of plenty has a sweet earthy richness that goes a long way to flavour soups, stews and casseroles. Its jet black appearance does not bleed, even after lengthy cooking.

Flammulina velutipes
Enokitake
These long-stemmed pinhead mushrooms are grown commercially on the stumps of the enoki or Chinese hackberry tree. They have a delicate flavour reminiscent of white pepper and lemon. Serve them raw or cooked in a light broth. Enokitake are available in Oriental grocers.

Hydnum repandum
Hedgehog Fungus or Pied de Mouton
Young hedgehog fungus has a peppery watercress quality that is appreciated raw in salads. Mature specimens can be bitter and are best cooked with sweet butter and herbs.

Laccaria amethystea
Amethyst Deceiver
These distinctive grape coloured mushrooms have a subtle, gentle flavour, but provide colour and interest when put with paler mushrooms.

Lactarius deliciosus
Saffron Milk-cap
The saffron milk-cap is prized for its saffron orange colour and firm texture. It has little flavour. Mature specimens often harbour insect larvae in the stem and centre cap, so take care when selecting.

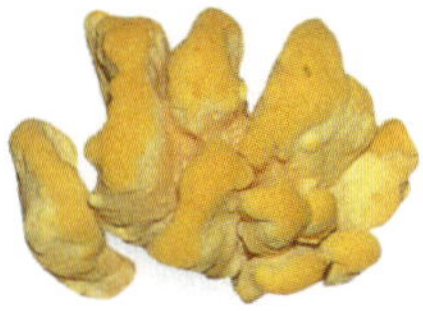

Laetiporus sulphureus
Chicken of the woods

Leccinum versipelle
Orange birch bolete

Marasmius oreades
Fairy ring champignon

Langermannia gigantea
Giant puffball

Macrolepiota procera
Parasol mushroom

Lentinus edodes
Shiitake

Lepista nuda
Wood blewit

Lepista saeva
Field blewit

Morchella esculenta and *elata*
Morels

Laetiporus sulphureus

Chicken of the Woods or Sulphur Polypore

Chicken of the woods has an intriguing flavour and texture of roast chicken. When fresh, moist and fragrant, the fungus can be used to replace chicken in many recipes.

Langermannia gigantea

Giant Puffball

When sliced open, the young giant puffball has a gentle meaty rich aroma similar in some ways to the cep. Older specimens discolour yellow when cut and should not be eaten.

Leccinum versipelle

Orange Birch Bolete

An attractive mushroom with a freckled mud-spattered stem. It has a tawny orange cap which fades with age. It softens when cooked and provides a good texture for soups and casseroles.

Lentinus edodes

Shiitake

Shiitake are grown commercially in the Far East on logs that are taken from the oak related *shii* tree. They have a robust beefy sweetness that remains even after lengthy cooking.

Lepista nuda (syn. *Tricholoma nuda*) and *Lepista saeva*

The Wood and Field Blewit

Both field and wood blewits have an assertive pine-rich perfume, that belongs with the pronounced flavour of game, toasted nuts and cheeses.

Macrolepiota procera

Parasol Mushroom

This handsome mushroom stands proudly on a tough inedible stem. Its cap offers a gamey rich flavour which strengthens when mature. Parasol mushrooms are best sautéed in butter with a few fresh herbs.

Marasmius oreades

Fairy Ring Champignon

One of the first mushrooms to appear in spring, the fairy ring champignon tastes just as good as it looks. Fresh and dried, this common mushroom has an oaky scent which is best cooked simply in sweet butter. Great care should be taken not to confuse the fairy ring champignon with the deadly poisonous *Clitocybe rivulosa*.

Morchella esculenta, vulgaris and *elata*

Morels

The morels are the most exciting springtime fungi. Both fresh and dried morels are prized for their tobacco-rich scent of sulphur and oak. This curious scent combines especially well with eggs, beef and game. A splash of Madeira will promote their flavour.

Pleurotus ostreatus
Oyster mushroom

Pleurotus citrinopileatus
Yellow oyster mushroom

Suillus luteus
Slippery jack

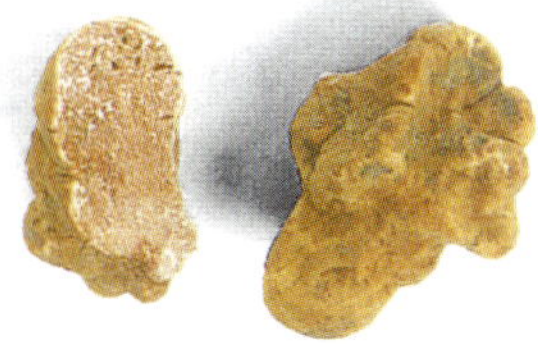

Tuber magnatum
White truffle

Russula cyanoxantha
Charcoal burner

Sparassis crispa
Cauliflower fungus

Tuber aestivum
Summer truffle

Pleurotus citrinopileatus

Yellow Oyster Mushroom

This pretty mushroom is designed by the mushroom cultivator to capture our attention in the supermarket. However, it tastes of very little and its colour disappears when cooked.

Pleurotus ostreatus

Oyster Mushroom

Both wild and cultivated oyster mushrooms have little flavour or aroma. Young specimens are best and provide good bulk when combining with stronger flavoured mushrooms.

Russula cyanoxantha

Charcoal Burner

The charcoal burner is an excellent mushroom to eat. However, it is a member of a very large genus and identification within the group can be very difficult. Correct identification is essential.

Sparassis crispa

Cauliflower Fungus

The cauliflower fungus is known more for its texture than its flavour. When raw and dried it has a curious scent of latex and ammonia which goes after brief cooking. The crisp texture of cauliflower fungus is appreciated when combined with other mushrooms.

Suillus luteus (syn. *Boletus luteus*)

Slippery Jack Pine Bolete or Sticky Bun

The slippery jack, so named because of its gluten covered cap, tends to absorb moisture in wet weather. When cooked, it softens to provide a basis for smooth soups and sauces.

Tuber aestivum

Summer Truffle

Less intensely flavoured than the white truffle, this warty black variety has a more delicate aroma associated with oak woodlands rather than the farm. More robust in texture than its white counterpart, the summer truffle should be pared before slicing raw. Truffles benefit from a few drops of truffle oil added towards the end of cooking.

Tuber magnatum

Piedmont or White Truffle

This rare and expensive tuber is found in very limited areas, mostly in northern Italy. It has a strong and curious aroma connected with the intensity of a pig sty! To touch, the white truffle has the fragility of firm fresh yeast. Unfortunately highly trained dogs or pigs are needed to find it. If you are fortunate enough to come by a white truffle, scrub it clean and shave over plainly cooked food. The flavour of the white truffle goes if it is cooked.

Drying Mushrooms

The process of drying mushrooms intensifies individual flavours and aromas. The cep develops a prolonged beefy rich aroma with a chamois leather sweetness. The bay boletus have a more pronounced sweetness and a less complex aroma. The morel develops a sulphur-rich, beefy, almost smoky quality, while fairy rings have a gentle sweetness. The cauliflower fungus has a strong latex vinegar smell which disappears with cooking. The saffron milk-cap and chanterelle have a fruity richness and the horn of plenty has a dark sweet woodland flavour.

When fully dried, mushrooms will keep through the winter in air-tight jars, providing a useful and nutritious source of flavour for soups, stews and casseroles.

1 To make sure the mushrooms are free from infestation, wipe them with a damp cloth, but avoid washing and cut away damaged parts. Slice the mushrooms thinly. When drying chanterelles, remove the stems of small specimens as they tend to toughen.

2 Lay the mushrooms on a basket tray, or baking sheet lined with several layers of newspaper and a final layer of baking parchment. Put in a warm and well-ventilated place for two days. For fast drying, preheat a fan oven to 80°C/150°F/Gas low, keep the door ajar and dry the mushrooms for 2 hours. If you have a small quantity of mushrooms, consider drying them on a needle and thread.

3 *(Right)* When mushrooms are completely dry, place each variety in an air-tight jar, label and store in a dark place. If mushrooms are not fully dry before storing, moulds will grow and spoil your work.

Mushroom Powder

The intense flavour of dried mushrooms can be used in powder form to enliven winter soups, stews and curries. The curry-scented milk-cap, *Lactarius camphoratus*, offers a pungent reminder of fenugreek and should always be used sparingly. The aniseed toadstool, *Clitocybe odora* is another powerful substitute for spices and can be used in sweet and savoury cooking. Other mushrooms suitable for powdering include many of the boletes and field and horse mushrooms.

1 Wipe clean the inside of a coffee grinder with a dry cloth. Put in the well-dried mushrooms and reduce to a fine powder.

2 Transfer to an air-tight jar, label and keep in a dark place. Use sparingly.

To Reconstitute Dried Mushrooms

To bring dried mushrooms back to life, they need to be soaked in warm water for 20 minutes. Boiling water will make them tough. The water used to soak dried mushrooms should be saved and added to stocks.

1 Place the mushrooms in a bowl. Cover with warm water and leave for 20 minutes.

Salt Preserving

Salt preserving is an age-old method of keeping mushrooms, and is still used in countries of the former Soviet Union. The method eliminates bacterial growth by packing mushrooms with layers of salt. The salt draws out the moisture in the mushrooms, forming a brine. Before using, the mushrooms need to be soaked in plenty of cold water to reduce saltiness. After soaking, salt preserved mushrooms can be added to braised meats such as beef, pork and tripe.

Suitable mushrooms for salting include: hedgehog fungus, oyster mushroom, bay boletus, winter chanterelle, saffron milk-cap, field and wood blewit.

The proportion of salt to mushrooms is 3–1.

1 *(Right)* Wipe the mushrooms clean with a damp cloth, trim and ensure that they are free from grit and infestation. Slice the mushrooms thickly with a stainless steel knife. Place a layer of rock or sea salt in the bottom of a covered glass or stoneware jar, layer with mushrooms. Alternate with more salt and mushrooms until full.

2 After 3–4 hours, you will find the volume of mushrooms will drop as the salt draws out their moisture. At this stage additional layers of salt and mushrooms can be added. Salted mushrooms will keep safely in a cool place for up to 12 months.

Freezing Mushrooms

To preserve mushrooms quickly and effectively, consider freezing them. Firmer varieties are best, such as shiitake, blewits, horn of plenty, chanterelle, closed field and horse mushrooms. To thaw, take Antonio Carluccio's advice and immerse briefly in boiling water before using.

1 Bring a saucepan of salted water to the boil and line a tray with greaseproof paper. Ensure mushrooms are free from grit and infestation then trim and slice thickly if large. Drop the mushrooms into the boiling water and simmer for 1 minute.

2 Drain well and open freeze for 30–40 minutes on a paper-lined tray. When frozen, turn loosely into plastic bags, label and return to the freezer for up to 6 months.

Preserving Mushrooms in Butter

Capturing the flavour and aroma of wild mushrooms in butter is a favourite method of preserving. The finest *Boletus, edulis, badius* and *pruinatus*, retain their qualities best of all when softened and combined with unsalted butter. If you are lucky enough to chance upon a few fresh truffles, these also keep well, peeled, chopped and concealed raw in butter. Other mushrooms that keep well in butter include the morel, chanterelle, saffron milk-cap and Caesar's mushroom. Wild mushroom butter is delicious melted over simply cooked meat or fish. It is also good over pasta, or with soups, sauces and gravies.

450 g / 1 lb mushrooms

175 g / 6 oz / 3/4 cup unsalted butter

15 g / 1/2 oz fresh black or white truffle, peeled and chopped (optional), or 3 drops truffle oil (optional)

1 Ensure the mushrooms are free from grit and infestation. Trim, slice and chop. Melt 50 g / 2 oz of the butter in a large non-stick frying pan. Add the mushrooms and soften over a gentle heat to reduce volume, then simmer in their own juices for 2–3 minutes. Cool.

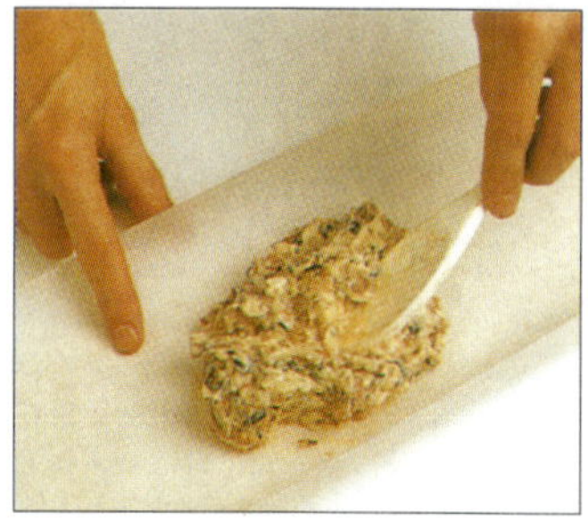

2 Combine the cooked mushrooms and truffles, or oil if you are using this instead, with the remaining butter and spoon the mixture onto a square of greaseproof paper.

3 *(Right)* Roll into a cigar shape, twist each end and label. Refrigerate for up to 10 days or freeze for up to 8 weeks.

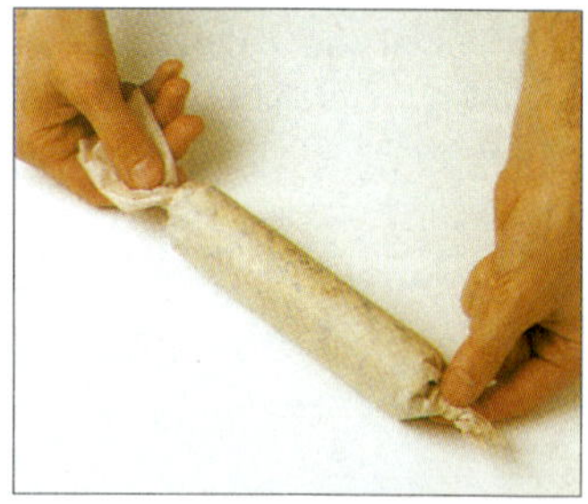

Duxelle

Duxelle is a preparation known to classical French cooking. It consists of finely chopped mushrooms and shallots cooked in butter, wine and herbs, and forms the basis for many well-known soups, sauces, stuffings, gratins and fillings. The name, according to Larousse, derives from a small town in the north east of France called Uxel. The preparation may be credited to La Varenne who cooked for the household of the Marquis d'Uxelles in the 17th century. Duxelle can be made from wild or cultivated mushrooms and refrigerated or frozen in ice cube portions for 10 days or 8 weeks respectively.

50 g / 2 oz / 4 tbsp unsalted butter

2 shallots, chopped

450 g / 1 lb wild and/or cultivated mushrooms, trimmed and finely chopped

1 sprig thyme, chopped

50 ml / 3 1/2 tbsp white wine or sherry

celery salt

freshly ground black pepper

1 Melt the butter in a large non-stick frying pan over a gentle heat, add the shallots and fry for 2–3 minutes to soften without browning.

2 *(Right)* Add the mushrooms, thyme and wine and simmer so that the mushroom juices run, then increase the heat to boil off moisture. When quite dry, season with celery salt and pepper, if using straight away. Otherwise, cool and refrigerate or freeze.

Mushroom Purée

Mushroom purée takes Duxelle a stage further and reduces it to a fine purée. Mushroom purée is used mainly for the enrichment of soups, and sauces, although a spoonful works wonders in a casserole of beef or game. As with the Duxelle, mushroom purée freezes conveniently in ice cube portions.

1 Prepare the Duxelle as shown in the previous recipe. Spoon into a food processor and blend until smooth.

2 Allow to cool, transfer into an airtight jar and refrigerate for up to 10 days or freeze for up to 8 weeks.

Mushroom Extract

The finest edible mushrooms are best preserved whole or sliced. More common although less elegant species such as the field, horse and parasol mushroom lend their flavour and colour to a dark extract. It is very important to ensure mushrooms are properly identified before using. An incorrectly identified mushroom put among the others can cause fatal illness. Shaggy ink caps are worth putting in, as are any overgrown boletus mushrooms providing they are free from infestation and are in good condition. Any deterioration can cause the extract to ferment at a later date. The flavour extracted from the mushrooms will keep in the refrigerater in a screw-top jar or bottle for 8–10 weeks. Use readily to enliven and enrich winter soups, stews and game dishes.

450 g / 1 lb field, horse and parasol mushrooms, shaggy ink caps, orange birch bolete, slippery jack and/or winter chanterelles, trimmed and roughly chopped

300 ml / 1/2 pint / 1 1/4 cups water

200 ml / 7 fl oz / 7/8 cup red wine

60 ml / 4 tbsp dark soy sauce

5 ml / 1 tsp salt

1 sprig thyme

1 Place all of the ingredients in a large stainless steel pan. Bring to the boil and simmer uncovered for 45 minutes.

2 Strain the mushrooms through a nylon sieve, pressing as much liquid as possible back into the pan. Return the extract to the boil and reduce until half its volume.

3 *(Left)* Sterilize a preserving jar or bottle by immersing in boiling water for a few minutes. Drain. Fill the jar or bottle with the mushroom liquid, cover and allow to cool. When cool, label and store in the refrigerator. Mushroom extract can be frozen and used in ice cube portions.

Pickled Mushrooms

The principle of pickling eliminates the chance of bacterial growth by immersing mushrooms in vinegar. Vinegar can be flavoured and diluted to lessen the sharp taste. In this recipe shiitake mushrooms take on an oriental flavour, although other firm mushrooms and spices can also be used. It is best to dress pickled mushrooms with olive oil when serving, to restore balance. Serve as an appetizer or buffet style lunch item.

250 ml / 8 fl oz / 1 cup white wine vinegar

150 ml / 1/4 pint / 2/3 cup water

5 ml / 1 tsp salt

1 red chilli

10 ml / 2 tsp coriander seeds

10 ml / 2 tsp szechuan pepper or anise-pepper

250 g / 9 oz shiitake mushrooms, halved if large

1 Bring the wine vinegar and water to a simmer in a stainless steel pan. Add the salt, chilli, coriander, szechuan pepper or anise-pepper and mushrooms and cook for 10 minutes.

2 Sterilize a 500 ml / 18 fl oz / 2 1/4 cup preserving jar by immersing in boiling water. Drain until dry.

Transfer mushrooms and liquid to the jar, seal, label and leave for at least 10 days before trying.

Chanterelle Vodka

If you manage to find a few chanterelles on your mushroom foray, consider steeping them in vodka. Vodka has a neutral flavour and allows the apricot quality of the chanterelles to shine. Chill thoroughly before serving as an aperitif.

375 ml / 13 fl oz / 1 1/2 cups vodka

75 g / 3 oz young chanterelle mushrooms, trimmed

1 Place the chanterelle mushrooms in a clean preserving bottle or jar.

2 Pour in the vodka, cover and leave at room temperature. Chanterelle vodka is ready when the mushrooms have dropped to the bottom.

Preserving Mushrooms in Oil

The method of preserving in oil is ideally suited to good quality firm mushrooms. The process can seem expensive, but the oil used takes on a delicious mushroom flavour which can then be used to make special salad dressings.

250 ml / 8 fl oz / 1 cup white wine vinegar

150 ml / ¼ pint / ⅔ cup water

5 ml / 1 tsp salt

1 sprig thyme

½ bay leaf

1 red chilli (optional)

450 g / 1 lb assorted wild mushrooms, including young bay boletus, chanterelles, saffron milk-caps and horn of plenty, trimmed and halved if large

400 ml / 14 fl oz / 1⅔ cups virgin olive oil

1 Bring the vinegar and water to a simmer in a stainless steel pan. Add the salt, thyme, bay leaf and chilli if using, and infuse for 15 minutes.

2 Add the mushrooms and simmer for 10 minutes. Sterilize a 500 ml / 18 fl oz / 2¼ cup preserving jar in boiling water. Drain until dry. Lift the cooked mushrooms out of the liquid, drain well and place in the jar.

3 (*Right*) Cover the mushrooms with oil, close the lid and label. Mushrooms in oil will keep in a cool place for up to 12 months.

Spiced Mushrooms in Alcohol

Winter chanterelles and oyster mushrooms combine with caraway seeds, lemon and chilli to make this unusual and warming infusion.

75 g / 3 oz winter chanterelle and oyster mushrooms

5 ml / 1 tsp caraway seeds

1 lemon

1 red chilli

375 ml / 13 fl oz / 1½ cups vodka

1 Place the mushrooms, caraway seeds, lemon and chilli in a clean preserving jar or bottle.

2 Pour in the vodka and leave for 2–3 weeks until the mushrooms no longer float. Chill thoroughly and serve as an aperitif.

Wild Mushroom Breakfasts

Kedgeree of Oyster and Chanterelle Mushrooms

Providing breakfast for an army of late risers is quite a challenge. This delicious kedgeree combines the rich woodland flavour of oyster and chanterelle mushrooms with eggs, rice and a touch of curry seasoning.

SERVES 4

250 g / 1 oz / 2 tbsp butter

1 medium onion, chopped

400 g / 14 oz / 2 cups long grain rice

1 small carrot, cut into julienne strips

900 ml / 1½ pints / 3¾ cups chicken or vegetable stock, boiling

1 pinch saffron

225 g / 8 oz oyster and chanterelle mushrooms, trimmed and halved

115 g / 4 oz floury potato, peeled and grated

450 ml / ¾ pint / 1⅞ cup milk

½ chicken or vegetable stock cube

2.5 ml / ½ tsp curry paste

30 ml / 2 tbsp double cream

4 eggs

60 ml / 4 tbsp chopped fresh parsley

1 Melt the butter in a large saucepan, add the onion and fry it gently without letting it colour.

2 Turn half of the softened onion into a medium-sized saucepan. Put the rice, carrot and stock in the large pan, add a pinch of saffron, stir and simmer, uncovered for 15 minutes. Remove the pan from the heat, cover and stand for 5 minutes.

3 Add the oyster and chanterelle mushrooms to the pan with the onion and cook gently for a few minutes to soften. Add the grated potato, milk, stock cube and curry paste and simmer for 15 minutes until the potatoes have thickened the liquid.

4 Place the eggs in a pan of boiling water and cook for 10 minutes. Run them under cold water to cool, then peel and cut into quarters.

5 Fork the rice onto a warmed serving platter. Spoon the mushrooms and sauce into the centre and garnish with the egg quarters and chopped parsley.

Cook's Tip
Kedgeree will keep warm without spoiling in a covered dish for up to 2 hours.

Cook's Tip
There are many varieties of long grain rice available. The least flavoursome are the non-stick brands that have been part cooked to remove a proportion of starch. The notion that every grain of rice must be separate undermines the nature and flavour of good rice.

Apricot Chanterelle Breakfast Muffins

Smell a chanterelle and you will be reminded of apricots. To encourage this association, here is a recipe for chanterelle muffins flecked with dried apricots and topped with pine nuts.

MAKES 12

- *6 oz / 175 g / 1⅓ cups self-raising flour*
- *2.5 ml / ½ tsp fine salt*
- *15 g / ½ oz / 1 tbsp chopped dried apricots*
- *75 g / 3 oz chanterelle mushrooms, trimmed and chopped*
- *5 ml / 1 tsp chopped fresh thyme*
- *1 egg*
- *50 g / 2 oz / 4 tbsp butter, melted*
- *120 ml / 4 fl oz / ½ cup milk*
- *25 g / 1 oz / ¼ cup pine nuts or flaked almonds*
- *melted butter or oil for brushing*

1 Preheat the oven to 220°C / 425°F / Gas 7. Grease 12 deep muffin tins with butter or oil and set aside.

2 Sift the flour and salt into a bowl. Add the apricots, mushrooms, thyme, egg, butter and milk, then stir to make a thick batter.

3 Spoon the mixture into the prepared muffin tins, so they are about two-thirds full. Sprinkle with pine nuts and bake near the top of the oven for 12 minutes until golden, then turn out and serve warm. They are particularly delicious cut in half and spread with butter.

Egg, Bacon and Wild Mushroom Fry Up

When you arrive home tired and hungry after a mushroom hunt, a quick fry up will restore your strength and vitality.

SERVES 4

- *75 g / 3 oz / 6 tbsp goose fat or lard*
- *350 g / 12 oz unsmoked bacon*
- *450 g / 1 lb pork sausages*
- *350 g / 12 oz assorted wild mushrooms* PALE: *oyster and parasol mushrooms, hedgehog fungus, St George's and Caesar's mushrooms, ceps, chanterelles and chicken of the woods.* DARK: *field mushrooms, shaggy ink caps, horn of plenty and orange birch bolete*
- *1 sprig thyme*
- *salt and freshly ground black pepper*
- *4 eggs*
- *4 slices brown or white bread*
- *butter for spreading*

1 Preheat the oven to 150°C / 300°F / Gas 2. Melt 25 g / 1 oz / 2 tbsp of the fat in a large non-stick frying pan and fry the bacon and sausages. Transfer to a serving dish and keep warm.

2 Clean the mushrooms and slice if necessary. Add to the pan and toss in the fat, then add the thyme and cook for 2–3 minutes. Season with salt and pepper, transfer to a bowl, cover and keep warm.

Cook's Tip

If using both pale and dark mushrooms, it is best to cook them separately, one batch at a time.

3 Melt the remaining fat in the pan and fry the eggs. Meanwhile toast the bread and spread with butter. Serve with the bacon, sausages and mushrooms.

Toasted Brioche, Scrambled Eggs and Morels

Morels have a rich flavour that combines well with other rich ingredients such as eggs, cream and Madeira. This simple breakfast dish can be made with fresh or dried morels.

SERVES 4

150 g / 5 oz fresh morels or 15 g / ½ oz / ¼ cup dried

25 g / 1 oz / 2 tbsp unsalted butter

1 shallot, finely chopped

60 ml / 4 tbsp Madeira

60 ml / 4 tbsp crème fraîche

4 small brioches

For the Scrambled Eggs

8 eggs

60 ml / 4 tbsp crème fraîche

salt and freshly ground black pepper

25 g / 1 oz / 2 tbsp unsalted butter

1 If using dried morels, cover with warm water, soak for 20 minutes and drain. Melt the butter in a non-stick frying pan and gently fry the shallot until it is softened. Add the morels and cook briefly, then stir in the Madeira and cook until the liquid is syrupy. Stir in the crème fraîche and simmer briefly. Season, transfer to a bowl and keep warm.

2 Remove the tops from the brioches and toast under a moderate grill.

Cook's Tip
Madeira provides an oaky hazelnut flavour to balance stronger-tasting mushrooms. You can also use a medium dry sherry.

3 Break the eggs into a jug, add the crème fraîche, season and beat with a fork. Melt the butter in the frying pan, pour in the eggs and cook, stirring gently but continuously until the eggs are slightly cooked. Remove from the heat: the eggs will continue cooking in their own heat.

4 Spoon the scrambled eggs over the brioches and top with morels.

English Muffins with a Florentine Parasol Topping

The parasol mushroom is prized for its delicate texture and rich flavour. The stems of open specimens are tough but both the stem and cap of closed parasols are delicious with a creamy spinach topping.

SERVES 4

400 g / 14 oz young leaf spinach, stems removed

salt and freshly ground black pepper

350 g / 12 oz parasol mushroom caps

50 g / 2 oz / 4 tbsp unsalted butter, plus extra for spreading

½ garlic clove, crushed

5 sprigs thyme

200 ml / 7 fl oz / 1 cup crème fraîche

pinch of grated nutmeg

4 English muffins, split

1 Rinse the spinach in plenty of water, then place in a large saucepan with a pinch of salt. Cover and cook over a steady heat for 6–8 minutes, then drain in a colander, pressing out as much water as you can with the back of a spoon. Chop the spinach finely.

2 Chop the mushrooms very finely, then melt the butter in a frying pan and add the mushrooms together with the garlic and 1 sprig of thyme. Cook for 3–4 minutes then add the chopped spinach and 150 ml / ¼ pint / ⅔ cup of the crème fraîche. Season with salt, pepper and a pinch of nutmeg. Toast the muffins, split and spread lightly with butter.

3 Spoon the spinach mixture onto the muffins, top with the remaining crème fraîche and garnish with thyme.

Cook's Tip
If using frozen chopped spinach, allow half the weight of fresh spinach, thaw thoroughly and squeeze dry.

Parsley, Lemon and Garlic Mushrooms on Toast

Field mushrooms have a long and happy relationship with garlic, but too often the intense flavour of the garlic takes over. With respect for the mushroom, the garlic in this recipe is tempered with a generous amount of fresh parsley and a touch of lemon.

SERVES 4

25 g / 1 oz / 2 tbsp unsalted butter, plus extra for spreading
1 medium onion, chopped
1 garlic clove, crushed
350 g / 12 oz assorted wild mushrooms such as field mushrooms, shaggy ink caps and orange birch bolete, trimmed and sliced
45 ml / 3 tbsp dry sherry
75 ml / 5 tbsp chopped fresh parsley
15 ml / 1 tbsp lemon juice
salt and freshly ground black pepper
4 slices brown or white bread

1 Melt the butter in a large non-stick frying pan and gently fry the onion without letting it colour.

2 Add the garlic and mushrooms, cover and cook for 3–5 minutes. Add the sherry, cook uncovered to evaporate the liquid.

3 Stir in the parsley and lemon juice, and then season to taste with salt and pepper.

4 Toast the bread and spread with butter. Spoon the mushrooms over the toast and serve.

Cook's Tip
Flat-leaved parsley has a good flavour and keeps well in the refrigerator. To keep it fresh, stand in a jar of water and cover with a plastic bag.

Hedgehog Mushroom Pancakes with Chive Butter

Pancakes are an ideal base for subtly flavoured wild mushrooms. Pale varieties, in particular the peppery hedgehog fungus, work best and should be softened in butter before they are added to the batter.

MAKES 12 PANCAKES

50 g / 2 oz / 4 tbsp unsalted butter

250 g / 9 oz hedgehog fungus, trimmed and chopped

50 g / 2 oz hedgehog fungus, sliced

For the Pancakes

175 g / 6 oz / 1½ cups self-raising flour

salt and white pepper

2 eggs

200 ml / 7 fl oz / ⅞ cup milk

For the Chive Butter

15 g / ½ oz / scant 1 cup fresh finely snipped chives

115 g / 4 oz / ½ cup unsalted butter, softened

5 ml / 1 tsp lemon juice

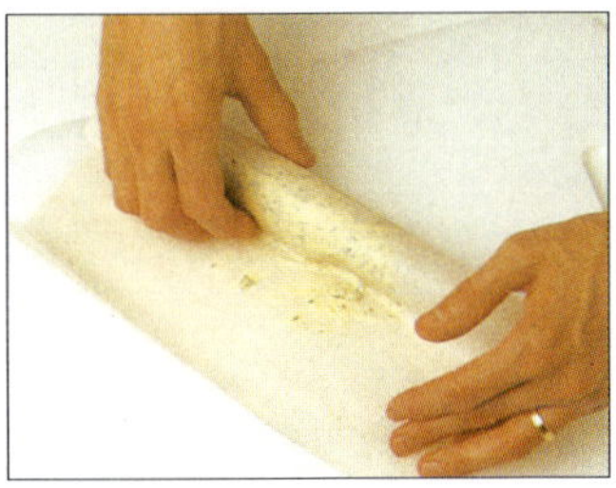

1 First make the chive butter. Stir the snipped chives and lemon juice into the butter. Turn out onto a 25cm / 10 in square of greaseproof paper and form into a sausage. Roll up, twist both ends of the paper and chill for about an hour until it is firm.

2 Melt half of the butter in a large pan, add the chopped mushrooms and fry over a moderate heat, allowing the mushrooms to soften and the moisture to evaporate. Spread onto a tray and cool. Cook the sliced mushrooms in a knob of butter and set aside.

3 To make the batter, sift the flour and salt and pepper into a bowl. Beat the eggs into the milk and add to the flour, stirring to make a thick batter. Add the chopped mushrooms.

4 Heat the remaining butter in the pan, arrange five slices of mushrooms at a time in the bottom, then spoon the batter into 5 cm / 2 in circles over each mushroom. When bubbles appear on the surface, turn the pancakes over and cook for a further 10–15 seconds. Serve warm with slices of chive butter.

Miso Shiitake Breakfast Soup

This Japanese breakfast soup provides a light nourishing start to the day. It is flavoured with shiitake mushrooms and a soy protein called miso. Both are available from health food stores.

SERVES 4

3 shiitake mushrooms, fresh or dried

1.2 litres / 2 pints / 5 cups water, boiling

45 ml / 3 tbsp light miso paste

115 g / 4 oz bean curd (tofu), cut into large dice

1 spring onion, green part only, sliced

1 If using dried mushrooms, soak in warm water for 20 minutes then drain. Slice the mushrooms thinly. Pour the boiling water into a saucepan. Stir in the miso, add the mushrooms and simmer for 5 minutes.

2 Divide the bean curd among four warmed soup bowls, ladle in the broth, scatter with sliced spring onion and serve.

Cook's Tip
Miso is a fermented soy bean paste that varies in strength and colour according to the maturity of the soy beans.

Home-baked Chanterelle Croissant

Chanterelle mushrooms will make a delicious filling and can be added to easy-bake croissants for an unusual and satisfying breakfast. The filling can be made well in advance and goes a long way.

SERVES 4

25 g / 1 oz / 2 tbsp unsalted butter

115 g / 4 oz fresh chanterelle mushrooms, trimmed and sliced, or 15 g / ½ oz / ¼ cup dried, soaked in warm water, drained and sliced

60 ml / 4 tbsp double cream

15 ml / 1 tbsp medium sherry or Madeira

salt and freshly ground black pepper

1 packet easy-bake croissants

1 egg, beaten

1 Preheat the oven as directed on the packet for the croissants. Melt the butter in a saucepan, add the chanterelles and fry gently for 3–4 minutes to soften without letting them colour. Add the cream and sherry, increase the heat and allow the moisture to evaporate. Season to taste and cool.

Cook's Tip
Other firm mushrooms can be used as a filling for the croissants. They might include ceps, bay boletus, winter chanterelles, morel, saffron milk-caps hedgehog fungus, field mushrooms, oyster and St George's mushrooms.

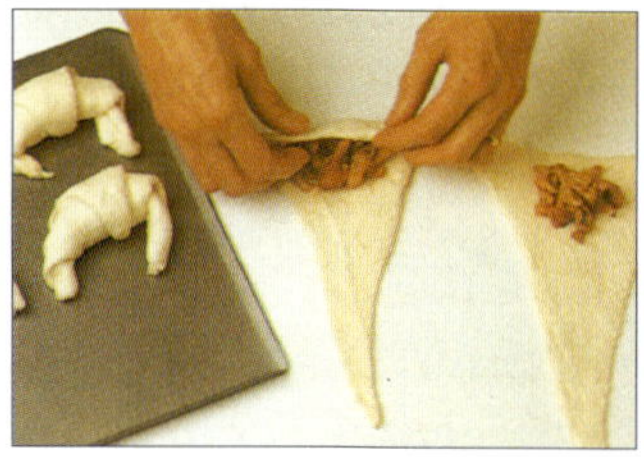

2 Lay the croissant dough shapes out on a floured surface. Place a spoonful of the mixture at the wide end of each triangle. Brush the pointed end of each triangle with beaten egg and roll up, enclosing the filling.

3 Arrange the croissants on a baking sheet, brush with a little more beaten egg and bake in the oven according to instructions on the packet. Serve warm.

Mushrooms in a Tarragon Cream Sauce

When your search for wild mushrooms yields only a few specimens and you have to provide breakfast for the proverbial five thousand, combine what you have with a few cultivated mushrooms – enhanced here in a creamy tarragon sauce.

SERVES 4

50 g / 2 oz / 4 tbsp unsalted butter, plus extra for spreading

2 shallots, finely chopped

50 g–225 g / 2–8 oz wild mushrooms such as St George's or Caesar's mushrooms, chanterelles, winter chanterelles, ceps, chicken of the woods, parasol mushrooms or hedgehog fungus, trimmed and sliced

350 g / 12 oz Paris mushrooms, trimmed and sliced

150 ml / ¼ pint / ⅔ cup double cream

45 ml / 3 tbsp chopped fresh tarragon

4 slices brown or white bread

1 Melt the butter in a large non-stick frying pan, add the shallots and fry over a gentle heat until they are soft, without letting them colour.

Cook's Tip
Almost any variety of mushrooms can be used in a cream sauce, but do avoid dark specimens which can turn the sauce grey.

2 Add your chosen mushrooms and cook over a moderate heat to soften. Add the cream and tarragon, increase the heat and cook until thick and creamy.

3 Toast the bread and spread with butter. Spoon over the mushroom mixture and serve at once.

Saffron Milk-caps with Parsley, Butter and Pine Nuts

Serving wild mushrooms on toast is a quick, easy way to appreciate their individual flavours. Butter-fried saffron milk-caps are good, served with a handful of chopped parsley and a scattering of toasted pine nuts.

SERVES 4

25 g / 1 oz / ¼ cup pine nuts

5 ml / 1 tsp vegetable oil

50 g / 2 oz / 4 tbsp unsalted butter, plus extra for spreading

1 shallot, finely chopped

350 g / 12 oz saffron milk-caps, trimmed and sliced

45 ml / 3 tbsp double cream

75 ml / 5 tbsp chopped fresh parsley

salt and freshly ground black pepper

4 slices brown or white bread

1 Fry the pine nuts in the oil, tilting the pan, and brown over a moderate heat. Set aside.

2 Soften the shallot in half the butter. Add the mushrooms and remaining butter and cook until soft. Stir in the cream and cook until thick. Stir in the parsley and season to taste.

3 Toast the bread and spread with butter. Spoon the mushroom mixture over the toast, scatter with toasted pine nuts and serve.

Cook's Tip
Saffron milk-caps have hollow stems which can harbour insect larvae. Be sure to avoid any that are infested.

Bacon, Egg and Chanterelle Sandwiches

When mid-morning hunger strikes, few mushroom hunters can resist a plate of egg and bacon sandwiches stuffed with chanterelles.

SERVES 4

350 g / 12 oz unsmoked bacon

50 g / 2 oz / 4 tbsp unsalted butter, plus extra for spreading

115 g / 4 oz chanterelle mushrooms, trimmed and halved

60 ml / 4 tbsp groundnut oil

4 eggs

4 large baps, split

salt and freshly ground black pepper

1 Place the bacon in a large non-stick frying pan and fry in its own fat until crisp. Transfer to a plate, cover and keep warm.

Cook's Tip

For best effect, let the aroma of frying bacon and mushrooms fill the breakfast room.

2 Melt 25 g / 1 oz / 2 tbsp of the butter in the pan, add the chanterelles and fry gently until soft without letting them colour. Transfer to a plate, cover and keep warm.

3 Melt the remaining butter, add the oil and heat to a moderate temperature. Break the eggs into the pan and fry as you like them, sunny side up or over easy.

4 Toast the baps, spread with butter, then layer with bacon, chanterelles and a fried egg. Season, top with the second half of the bap and serve.

Chicken of the Woods Cornbread with Bacon and Tomatoes

Savoury cornbread is a welcome sight at breakfast time and is really delicious with crispy grilled bacon and tomatoes.

SERVES 4

25 g / 1 oz / 2 tbsp butter

50 g / 2 oz chicken of the woods, trimmed and finely chopped

115 g / 4 oz / 1 cup plain flour

115 g / 4 oz / 3/4 cup fine cornmeal

10 ml / 2 tsp baking powder

2.5 ml / 1/2 tsp salt

2.5 ml / 1/2 tsp sugar

150 ml / 1/4 pint / 2/3 cup milk

2 eggs

75 g / 3 oz sweetcorn, canned or frozen

350 g / 12 oz unsmoked bacon

4 tomatoes, halved

salt and freshly ground black pepper

1 bunch watercress, to garnish

1 Preheat oven to 200°C / 400°F / Gas 6. Melt the butter in a frying pan, add the chicken of the woods and fry over a gentle heat for 5 minutes, then set aside to cool. Lightly oil a 900 ml / 1 1/2 pint / 3 3/4 cup loaf tin then line with greaseproof paper.

2 Sift the flour, cornmeal, baking powder, salt and sugar into a bowl. Add the milk, eggs, sweetcorn and mushrooms. Stir to make batter.

3 Preheat the grill to a moderate temperature. Meanwhile, turn the batter into the prepared tin and bake near the top of the oven for 25 minutes. Allow to cool slightly.

Cook's Tip

For individual shapes, spoon the cornbread mixture into greased muffin tins and bake for 10–12 minutes at 220°C/425°F/Gas 7.

4 Arrange the bacon and tomato halves on a tray or grill pan and season the tomatoes with salt and pepper. Grill until the bacon is golden, turning once.

5 Lift the cornbread out of the tin and cut into thick slices. Serve with the grilled bacon and tomatoes, garnished with watercress.

Champagne Truffle Breakfast

When you have something to celebrate, start the day with a stylish breakfast. Scrambled eggs with fresh truffles are a treat with toasted brioche and Champagne. For the best flavour, it is worth tracking down fresh black and white truffles. Preserved truffles offer little if any flavour and benefit from a drop or two of truffle oil.

SERVES 4

4 brioches

8 free-range eggs

60 ml / 4 tbsp crème fraîche

3 drops truffle oil (optional)

salt and freshly ground black pepper

1 fresh black truffle

25 g / 1 oz / 2 tbsp unsalted butter, plus extra for spreading

Champagne or Bucks Fizz, to serve

1 Preheat a moderate grill. Slice the buns, toast and keep warm.

2 Break the eggs into a jug, add the crème fraîche and truffle oil, if using, season and beat with a fork. Then slice half of the truffle finely into the egg mixture.

3 Melt the butter in the frying pan, pour in the eggs and with a flat wooden spoon stir the base of the pan until lightly scrambled.

4 Butter the toasted brioches and arrange on four plates.

5 Spoon the scrambled egg onto each slice of brioche and scatter with truffle shavings. Serve with Champagne or Bucks Fizz (Champagne and orange juice).

Cook's Tip
To ensure scrambled eggs are soft and creamy, they should be a little underdone and always cooked to order.

Cook's Tip
When using truffle oil, never be tempted to add more than a few drops. If too much of this precious oil is used its flavour will become bitter to taste.

Soups, Starters & Salads

Buckwheat Blinis with Mushroom Caviar

These little Russian pancakes are traditionally served with fish roe caviar and soured cream. The term caviar is also given to fine vegetable mixtures called ikry. This wild mushroom ikry caviar is popular in the autumn and has a silky rich texture.

SERVES 4

115 g / 4 oz / 1 cup strong white bread flour

50 g / 2 oz / 1/3 cup buckwheat flour

2.5 ml / 1/2 tsp salt

300 ml / 1/2 pint / 1 1/4 cups milk

5 ml / 1 tsp dried yeast

2 eggs, separated

For the Caviar

350 g / 12 oz mixed assorted wild mushrooms such as field mushrooms, orange birch bolete, bay boletus, oyster and St George's mushrooms

5 ml / 1 tsp celery salt

30 ml / 2 tbsp walnut oil

15 ml / 1 tbsp lemon juice

45 ml / 3 tbsp chopped fresh parsley

freshly ground black pepper

200 ml / 7 fl oz / scant 1 cup soured cream or crème fraîche

1 To make the caviar, trim and chop the mushrooms, then place them in a glass bowl, toss with the celery salt and cover with a weighted plate.

2 Leave the mushrooms for 2 hours until the juices have run out into the bottom of the bowl. Rinse the mushrooms thoroughly to remove the salt, drain and press out as much liquid as you can with the back of a spoon. Return them to the bowl and toss with walnut oil, lemon juice, parsley and a twist of pepper. Chill until ready to serve.

3 Sift the two flours together with the salt in a large mixing bowl. Warm the milk to approximately blood temperature. Add the yeast, stirring until dissolved, then pour into the flour, add the egg yolks and stir to make a smooth batter. Cover with a damp cloth and leave in a warm place.

4 Whisk the egg whites in a clean bowl until stiff then fold into the risen batter.

5 Heat an iron pan or griddle to a moderate temperature. Moisten with oil, then drop spoonfuls of the batter onto the surface. When bubbles rise to the surface, turn them over and cook briefly on the other side. Spoon on the soured cream, top with the mushroom caviar and serve.

Wild Mushroom Tapenade Toasts

Tapenade is a paste made from black olives, garlic, anchovies, capers, olive oil and lemon. A little goes a long way. Here it is spread on bread, toasted and topped with wild mushrooms and hard boiled eggs.

SERVES 4

350 g / 12 oz strongly flavoured wild mushrooms such as ceps, bay boletus, chicken of the woods, saffron milk-caps and chanterelles, trimmed and sliced

50 g / 2 oz / 4 tbsp unsalted butter

½ lemon

salt and freshly ground black pepper

4 small eggs

1 narrow French loaf, sliced

1 small bunch parsley, to garnish

For the Tapenade

150 g / 5 oz / 1 cup Kalamata olives, stoned

1 garlic clove, peeled

5 anchovy fillets

15 ml / 1 tbsp capers

30 ml / 2 tbsp olive oil

juice of ½ lemon

Cook's Tip

If you don't have time to make your own tapenade, buy it ready prepared from delicatessens and specialist food stores.

1 Fry the mushrooms gently in butter for 6–8 minutes to soften, then increase heat to evaporate the juices. Add a generous squeeze of lemon and season to taste. Transfer to a bowl, cover and keep warm.

2 To make the tapenade, place all the tapenade ingredients in a food processor and blend to a fine paste. Boil the eggs for 10 minutes.

3 Preheat a grill to a moderate temperature. Meanwhile cool the eggs under running cold water, peel and cut into quarters. Then slice the French loaf diagonally and toast on one side. Spread the other side thinly with tapenade and toast again.

4 Heap each piece of toast with wild mushrooms, top with a section of hard boiled egg and garnish with a sprig of parsley.

French Onion and Morel Soup

French onion soup is appreciated for its light beefy taste. Few improvements can be made to this classic soup, but a few richly scented morel mushrooms will impart a worthwhile flavour.

SERVES 4

- *50 g / 2 oz / 4 tbsp unsalted butter, plus extra for spreading*
- *15 ml / 1 tbsp vegetable oil*
- *3 medium onions, sliced*
- *900 ml / 1½ pints / 3¾ cups beef stock*
- *75 ml / 5 tbsp Madeira or sherry*
- *8 medium dried morel mushrooms*
- *4 slices French bread*
- *75 g / 3 oz / 1 cup Gruyère, Beaufort or Fontina cheese, grated*
- *30 ml / 2 tbsp chopped fresh parsley*

1 Melt the butter and oil in a large frying pan, add the onions and cook for 10–15 minutes until the onions are a rich mahogany brown colour.

Cook's Tip
The flavour and richness of this soup will improve with keeping. Refrigerate for up to 5 days.

2 Transfer the browned onions to a large saucepan, cover with beef stock, add the Madeira and the morels, then simmer for 20 minutes.

3 Preheat the grill to a moderate temperature and toast the French bread on both sides. Spread one side with butter and heap with grated cheese. Ladle the soup into four flameproof bowls, float the cheesy toasts on top and grill until crisp and brown. Alternatively, grill the cheese-topped toast, place one slice in each warmed soup bowl and ladle the hot soup over. The toast will float to the surface. Scatter with chopped parsley and serve.

Cep Soup with Parsley Sippets

The lasting aroma of the cep mushroom is caught in this delicious soup.

SERVES 4

- *50 g / 2 oz / 4 tbsp unsalted butter*
- *2 medium onions, finely chopped*
- *1 garlic clove*
- *225 g / 8 oz fresh ceps or bay bolete, sliced, or 25 g / 1 oz / ½ cup dried*
- *75 ml / 5 tbsp dry white wine*
- *900 ml / 1½ pints / 3¾ cups boiling chicken stock*
- *115 g / 4 oz floury potatoes, peeled and diced*
- *1 sprig thyme*
- *15 ml / 1 tbsp lemon juice*
- *salt and freshly ground black pepper*

For the Sippets

- *3 slices day-old bread*
- *50 g / 2 oz / 4 tbsp butter*
- *45 ml / 3 tbsp finely chopped fresh parsley*

Cook's Tip
A variation on this soup can be made with the same quantity of dried saffron milk-caps or half the quantity of dried morel mushrooms.

1 Melt the butter in a large saucepan, add the onions and brown lightly. Add the garlic, ceps and wine. Add the stock, potatoes and thyme. Simmer gently for 45 minutes.

2 Liquidize the soup in just a few short bursts so that pieces of mushroom are left intact. Sharpen with lemon juice and season to taste.

3 To make the sippets, cut the bread into 2.5 cm / 1 in fingers. Melt the butter in a large frying pan, toss in the fingers of bread and fry until golden. Add the parsley and combine. Ladle the soup into warmed soup bowls, strew with parsley sippets and serve.

Tortellini Chanterelle Broth

The savoury-sweet quality of chanterelle mushrooms combines well in a simple broth with spinach-and-ricotta-filled tortellini. Serve as a starter or light main course.

SERVES 4

350 g / 12 oz fresh spinach and ricotta tortellini, or 175 g / 6 oz dried

1.2 litres / 2 pints / 5 cups chicken stock

75 ml / 5 tbsp dry sherry

175 g / 6 oz fresh chanterelle mushrooms, trimmed and sliced, or 15 g / ½ oz / ¼ cup dried

chopped fresh parsley, to garnish

1 Cook the tortellini according to the packet instructions.

2 Bring the chicken stock to the boil, add the sherry and mushrooms and simmer for 10 minutes.

3 Strain the tortellini, add to the stock, ladle into four warmed soup bowls and garnish with the chopped parsley.

Cook's Tip

For a lighter version, replace the tortellini with 115 g / 4 oz / 2 cups dried vermicelli pasta.

Champignons de Paris à la Grècque

Cultivated mushrooms are often criticized by serious mushroom pickers for a lack of flavour, but the *champignon de Paris* or chestnut mushroom is an improvement on the ubiquitous button mushroom.

SERVES 4

45 ml / 3 tbsp olive oil

15 button onions, peeled

½ garlic clove, crushed

675 g / 1½ lb Paris mushrooms or closed field mushrooms, halved or quartered if large

300 ml / ½ pint / 1¼ cups chicken stock, boiling

75 ml / 5 tbsp white wine

10 ml / 2 tsp black peppercorns

20 ml / 4 tsp coriander seeds

1 sprig thyme

1 small bay leaf

salt and freshly ground black pepper, if necessary

15 ml / 1 tbsp wine vinegar

15 cherry tomatoes

1 Heat the olive oil in a large non-stick frying pan. Add the onions and brown gently over a low heat. Add the garlic and the mushrooms, stir and fry gently until the mushrooms soften and the juices begin to run. Transfer to a large saucepan.

2 Add the stock, wine, peppercorns, coriander seeds, thyme and bay leaf. Cover the surface with a round of greaseproof paper. Simmer for 15 minutes. Add the vinegar and season if required.

Cook's Tip

The flavour of these mushrooms will improve if kept refrigerated for up to a week. To peel button onions, cover with boiling water to soften their skins.

3 Cover the cherry tomatoes with boiling water to loosen their skins, peel and add to the onion and mushroom mixture. Allow to cool to room temperature and serve with a basket of open textured bread.

Salad of Fresh Ceps with a Parsley, Egg and Walnut Dressing

To capture the just picked flavour of a cep or bay boletus, consider this delicious salad enriched with an egg yolk and walnut oil dressing. Choose small ceps and bay boletus for a firm texture and a fine flavour.

SERVES 4

350 g / 12 oz fresh ceps or bay boletus

175 g / 6 oz mixed salad leaves, to include: bativia, young spinach and frisée

salt and freshly ground black pepper

50 g / 2 oz / ½ cup broken walnut pieces, toasted

50 g / 2 oz fresh Parmesan cheese

For the Dressing

2 egg yolks

2.5 ml / ½ tsp French mustard

75 ml / 5 tbsp groundnut oil

45 ml / 3 tbsp walnut oil

30 ml / 2 tbsp lemon juice

30 ml / 2 tbsp chopped fresh parsley

1 pinch caster sugar

Cook's Tip
For special occasions, 2–3 drops of truffle oil will impart a deep and mysterious flavour of the forests.

1 Place the egg yolks in a screw top jar with the mustard, groundnut and walnut oil, lemon juice, parsley and sugar. Shake well.

2 Slice the mushrooms thinly.

3 Place the mushrooms in a large salad bowl and combine with the dressing. Leave for 10–15 minutes for the flavours to mingle.

4 Wash and spin the salad leaves, then toss with the mushrooms.

5 Turn out onto four large plates, season well then scatter with toasted walnuts and shavings of Parmesan cheese.

Cook's Tip
The dressing for this salad uses raw egg yolks. Be sure to use only the freshest eggs from a reputable supplier. Expectant mothers, young children and the elderly are not advised to eat raw egg yolks. If this presents a problem the dressing can be made without the egg yolks.

Shaggy Ink Cap and Parasol Mushroom Soup

The shaggy ink cap forms the basis of this creamy soup and the parasol mushrooms provide additional flavour.

SERVES 4

50 g / 2 oz / 4 tbsp unsalted butter

4 shallots or 1 medium onion, chopped

225 g / 8 oz shaggy ink caps, closed specimens, trimmed and chopped

1 garlic clove, crushed

900 ml / 1½ pints / 3¾ cups chicken stock, boiling

175 g / 6 oz parasol mushrooms, caps and young stems, trimmed and sliced

60 ml / 4 tbsp double cream

30 ml / 2 tbsp lemon juice

salt and freshly ground black pepper

45 ml / 3 tbsp chopped fresh parsley

1 Melt half of the butter in a saucepan, add the shallots or onion and soften over a gentle heat.

2 Add the ink caps and garlic, and fry gently until the mushrooms soften and the juices begin to run.

3 Add the chicken stock, bring back to the boil and simmer for 15 minutes. Liquidize and return to the saucepan.

4 Melt the remaining butter in a non-stick frying pan, add the parasol mushrooms and fry to soften without letting them colour. Add to the saucepan and simmer for a minute.

5 Stir in the cream, sharpen with lemon juice, then season to taste. Ladle into four warmed soup bowls, scatter with parsley and serve with broken bread.

Cook's Tip

For best results, use closed ink caps that haven't started to blacken. Once they have begun to blacken they are quite safe to eat, but they will darken the colour of the soup.

An Artichoke Lover's Feast

Artichokes are a rich earthy vegetable which make a wonderful starter stuffed to the brim with a variety of cultivated and woodland mushrooms.

SERVES 4

4 large globe artichokes

1 lemon, sliced

25 g / 1 oz / 2 tbsp butter

2 shallots or 1 small onion, chopped

225 g / 8 oz assorted wild and cultivated mushrooms such as ceps, bay boletus, chanterelles, saffron milk-caps, oyster mushrooms, St George's, Caesar's and closed field mushrooms, trimmed and chopped

15 ml / 1 tbsp chopped fresh thyme

For the Hollandaise Sauce

175 g / 6 oz / ¾ cup unsalted butter

2 egg yolks

juice of ½ lemon

salt and freshly ground black pepper

1 Bring a large saucepan of salted water to the boil. With a serrated knife remove one third from the top of each artichoke. Pull off the outer leaves and discard. Break off the artichoke stems at the base, then trim about 5 mm / ¼ in from the base. To prevent the artichokes from darkening tie a slice of lemon to the base. Place in the boiling water and cook for 25 minutes.

2 To make the mushroom filling, fry the shallots gently in butter to soften without letting them colour. Add the mushrooms and thyme, cover and cook until the juices begin to run. Increase the heat and allow the juices to evaporate. Keep warm.

3 When the artichokes are cooked (a small knife inserted in the base will indicate whether it is tender) drain and cool under running water. Remove the lemon slices and drain the artichokes upside down. To create a central cavity, pull out the small leaves from the middle of each artichoke then scrape out the fibrous choke.

4 To make the sauce, melt the butter skimming off any surface scum. Pour into a jug leaving behind the milky residue. Place the egg yolks in a glass bowl over a saucepan of 2.5cm / 1 in simmering water. Add 2.5 ml / ½ tsp water to the egg yolks and whisk until thick and foamy. Remove from the heat, then add the butter in a thin stream, whisking all the time. Add the lemon juice and a little boiling water to thin the sauce. Season to taste.

5 Combine one third of the sauce with the mushroom mixture and fill each of the artichokes. Serve at room temperature with the extra sauce.

Spinach with Wild Mushroom Soufflé

Wild mushrooms combine especially well with eggs and spinach in this sensational soufflé. Almost any combination of mushrooms can be used for this recipe although the firmer varieties provide the best texture.

SERVES 4

225 g / 8 oz fresh spinach, washed, or 115 g / 4 oz frozen chopped spinach

50 g / 2 oz / 4 tbsp unsalted butter, plus extra for greasing

1 garlic clove, crushed

175 g / 6 oz assorted wild mushrooms such as ceps, bay boletus, saffron milk-caps, oyster, field and Caesar's mushrooms

200 ml / 7 fl oz / 1 cup milk

45 ml / 3 tbsp plain flour

6 eggs, separated

salt and freshly ground black pepper

pinch grated nutmeg

25 g / 1 oz / ⅛ cup freshly grated Parmesan cheese

Cook's Tip
The soufflé base can be prepared up to 12 hours in advance and reheated before the beaten egg whites are folded in.

1 Preheat the oven to 190°C / 375°F / Gas 5. Steam the spinach over a moderate heat for 3–4 minutes. Cool under running water, then drain. Press out as much liquid as you can with the back of a large spoon and chop finely. If using frozen spinach, defrost and squeeze dry in the same way.

2 Gently soften the garlic and mushrooms in butter. Turn up the heat and evaporate the juices. When dry, add the spinach and transfer to a bowl. Cover and keep warm.

3 Measure 45 ml / 3 tbsp of the milk into a basin. Bring the remainder to the boil. Stir the flour and egg yolks into the milk in the basin and blend well. Stir the boiling milk into the egg and flour mixture, return to the pan and simmer to thicken. Add the spinach mixture. Season to taste with salt, pepper and nutmeg.

4 Butter a 900 ml / 1½ pint / 3¾ cups soufflé dish, paying particular attention to the sides. Sprinkle with a little of the cheese. Set aside.

5 Whisk the egg whites until they hold their weight on the whisk. Bring the spinach mixture back to the boil. Stir in a spoonful of beaten egg white, then fold the mixture into the remaining egg white. Turn into the soufflé dish, spread level, scatter with the remaining cheese and bake in the oven for about 25 minutes until well risen and golden.

Alsatian Tart

Alsace is renowned for its abundance of wild mushrooms. This tart is good with a cool Alsatian wine.

SERVES 4

350 g / 12 oz shortcrust pastry, thawed if frozen

50 g / 2 oz / 4 tbsp unsalted butter

3 medium onions, halved and sliced

350 g / 12 oz assorted wild mushrooms such as ceps, bay boletus, morels, chanterelles, saffron milk-caps, oyster, field and Caesar's mushrooms

leaves of 1 sprig thyme, chopped

salt and freshly ground black pepper

pinch of grated nutmeg

50 ml / 3½ tbsp full-fat milk

50 ml / 3½ tbsp single cream

1 egg and 2 egg yolks

1 Preheat the oven to 190°C / 375°F / Gas 5 and lightly grease a 23 cm / 9 in loose bottomed flan tin with butter. Roll out the pastry on a lightly floured board and line the tin. Rest the pastry in the fridge for 1 hour.

Cook's Tip
To prepare ahead, the flan case can be part baked and the filling made in advance. Continue from step 3.

2 Place three squares of tissue paper in the flan case, fill with rice and bake blind for 25 minutes. Lift out the paper and rice and leave to cool.

3 Melt the butter in a frying pan, add the onions, cover and cook slowly for 20 minutes. Add the mushrooms and thyme, and continue cooking for a further 10 minutes. Season with salt, pepper and nutmeg.

4 Place the milk and cream in a jug and beat in the egg and egg yolks. Place the mushroom mixture in the flan case and then pour over the milk and egg mixture. Bake for 15–20 minutes until the centre is firm to the touch.

Stuffed Garlic Mushrooms with Prosciutto and Herbs

SERVES 4

- *1 medium onion, chopped*
- *75 g / 3 oz / 6 tbsp unsalted butter*
- *8 medium field mushrooms*
- *15 g / ½ oz / ¼ cup dried ceps, bay boletus or saffron milk-caps, soaked in warm water for 20 minutes*
- *1 garlic clove, crushed*
- *75 g / 3 oz / ¾ cup fresh breadcrumbs*
- *1 egg*
- *75 ml / 5 tbsp chopped fresh parsley*
- *15 ml / 1 tbsp chopped fresh thyme*
- *salt and freshly ground black pepper*
- *115 g / 4 oz prosciutto di Parma or San Daniele, thinly sliced*
- *fresh parsley, to garnish*

1 Preheat the oven to 190°C / 375 °F / Gas 5. Fry the onion gently in half the butter for 6–8 minutes until soft but not coloured. Meanwhile, break off the stems of the field mushrooms, setting the caps aside. Drain the dried mushrooms and chop these and the stems of the field mushrooms finely. Add to the onion together with the garlic and cook for a further 2–3 minutes.

Cook's Tip
Garlic mushrooms can be easily prepared in advance ready to go into the oven.

2 Transfer the mixture to a bowl, add the breadcrumbs, egg, herbs and seasoning. Melt the remaining butter in a small pan and generously brush over the mushroom caps. Arrange the mushrooms on a baking sheet and spoon in the filling. Bake in the oven for 20–25 minutes until well browned.

3 Top each with a strip of prosciutto, garnish with parsley and serve.

Mushroom Salad with Parma Ham

SERVES 4

- *40 g / 1½ oz / 3 tbsp unsalted butter*
- *450 g / 1 lb assorted wild and cultivated mushrooms such as chanterelles, ceps, bay boletus, Caesar's mushrooms, oyster, field and Paris mushrooms, trimmed and sliced*
- *60 ml / 4 tbsp Madeira or sherry*
- *juice of ½ lemon*
- *½ oak leaf lettuce*
- *½ frisée lettuce*
- *30 ml / 2 tbsp walnut oil*

For the Pancake Ribbons

- *30 g / 1 oz / 3 tbsp plain flour*
- *75 ml / 5 tbsp milk*
- *1 egg*
- *60 ml / 4 tbsp freshly grated Parmesan cheese*
- *60 ml / 4 tbsp chopped fresh herbs such as parsley, thyme, marjoram or chives*
- *salt and freshly ground black pepper*
- *175 g / 6 oz Parma ham, thickly sliced*

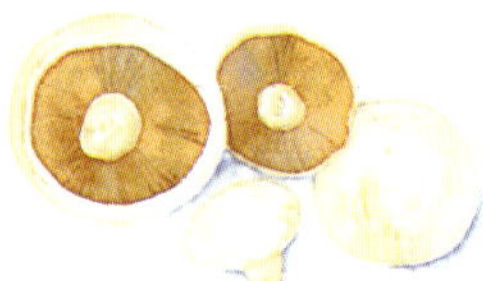

1 To make the pancakes, blend the flour and the milk. Beat in the egg, cheese, herbs and seasoning. Pour enough of the mixture into a frying pan to coat the bottom of it. When the batter has set, turn the pancake over and cook briefly on the other side.

2 Turn out and cool. Roll up the pancake and slice thinly to make 1 cm / ½ in ribbons. Cook the remaining batter in the same way and cut the ham into similar sized ribbons. Toss with the pancake ribbons.

3 Gently soften the mushrooms in the remaining butter for 6–8 minutes until the moisture has evaporated. Add the Madeira and lemon juice, and season to taste.

4 Toss the salad leaves in the oil and arrange on four plates. Place the ham and pancake ribbons in the centre, spoon on the mushrooms and serve.

Woodland Salsa Dip

This recipe makes good use of mushrooms that soften when cooked. Firmer-fleshed mushrooms can be added to provide texture and flavour.

SERVES 4

75 ml / 5 tbsp olive oil

1 medium onion, chopped

1 garlic clove, crushed

450 g / 1 lb aubergines, chopped

350 g / 12 oz shaggy ink caps, orange birch bolete and slippery jacks, trimmed and chopped

75 g / 3 oz chanterelles, charcoal burner or saffron milk caps, trimmed and chopped

45 ml / 3 tbsp chopped fresh parsley, chervil and chives

15 ml / 1 tbsp balsalmic vinegar

salt and freshly ground black pepper

For Dipping

sesame bread sticks, celery, carrot, baby sweetcorn, strips of toasted pitta bread

1 Heat 15 ml / 1 tbsp of the olive oil in a heavy saucepan over a moderate heat, add the onion and cook gently to soften without colouring.

2 Stir in the remaining oil, the garlic and aubergines, then cover and cook for 10 minutes. Add the mushrooms and cook uncovered for a further 15 minutes.

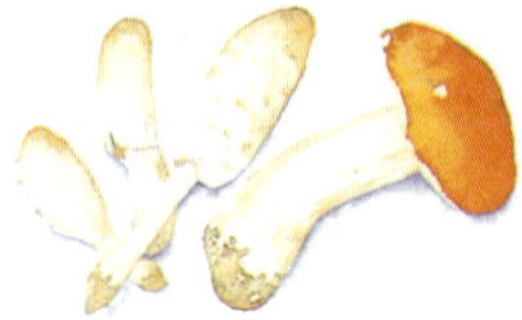

3 Stir in the herbs and vinegar and season to taste. Allow to cool and serve with bread sticks, pitta bread and raw vegetables.

Cook's Tip
Woodland salsa dip will keep in the fridge in a covered container for 10 days. Do not freeze it.

Spinach and Wild Mushroom Soup

SERVES 4

25 g / 1 oz / 2 tbsp unsalted butter

1 medium onion, chopped

350 g / 12 oz assorted wild and cultivated mushrooms such as ceps, bay boletus, orange birch bolete, shaggy ink caps, field, oyster and shiitake mushrooms, trimmed and chopped

1 garlic clove, crushed

10 ml / 2 tsp chopped fresh thyme or 5 ml / 1 tsp dried

1.2 litres / 2 pints / 5 cups boiling chicken or vegetable stock

75 g / 3 oz floury potato, finely chopped

400 g / 14 oz fresh spinach, trimmed, or 200 g / 7 oz frozen chopped spinach, defrosted and drained

salt and freshly ground black pepper

pinch of grated nutmeg

60 ml / 4 tbsp double or soured cream, to serve

Cook's Tip
If fresh wild mushrooms are unavailable, use 225 g / 8 oz cultivated field mushrooms with 10 g / ½ oz / ¼ cup dried ceps, bay boletus or saffron milk-caps.

1 Melt the butter in a large pan, add the onion and fry gently without colouring for 6–8 minutes. Add the mushrooms, garlic and herbs, cover and allow the moisture to run.

2 Add half of the stock, the potato and spinach. Bring back to the boil and simmer for 10 minutes.

3 Liquidize the soup and return to the saucepan. Add the remaining stock and season to taste with salt, pepper and a little nutmeg. Serve with a dollop of cream stirred into the soup.

Poultry & Game Dishes

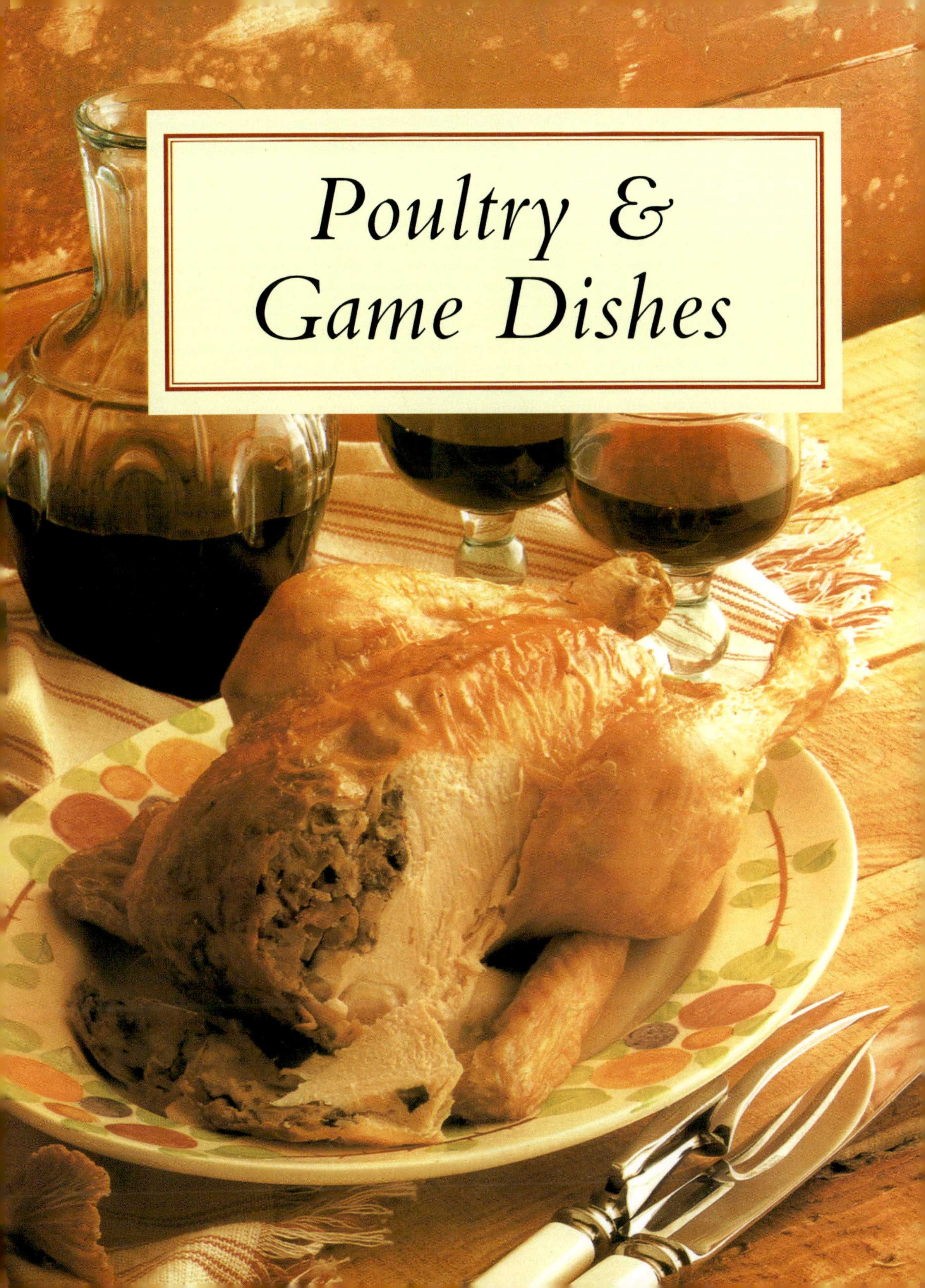

Mushroom Picker's Chicken Paella

A good paella is based on a few well chosen ingredients. Here, wild mushrooms combine with chicken and vegetables.

SERVES 4

45 ml / 3 tbsp olive oil

1 medium onion, chopped

1 small bulb fennel, sliced

225 g / 8 oz assorted wild and cultivated mushrooms such as ceps, bay boletus, chanterelles, saffron milk-caps, hedgehog fungus, St George's, Caesar's and oyster mushrooms, trimmed and sliced

1 garlic clove, crushed

3 free range chicken legs, chopped through the bone

350 g / 12 oz / 1⅔ cups short-grain Spanish or Italian rice

900 ml / 1½ pints / 3¾ cups chicken stock, boiling

1 pinch saffron strands or 1 sachet of saffron powder

1 sprig thyme

400 g / 14 oz can butter beans, drained

75 g / 3 oz / ¾ cup frozen peas

Cook's Tip
For a vegetarian mushroom paella, omit the chicken, replace the chicken stock with vegetable stock and if you can, include chicken of the woods in your choice of mushrooms.

1 Heat the olive oil in a 35 cm / 14 in paella pan or a large frying pan. Add the onion and fennel and fry over a gentle heat for 3–4 minutes.

2 Add the mushrooms and garlic, and cook until the juices begin to run, then increase the heat to evaporate the juices. Push the onion and mushrooms to one side. Add the chicken pieces and fry briefly.

3 Stir in the rice, add the stock, saffron, thyme, butter beans and peas. Bring to a simmer and then cook gently for 15 minutes without stirring.

4 Remove from the heat and cover the surface of the paella with a circle of greased greaseproof paper. Cover the paper with a clean tea towel and allow the paella to finish cooking in its own heat for about 5 minutes. Bring to the table, uncover and serve.

"Chicken" of the Woods Polenta with a Cauliflower Fungus Cream

This dish contains no chicken at all and will please both meat eaters and vegetarians alike. So convincing is the flavour and texture of chicken of the woods, that many people will find it difficult to believe that they're not actually eating chicken.

SERVES 4

450 g / 1 lb small new potatoes

1.3 litres / 2¼ pints / 5½ cups light vegetable stock, boiling

175 g / 6 oz young carrots, trimmed and peeled

175 g / 6 oz sugar snap peas

50 g / 2 oz / 4 tbsp unsalted butter

75 g / 3 oz Caesar's mushrooms or hedgehog fungus, trimmed and sliced

5 horn of plenty, fresh or dried, chopped

250 g / 9 oz / 1½ cups fine polenta or cornmeal

2 shallots or 1 small onion, chopped

2 fist-sized pieces cauliflower fungus or 15 g / ½ oz / ¼ cup dried

115 g / 4 oz chicken of the woods, trimmed and sliced

150 ml / ¼ pint / ⅔ cup single cream

3 egg yolks

10 ml / 2 tsp lemon juice

celery salt and cayenne pepper

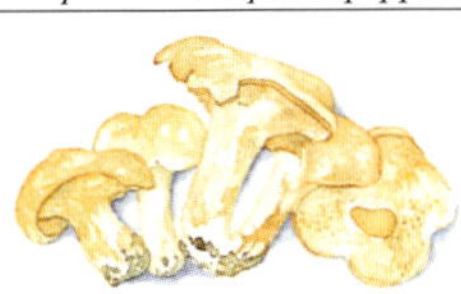

Cook's Tip

If preparing this recipe in advance, make the polenta loaf and mushroom and vegetable sauce then allow to cool. When ready to serve, reheat the polenta and sauce, then thicken the sauce with egg yolks, season and serve.

1 Lightly oil a 23 cm / 9 in loaf tin and line with a single sheet of greaseproof paper. Set aside. Cover the potatoes with boiling water, add a pinch of salt and cook for 20 minutes. Bring the vegetable stock to the boil, add the carrots and peas and cook for 3–4 minutes. Remove with a slotted spoon and keep warm.

2 Add 25 g / 1 oz / 2 tbsp of the butter and the Caesar's mushrooms or hedgehog fungus and horn of plenty to the stock and simmer for 5 minutes. Introduce the polenta in a steady stream and stir for 2–3 minutes until thickened. Turn the polenta into the prepared tin, cover and allow to become firm.

3 To make the sauce, melt the remaining butter, add the shallots or onion and cook gently without colouring. Add the cauliflower fungus cut into thumb-sized pieces, with the chicken of the woods, and cook for 2–3 minutes. Add the cream and the reserved cooked vegetables and simmer to eliminate excess moisture.

4 Remove from the heat, stir in the egg yolks and allow residual heat to slightly thicken the sauce. The sauce must not boil at this stage. Add the lemon juice, then season with celery salt and a dash of cayenne pepper.

5 To serve, turn the warm polenta out onto a board, slice with a wet knife and arrange on four serving plates. Spoon the mushroom and vegetable sauce over the polenta.

St George's Chicken Cobbler

The St George's mushroom, so named because it emerges near to St George's day, 23rd April, combines especially well with chicken in this traditional English cobbler. If St George's mushrooms are not available, use a mixture of bay boletus, saffron milk-caps, parasol mushroom, yellow russula, oyster or closed field mushrooms.

SERVES 4

60 ml / 4 tbsp vegetable oil

1 medium onion, chopped

1 celery stick, sliced

1 small carrot, peeled and cut into julienne strips

3 chicken breasts, skin and bone removed

450 g / 1 lb St George's mushrooms or a selection of others mentioned above, trimmed and sliced

75 g / 3 oz / 6 tbsp plain flour

500 ml / 18 fl oz / 2¼ cups chicken stock, boiling

10 ml / 2 tsp Dijon mustard

30 ml / 2 tbsp medium sherry

10 ml / 2 tsp wine vinegar

salt and freshly ground black pepper

For the Cobbler Topping

275 g / 10 oz / 2½ cups self-raising flour

pinch of celery salt

pinch of cayenne pepper

115 g / 4 oz / ½ cup firm unsalted butter, diced

50 g / 2 oz / ½ cup Cheddar cheese, grated

150 ml / ¼ pint / ⅔ cup cold water

1 beaten egg, to glaze, optional

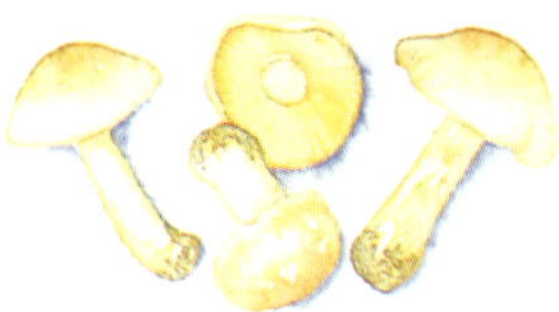

1 Preheat the oven to 200°C / 400°F / Gas 6. Heat the oil in a large heavy saucepan, add the onion, celery and carrot and fry gently without colouring, to soften. Cut the chicken breasts into bite-sized pieces, add to the vegetables and cook briefly. Add the mushrooms, fry until the juices run, then stir in the flour.

2 Remove the pan from the heat and stir in the stock gradually so that the flour is completely absorbed. Return the pan to the heat, and simmer gently to thicken, stirring all the time. Add the mustard, sherry, vinegar and seasoning. Cover and keep warm.

Cook's Tip

This recipe can easily be made as a pie by replacing the cobbler topping with a layer of flaky or shortcrust pastry.

3 To make the topping, sift the flour, celery salt and cayenne pepper into a bowl or a food processor fitted with a metal blade. Add the butter and half of the cheese, then either rub the mixture together with your fingers or process until it resembles large fresh breadcrumbs. Add the water and combine without over mixing.

4 Turn out onto a floured board, form into a round and flatten to about a 1.5 cm / ½ in thickness. Cut out as many 5 cm / 2 in shapes as you can, using a plain cutter.

5 Transfer the chicken mixture to a 1.2 litre / 2 pint / 5 cup pie dish, then overlap the cobbler shapes around the edge. Brush with beaten egg, scatter with the remaining cheese and bake in the oven for 25–30 minutes until the topping is well risen and golden.

Main course Soup of Duck, Beetroot and Ceps

SERVES 4

50 g / 2 oz / 4 tbsp butter

2 medium onions, halved and sliced

2 duck legs or breasts

1.2 litres / 2 pints / 5 cups chicken stock

175 g / 6 oz white cabbage, sliced

675 g / 1½ lb raw beetroot, chopped

15 g / ½ oz / ¼ cup dried ceps or bay boletus

1 sprig thyme

400 g / 14 oz can butter beans

30 ml / 2 tbsp wine vinegar

salt and freshly ground black pepper

For the Garnish

150 ml / ¼ pint / ⅔ cup soured cream

30 ml / 2 tbsp creamed horseradish

60 ml / 4 tbsp chopped fresh parsley

1 Melt the butter in a heavy saucepan, add the onions and brown lightly. Add the duck, cover with stock, then add the cabbage, beetroot, ceps, thyme and butter beans. Cover and simmer for 1¼ hours.

2 Skim off as much fat as you can. Remove the pieces of duck, slice into thick pieces and return to the pan. Add the vinegar and season to taste.

3 Blend the soured cream with the horseradish. Ladle the soup into bowls, and add a dollop of horseradish and some parsley. Serve with rye bread.

Roly Poly Chicken and Chanterelle Pudding

SERVES 4

1 medium onion, chopped

1 celery stick, sliced

10 ml / 2 tsp chopped fresh thyme

30 ml / 2 tbsp vegetable oil

2 chicken breasts, skinned and boned

115 g / 4 oz fresh chanterelles, trimmed and sliced, or 15 g / ½ oz / ¼ cup dried, soaked in warm water for 20 minutes

40 g / 1½ oz / 4 tbsp plain flour

300 ml / ½ pint / 1¼ cups chicken stock, boiling

5 ml / 1 tsp Dijon mustard

10 ml / 2 tsp wine vinegar

salt and freshly ground black pepper

For the Roly Poly Dough

350 g / 12 oz / 3 cups self-raising flour

2.5 ml / ½ tsp salt

150 g / 5 oz / ⅔ cup chilled unsalted butter, diced

75 ml / 5 tbsp cold water

1 Fry the onion, celery and thyme gently in oil without colouring. Cut the chicken into bite-sized pieces, add to the pan with the mushrooms and cook briefly. Stir in the flour, then remove from the heat.

2 Stir in the chicken stock gradually so that the flour is completely absorbed by the stock. Return to the heat, simmer to thicken, then add the mustard, vinegar and seasoning. Set aside to cool.

3 To make the dough, sift the flour and salt into a bowl. Add the butter, then rub together with the fingers until it resembles coarse breadcrumbs. Add the water all at once and combine without over mixing. Roll out the dough on a floured surface into a rectangle 25 × 30 cm / 10 × 12 in. Rinse a piece of muslin about twice as big as the dough, in a little water. Place the dough on the muslin. Spread the cool chicken filling over the dough and roll up from the short end using the muslin to help, to make a fat sausage. Enclose in muslin and tie each end with string.

4 Lower the pudding into a pan of boiling water, cover and simmer for 1½ hours. Lift out, untie, slice and serve.

Wild Rabbit in a Mushroom Pot

The rich flavour of wild rabbit echoes the qualities of wild mushrooms.

SERVES 4

- *45 ml / 3 tbsp olive oil*
- *12 button onions, peeled*
- *1 celery stick, cut into batons*
- *1 medium carrot, cut into batons*
- *900 g / 2 lb wild rabbit portions, trimmed*
- *salt and freshly ground black pepper*
- *30 ml / 2 tbsp plain flour*
- *115 g / 4 oz Jerusalem artichokes, peeled and chopped*
- *500 ml / 18 fl oz / 2¼ cups chicken stock, boiling*
- *75 g / 3 oz fresh horn of plenty, trimmed*
- *15 g / ½ oz / ¼ cup dried ceps or bay boletus*
- *15 ml / 1 tbsp green olive paste*
- *8 green olives*
- *15 ml / 1 tbsp lemon juice*

1 Heat the olive oil in a heavy skillet, add the onions, celery and carrots and brown lightly for 6–8 minutes. Push to one side of the pan. Season the rabbit, add to the pan and seal. Stir in the flour, add the Jerusalem artichokes, then remove from the heat.

2 Add the chicken stock gradually so that the flour is absorbed.

3 Add the mushrooms and the olive paste, cover and simmer over a gentle heat for 1 hour. Add the green olives and lemon juice and adjust the seasoning. Serve with parsley potatoes.

Cook's Tip
Trim away as many of the small rabbit bones as you can.

Stuffed Fennel

Vegetable fennel divides into neat boat shapes. In this recipe the shapes are baked with a creamy chicken and oyster mushroom filling and served on a bed of rice.

SERVES 4

- *2 large bulbs fennel*
- *3 eggs*
- *25 g / 1 oz / 2 tbsp butter*
- *1 medium onion, chopped*
- *2 chicken breasts, skinned and boned*
- *225 g / 8 oz oyster mushrooms, trimmed and chopped*
- *40 g / 1½ oz / 4 tbsp plain flour*
- *300 ml / ½ pint / 1¼ cups chicken stock, boiling*
- *5 ml / 1 tsp Dijon mustard*
- *30 ml / 2 tbsp sherry*
- *salt and freshly ground black pepper*
- *parsley sprigs, to garnish*

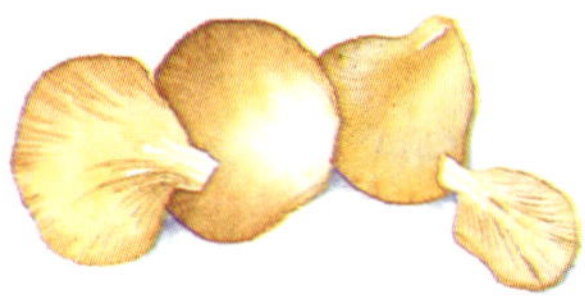

1 Preheat the oven to 190°C / 375 °F / Gas 5. Trim the base of the fennel and pull each bulb apart into four pieces (save the central part). Boil the fennel in salted water for 3–4 minutes, then drain and leave to cool. Boil the eggs for 10 minutes. Cool, peel and set aside.

2 Finely chop the central part of the fennel. Fry the fennel and onion gently in butter for 3–4 minutes.

3 Cut the chicken into pieces and add to the pan, with the mushrooms. Cook over a moderate heat for 6 minutes stirring frequently. Add the flour and remove from the heat.

4 Gradually add the chicken stock making sure the flour is completely absorbed by the stock. Return to the heat and simmer until thickened, stirring all the time. Grate one of the eggs into the chicken mixture, add the mustard, sherry and seasoning to taste.

5 Arrange the fennel in a baking dish. Spoon the filling into each one, cover with foil and bake for 20–25 minutes. Serve on a bed of rice, garnished with eggs and parsley.

Sherry Braised Guinea Fowl with Saffron Milk-caps

SERVES 4

2 young guinea fowl, tied

salt and freshly ground black pepper

50 g / 2 oz / 4 tbsp unsalted butter

75 ml / 5 tbsp dry sherry

2 medium onions, sliced

1 small carrot, peeled and chopped

½ celery stick, chopped

225 g / 8 oz assorted wild mushrooms such as saffron milk-caps or chanterelles, oyster, St George's, parasol and field mushrooms, trimmed and sliced

450 ml / ¾ pint / 1⅞ cup chicken stock, boiling

1 sprig thyme

1 bay leaf

15 ml / 1 tbsp lemon juice

1 Preheat the oven to 190°C / 375°F / Gas 5. Season the guinea fowl with salt and pepper. Melt half of the butter in a flameproof casserole, add the birds and turn until browned all over. Transfer to a shallow dish, heat the sediment in the pan, pour in the sherry and bring to the boil, stirring to deglaze the pan. Pour this liquid over the birds and set aside.

Cook's Tip

If fresh wild mushrooms are unavailable substitute with 15 g / ½ oz / ¼ cup of dried saffron milk-caps or ceps, with 75 g / 3 oz cultivated oyster or field mushrooms.

2 Wipe the casserole clean, then melt the remaining butter. Add the onions, carrots and celery. Place the birds on top, cover and cook in the oven for 40 minutes.

3 Add the chicken stock and the thyme and bay leaf. Tie the mushrooms into a 30 cm / 12 in square of muslin. Place in the casserole, cover and return to the oven for a further 40 minutes.

4 Transfer the birds to a serving platter, remove the thyme and bay leaf and set the mushrooms in the bag aside. Liquidize the braising liquid and pour back into the casserole. Add the mushrooms from the muslin to the sauce. Season with salt and pepper and add lemon juice to taste. Heat until simmering and serve over the guinea fowl or pour into a serving jug.

Braised Pheasant with Ceps, Chestnuts and Bacon

Pheasant at the end of their season are not suitable for roasting, so consider this delicious casserole enriched with wild mushrooms and chestnuts. Allow two birds for four people.

SERVES 4

2 mature pheasants

salt and freshly ground black pepper

50 g / 2 oz / 4 tbsp butter

75 ml / 5 tbsp brandy

12 button or pickling onions, peeled

1 celery stick, chopped

50 g / 2 oz unsmoked rindless bacon, cut into strips

45 ml / 3 tbsp plain flour

500 ml / 18 fl oz / 2¼ cups chicken stock, boiling

175 g / 6 oz peeled chestnuts

350 g / 12 oz fresh ceps or bay boletus, trimmed and sliced, or 15 g / ½ oz / ¼ cup dried, soaked in warm water for 20 minutes

15 ml / 1 tbsp lemon juice

watercress sprigs, to garnish

1 Preheat the oven to 170°C / 325°F / Gas 3. Season the pheasants with salt and pepper. Melt half of the butter in a large flameproof casserole and brown the pheasants over a moderate heat. Transfer to a shallow dish and pour off the cooking fat. Return the casserole to the heat and brown the sediment. Stand back and add the brandy, (the sudden flames will die down quickly). Stir to loosen the sediment with a flat wooden spoon and then pour the juices over the pheasant.

2 Wipe the casserole and melt the remaining butter. Lightly brown the onions, celery and bacon. Stir in the flour. Remove from the heat.

3 Stir in the stock gradually so that it is completely absorbed by the flour. Add the chestnuts, mushrooms, the pheasants and their juices. Bring back to a gentle simmer, then cover and cook in the oven for 1½ hours.

Cook's Tip

Cooking and peeling fresh chestnuts can be hard work, so look out for canned or vacuum packed varieties.

4 Transfer the pheasants and vegetables to a serving plate. Bring the sauce back to the boil, add the lemon juice and season to taste. Pour the sauce into a jug and garnish the birds.

Chicken Fricassée Forestier

The term fricassée is used to describe a light stew, usually of chicken that is first sauteed in butter. The accompanying sauce can vary, but here wild mushrooms and bacon provide a rich woodland flavour.

SERVES 4

3 free range chicken breasts, sliced

salt and freshly ground black pepper

50 g / 2 oz / 4 tbsp unsalted butter

15 ml / 1 tbsp vegetable oil

115 g / 4 oz unsmoked rindless streaky bacon, cut into pieces

75 ml / 5 tbsp dry sherry or white wine

1 medium onion, chopped

350 g / 12 oz assorted wild mushrooms such as chanterelles, ceps, bay boletus, horn of plenty, chicken of the woods, hedgehog fungus, saffron milk-caps, closed field mushrooms and cauliflower fungus, trimmed and sliced

40 g / 1½ oz / 3 tbsp plain flour

500 ml / 18 fl oz / 2¼ cups chicken stock

10 ml / 2 tsp lemon juice

60 ml / 4 tbsp chopped fresh parsley

1 Season the chicken with pepper. Heat half of the butter and the oil in a large heavy skillet or flameproof casserole and brown the chicken and bacon pieces. Transfer to a shallow dish and pour off any excess fat.

Cook's Tip
It is worth spending a little extra on properly reared free range chicken. Not only is it less fatty, but it also has a better flavour and texture.

2 Return the skillet to the heat and brown the sediment. Pour in the sherry or wine and stir with a flat wooden spoon to deglaze the pan. Pour the sherry liquid over the chicken and wipe the skillet clean.

3 Fry the onion in the remaining butter until golden brown. Add the mushrooms and cook, stirring frequently, for 6–8 minutes, until their juices begin to run. Stir in the flour then remove from the heat. Gradually add the chicken stock and stir well until the flour is completely absorbed.

4 Add the reserved chicken and bacon with the sherry juices, return to the heat and stir to thicken. Simmer for 10–15 minutes and then add the lemon juice, parsley and seasoning. Serve with plain boiled rice, carrots and baby sweetcorn.

Pan Fried "Chicken" of the Woods with a Sherry Cream Sauce

This dish doesn't use real chicken, the flavour, texture and aroma of *Laetiporus sulphureus* or chicken of the woods is so similar to roast chicken, that it can be used in place of the real thing. There's no doubt that both vegetarians and meat eaters will enjoy this dish.

SERVES 4

50 g / 2 oz / 4 tbsp unsalted butter
2 shallots or 1 small onion, chopped
1 celery stick, sliced
½ medium carrot, peeled and sliced
350 g / 12 oz chicken of the woods, trimmed and sliced
50 g / 2 oz / 5 tbsp plain flour
450 ml / ¾ pint / 1⅞ cups chicken or vegetable stock
75 ml / 5 tbsp sherry
30 ml / 2 tbsp chopped fresh tarragon
75 ml / 5 tbsp double cream
30 ml / 2 tbsp lemon juice
celery salt and cayenne pepper

1 Melt the butter in a large skillet or flameproof casserole, add the shallots or onion, celery and carrot and fry gently until soft but without colouring.

2 Add the chicken of the woods, let them absorb some of the pan juices, then cook for 3–4 minutes. Stir in the flour and remove from the heat.

3 Gradually add the stock, stirring well so that the flour is absorbed. Heat gently until simmering, stirring all the time, then add the sherry and tarragon and simmer for 6–8 minutes.

4 Just before serving, stir in the cream and lemon juice and season to taste with celery salt and a dash of cayenne pepper. Serve over tagliatelle or fettuccine pasta.

Cook's Tip
Instead of serving it over pasta, try this recipe as a delicious pie filling. Cover with puff or shortcrust pastry and bake for 45–50 minutes at 190°C / 375°F / Gas 5.

Wild Duck Roasted with Morels and Madeira

Wild duck has a rich autumnal flavour that combines well with stronger-tasting mushrooms.

SERVES 4

2 × 1.1 kg / 2½ lb mallards, dressed and barded weight

salt and freshly ground black pepper

50 g / 2 oz / 4 tbsp unsalted butter

75 ml / 5 tbsp Madeira or sherry

1 medium onion, halved and sliced

½ celery stick, chopped

1 small carrot, chopped

10 large dried morel mushrooms

225 g / 8 oz blewits, parasol and field mushrooms, trimmed and sliced

600 ml / 1 pint / 2½ cups chicken stock, boiling

1 sprig thyme

10 ml / 2 tsp wine vinegar

parsley sprigs and carrot juliennes, to garnish

game chips, to serve

1 Preheat the oven to 190°C / 375°F / Gas 5 and season the ducks with salt and pepper. Melt half of the butter in a heavy skillet and brown the birds evenly. Transfer to a shallow dish, heat the sediment in the pan, pour in the Madeira or sherry and bring to the boil, stirring, to deglaze the pan. Pour this liquid over the birds and set aside.

2 Heat the remaining butter in a large flameproof casserole and add the onion, celery and carrot. Place the birds on top and cook in the oven for 40 minutes, reserving the juices.

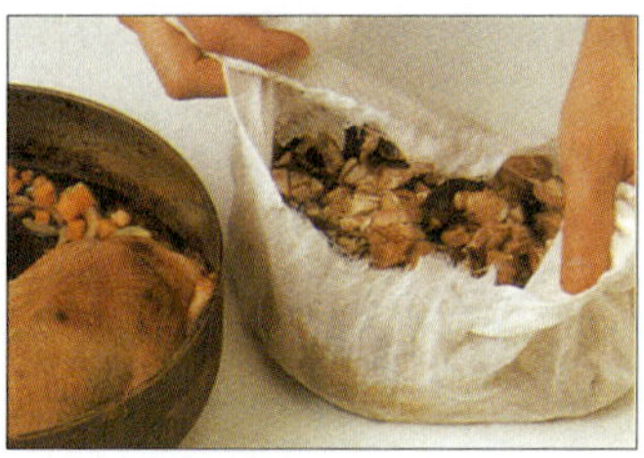

3 Tie the mushrooms in a 46 cm / 18 in square piece of muslin. Add the stock, pan liquid, thyme and the muslin bag to the casserole. Cover and return to the oven for 40 minutes.

Cook's Tip
Mallard is the most popular wild duck, although widgeon and teal are good substitutes. A widgeon will serve two but allow one teal per person.

4 Transfer the birds to a serving platter, remove and discard the thyme and set the mushrooms aside. Liquidize the braising liquid and pour back into the casserole. Break open the muslin bag and stir the mushrooms into the sauce. Add the vinegar, season to taste and heat through gently. Garnish the ducks with parsley and carrot. Serve with game chips or crisps and the Madeira or sherry sauce.

Roast Chicken Stuffed with Forest Mushrooms

A good roast chicken is a feast of flavour and succulence. Spend a little more money on a free range bird and let its flavour mingle with the wild aroma of woodland mushrooms.

SERVES 4

25 g / 1 oz / 2 tbsp unsalted butter, plus extra for basting and to finish gravy
1 shallot, chopped
225 g / 8 oz wild mushrooms such as chanterelles, ceps, bay boletus, oyster, chicken of the woods, saffron milk-caps, and hedgehog fungus, trimmed and chopped
45 g / 1½ oz / ⅔ cup fresh white breadcrumbs
salt and freshly ground black pepper
2 egg yolks
1.75 kg / 4–4½ lb free range chicken
½ celery stick, chopped
½ small carrot, chopped
75 g / 3 oz potato, peeled and chopped
200 ml / 7 fl oz / 1 cup chicken stock, plus extra if required
10 ml / 2 tsp wine vinegar
parsley sprigs, to garnish

1 Preheat the oven to 220°C / 425°F / Gas 7. Melt the butter in a saucepan and gently fry the shallot without letting it colour. Add half of the chopped mushrooms and cook for 2–3 minutes until the moisture appears. Remove from the heat, stir in the breadcrumbs, seasoning and egg yolks, to bind.

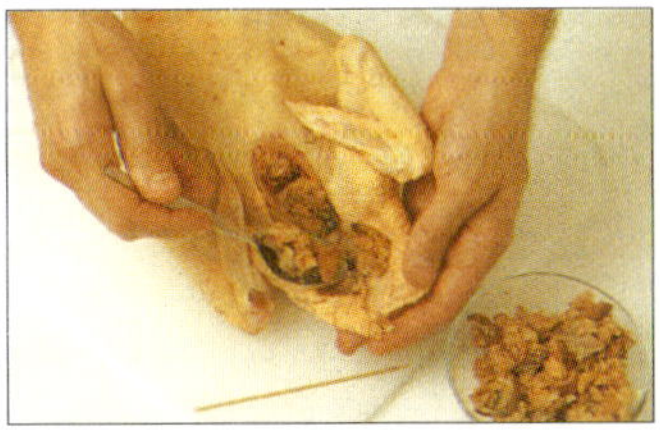

2 Spoon the stuffing into the neck of the chicken, enclose and fasten the skin on the underside with a skewer.

3 Rub the chicken with some extra butter and season well. Put the celery, carrot, potato and remaining mushrooms in the bottom of a roasting tin. Place the chicken on top of the vegetables, add the chicken stock and roast in the oven for 1¼ hours.

4 Transfer the chicken to a carving board or warmed serving plate, then liquidize the vegetables and mushrooms. Pour the mixture back into the tin and heat gently, adjusting the consistency with chicken stock if necessary. Taste and adjust seasoning then add the vinegar and a knob of butter and stir briskly. Pour the sauce into a serving jug and garnish the chicken with sprigs of parsley.

Cook's Tip

If fresh mushrooms are not available, replace with 15 g / ½ oz / ¼ cup of the dried equivalent and soak for 20 minutes before using.

Roast Turkey Flavoured with all Manner of Mushrooms

A roast turkey on the festive table tends to look better than it tastes. One sure way to boost its flavour and succulence is to stuff it with the season's wild mushrooms. The gravy too, can be flavoured with all manner of mushrooms.

SERVES 6–8

5 kg / 10 lb free range turkey, dressed weight

butter, for basting

watercress, to garnish

For the Mushroom Stuffing

50 g / 2 oz / 4 tbsp unsalted butter

1 medium onion, chopped

225 g / 8 oz wild mushrooms, such as chanterelle, ceps, bay boletus, chicken of the woods, saffron milk-caps, Caesar's mushrooms and hedgehog fungus, trimmed and chopped

75 g / 3 oz / 1½ cups fresh white breadcrumbs

115 g / 4 oz pork sausages, skinned

1 small fresh truffle, sliced (optional)

5 drops truffle oil (optional)

salt and freshly ground black pepper

For the Gravy

75 ml / 5 tbsp medium sherry

400 ml / 14 fl oz / 1⅔ cups chicken stock

15 g / ½ oz / ¼ cup dried ceps, soaked

20 ml / 4 tsp cornflour

5 ml / 1 tsp Dijon mustard

2.5 ml / ½ tsp wine vinegar

salt and freshly ground black pepper

1 Preheat the oven to 220°C / 425°F / Gas 7. To make the stuffing, melt the butter in a saucepan, add the onion and fry gently without colouring. Add the mushrooms and stir until their juices begin to flow. Remove from the heat, add the breadcrumbs, sausage meat and the truffle and truffle oil if using, season and stir well to combine.

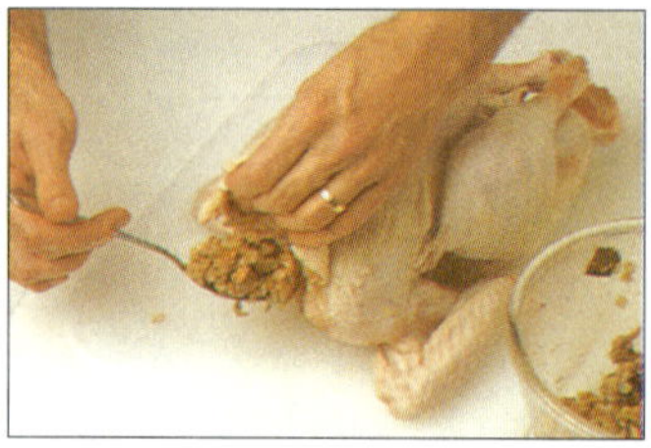

2 Spoon the stuffing into the neck cavity of the turkey and enclose, fastening the skin on the underside with a skewer.

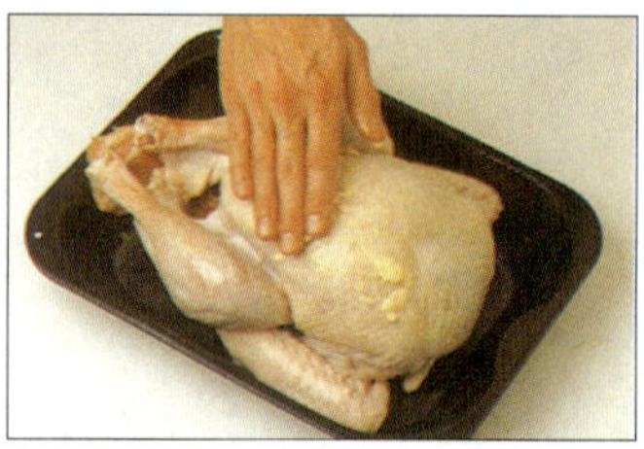

3 Rub the skin of the turkey with butter, place in a large roasting tin uncovered and roast in the oven for 50 minutes. Lower the temperature to 180°C / 350°F / Gas 4 and cook for a further 2 hours and 30 minutes.

4 To make the gravy, transfer the turkey to a carving board, cover loosely with foil and keep warm. Spoon off the fat from the roasting tin and discard. Heat the remaining liquid until reduced to a sediment. Add the sherry and stir briskly with a flat wooden spoon to loosen the sediment. Stir in the chicken stock.

5 Place the cornflour and mustard in a cup, and blend with 10 ml / 2 tsp water and the wine vinegar. Stir this mixture into the juices in the basting tin and simmer to thicken. Season with salt and pepper and then stir in a knob of butter.

6 Garnish the turkey with bunches of watercress. Turn the gravy into a serving jug and serve separately.

Cook's Tip

Other sizes of turkey can be cooked this way – allow 675 g / 1½ lb dressed weight of turkey per person and roast for 20 minutes per 450 g / 1 lb.

Beef, Pork & Lamb

Veal Stew with Mushrooms

The combination of ripe tomatoes and tangy orange in this dish brings to mind Mediterranean sunshine. Choose tomatoes grown outside for the very best sundrenched taste.

SERVES 6

60 ml / 4 tbsp plain flour

1.3 kg / 3 lb boneless veal shoulder, cut into 4 cm / 1½ in pieces

30–45 ml / 2–3 tbsp olive oil

4 or 5 shallots, finely chopped

2 garlic cloves, very finely chopped

300 ml / ½ pint / 1¼ cups dry white wine

450 g / 1 lb tomatoes, peeled, seeded and chopped

grated rind and juice of 1 unwaxed orange

bouquet garni

15 ml / 1 tbsp tomato purée

15 g / ½ oz / 1 tbsp butter

350 g / ¾ lb button mushrooms, quartered if large

salt and freshly ground black pepper

chopped fresh parsley, to garnish

1 Put the flour in a polythene bag and season with salt and pepper. Drop the pieces of meat into the bag a few at a time and shake to coat with flour, tapping off the excess. Discard the remaining flour.

2 Heat 30 ml / 2 tbsp of the oil in a flameproof casserole over a medium heat. Add enough meat to the pan to fit easily in one layer (do not overcrowd the pan or the meat will not brown). Cook, turning to colour all sides, until well browned, then transfer to a plate. Continue browning the meat in batches, adding more oil if needed.

3 In the same pan, cook the shallots and garlic over a medium heat, stirring, until just softened, then stir in the wine and bring to the boil. Return the meat to the pan and add the tomatoes, orange rind and juice, bouquet garni and tomato purée. Bring back to the boil, then reduce the heat to low, cover and simmer gently for approximately 1 hour.

4 Melt the butter in a frying pan over a medium heat and sauté the mushrooms until golden. Add the mushrooms to the casserole and cook, covered, for 20–30 minutes, or until the meat is very tender. Adjust the seasoning and discard the bouquet garni before serving. Garnish the stew with parsley.

Cook's Tip
If shallots are not available, use 1 or 2 mild-flavoured red onions instead.

Beef Goulash with Dark Mushrooms and Morels

A good Hungarian goulash is made rich and smooth with onions and paprika. In this recipe dark field mushrooms and morel mushrooms provide extra smoothness and a good depth of flavour.

SERVES 4

900 g / 2 lb chuck steak, diced

salt and freshly ground black pepper

60 ml / 4 tbsp vegetable oil

150 ml / 1/4 pint / 2/3 cup red wine

4 medium onions, halved and sliced

450 g / 1 lb field or horse mushrooms or closed shaggy ink caps, trimmed and chopped

45 ml / 3 tbsp mild paprika

600 ml / 1 pint / 2 1/2 cups beef stock

30 ml / 2 tbsp tomato purée

15 g / 1/2 oz / 1/4 cup dried morel mushrooms, soaked in warm water for 20 minutes

15 ml / 1 tbsp wine vinegar

1 Preheat the oven to 170°C / 325°F / Gas 3 and season the meat with pepper. Heat half of the oil in a large frying pan and fry the meat over a high heat. A quantity of liquid will appear which must be evaporated before the meat will brown and take on flavour. When the meat has browned, transfer to a flameproof casserole and pour off the fat. Return the frying pan to the heat, add the wine and stir with a flat wooden spoon to deglaze the pan. Pour the liquid over the meat and wipe the pan clean.

2 Heat the remaining oil in the pan, add the onions and brown lightly.

3 Add the mushrooms, paprika, stock, tomato purée, the morels and their liquid to the casserole. Bring to a simmer, cover and cook in the oven for about 1 1/2 hours.

Cook's Tip

Goulash can also be made with diced pork or veal. In this case use chicken stock in place of beef. To keep the goulash a good colour, select closed shaggy ink caps that have not started to blacken and deteriorate.

4 Just before serving, add the vinegar and adjust seasoning if necessary. Serve with jacket potatoes, Savoy cabbage and carrots.

Cep Meatballs with a Roquefort and Walnut Sauce

The salty rich acidity of Roquefort cheese enhances the flavour of good beef. In this recipe meatballs are flavoured with cep mushrooms. A Roquefort and walnut sauce makes it a dish to remember.

SERVES 4

- *15 g / ½ oz / ¼ cup dried ceps or bay boletus, soaked in warm water for 20 minutes*
- *450 g / 1 lb lean minced beef*
- *1 small onion, finely chopped*
- *2 egg yolks*
- *10 ml / 2 tsp chopped fresh thyme*
- *celery salt and freshly ground black pepper*
- *30 ml / 2 tbsp olive oil*

For the Roquefort Sauce

- *200 ml / 7 fl oz / ⅞ cup milk*
- *50 g / 2 oz walnuts, toasted*
- *3 slices white bread, crusts removed*
- *75 g / 3 oz Roquefort cheese*
- *60 ml / 4 tbsp chopped fresh parsley*

1 Drain the mushrooms, reserving the liquid, and chop finely. Place the beef, onion, egg yolks, thyme and seasoning in a bowl, add the mushrooms and combine well. Divide the mixture into thumb-sized pieces with wet hands and roll into balls.

2 To make the sauce, place the milk in a small pan and bring to a simmer. Put the walnuts in a food processor and grind smoothly, then add the bread and pour in the milk and reserved mushroom liquid. Add the cheese and parsley, then process smoothly. Transfer to a mixing bowl, cover and keep warm.

3 Heat the olive oil in a large non-stick frying pan. Cook the meatballs in two batches for 6–8 minutes. Add the sauce to the pan and heat very gently without allowing it to boil, then turn into a serving dish or serve over ribbon pasta.

Old English Steak and Mushroom Pudding

This pudding has been lost to the fast-food lifestyle. It takes five hours to cook but it is worth waiting for!

SERVES 4

- *450 g / 1 lb chuck steak, diced*
- *225 g / 8 oz assorted wild and cultivated mushrooms such as chanterelles, ceps, orange birch bolete, shaggy ink caps, horn of plenty, saffron milk-caps, blewits, oyster, field and St George's mushrooms and not more than 3 dried morels, trimmed and sliced*
- *1 medium onion, chopped*
- *45 ml / 3 tbsp plain flour*
- *celery salt and freshly ground black pepper*
- *3 shakes Worcestershire sauce*
- *120 ml / 4 fl oz / ½ cup beef stock*

For the Pastry Crust

- *225 g / 8 oz / 2 cups self-raising flour*
- *2.5 ml / ½ tsp salt*
- *75 g / 3 oz / 6 tbsp cold butter, grated*
- *150 ml / ¼ pint / ⅔ cup cold water*

1 To make the pastry, sift the flour and salt into a bowl and stir in the butter. Add all of the water and stir with a knife to form a loose dough. Turn out onto a floured surface and press together without over working.

2 Brush a 1.2 litre / 2 pint / 5 cup pudding basin with oil or butter. Roll out the dough with a dusting of flour to form a 25 cm / 10 in circle. Cut out a quarter section and save for the lid. Line the basin and set aside.

3 Mix the beef, mushrooms, onion, flour and seasoning in a large bowl. Transfer to the lined basin, add the Worcestershire sauce and top up with the beef stock. Bring overlapping pastry edges towards the centre, moisten with water and cover the top with the leftover pastry.

4 Place a circle of greaseproof paper on the pastry, then cover the whole basin with a 46 cm / 18 in piece of foil. Boil 5 cm / 2 in of water in a pan and lower the basin into the pan. Cover and steam for 2½ hours, making sure the water doesn't boil away.

5 When ready to serve, turn out onto a plate and serve with curly kale, carrots and boiled potatoes.

Rich Beef Stew with Cep Dumplings

As if the temptation of a rich beef stew isn't enough, here it is crowned with cep dumplings.

SERVES 4

60 ml / 4 tbsp vegetable oil

900 g / 2 lb chuck steak, diced

150 ml / ¼ pint / ⅔ cup red wine

2 medium onions, halved and sliced

½ celery stick, chopped

450 g / 1 lb open cap wild or cultivated field mushrooms, sliced

½ garlic clove, crushed

600 ml / 1 pint / 2½ cups beef stock

30 ml / 2 tbsp tomato purée

10 ml / 2 tsp black olive purée

15 ml / 1 tbsp wine vinegar

5 ml / 1 tsp anchovy sauce

1 sprig thyme

salt and freshly ground black pepper

For the Cep Dumplings

275 g / 10 oz / 2¼ cups self-raising flour

2.5 ml / ½ tsp salt

115 g / 4 oz / ½ cup cold butter, finely diced

45 ml / 3 tbsp chopped fresh parsley

5 ml / 1 tsp chopped fresh thyme

dried ceps, soaked in warm water for 20 minutes

250 ml / 8 fl oz / 1 cup cold milk

1 Preheat the oven to 170°C / 325°F / Gas 3. Season the meat with pepper then heat half of the oil in a pan, and seal the meat over a high heat. The liquid that appears must be evaporated before the meat will brown.

2 When the meat has browned, transfer to a flameproof casserole and pour off the fat from the pan. Add the wine to the pan and stir with a flat wooden spoon to loosen the sediment. Pour over the meat.

3 Wipe the pan clean then heat the remaining oil, add the onions and celery and brown lightly. Add to the casserole with the mushrooms, garlic, beef stock, tomato and olive purée, vinegar, anchovy sauce and thyme. Bring to a simmer, cover and cook in the oven for 1½–2 hours.

4 To make the dumplings, sift the flour and salt together, add the butter, then the parsley and thyme. Drain the ceps and chop finely. Add the ceps and milk to the mixture and stir with a knife to make a soft dough, taking care not to overmix.

5 Flour your hands and form the mixture into thumb-sized dumplings. Drop them into simmering water and cook uncovered for 10–12 minutes. When cooked, remove and arrange on top of the stew.

Braised Beef with Mushroom Gravy

Delicious gravy is an integral part of a good stew.

SERVES 4

900 g / 2 lb chuck steak, sliced

salt and freshly ground black pepper

60 ml / 4 tbsp vegetable oil

150 ml / ¼ pint / ⅔ cup red wine

2 medium onions, halved and sliced

½ celery stick, chopped

450 g / 1 lb open cap wild or cultivated field mushrooms, sliced

½ garlic clove, crushed

600 ml / 1 pint / 2½ cups beef stock

30 ml / 2 tbsp tomato purée

10 ml / 2 tsp black olive purée

5 ml / 1 tsp anchovy sauce

1 sprig thyme

15 ml / 1 tbsp wine vinegar

1 Preheat the oven to 170°C / 325°F / Gas 3. Season the meat with pepper. Heat half of the oil in a large frying pan, and seal the beef over a high heat. Liquid will appear, which must be evaporated before the meat will brown and take on flavour.

2 Transfer the meat to a flameproof casserole and pour off the fat from the pan. Return the pan to the heat, add the wine and stir briskly. Pour over the meat and wipe the pan clean.

3 Heat the remaining oil in the pan, add the onions and celery and brown lightly. Add the mushrooms, garlic, beef stock, tomato and olive purée, anchovy sauce and thyme to the casserole. Set over the heat and bring to a simmer. Cover and cook in the oven for about 2 hours until the meat is tender. Add the vinegar and adjust the seasoning. Serve with mashed potatoes, swede and cabbage.

Lamb Chop Sauté with a Sauce of Woodland Mushrooms

SERVES 4

4 × 175 g / 6 oz lamb chops
salt and freshly ground black pepper
30 ml / 2 tbsp olive oil
75 ml / 3 fl oz / ⅓ cup red wine
225 g / 8 oz assorted wild and cultivated mushrooms such as chanterelles, ceps, bay boletus, horn of plenty, saffron milk-caps, parasol mushrooms, oyster, Caesar's, St George's or field mushrooms, trimmed and sliced
½ garlic clove, crushed
200 ml / 7 fl oz / ⅞ cup chicken stock, boiling
10 ml / 2 tsp cornflour
5 ml / 1 tsp Dijon mustard
2.5 ml / ½ tsp black olive paste
5 ml / 1 tsp wine vinegar
25 g / 1 oz / 2 tbsp unsalted butter

1 Season the lamb with black pepper, then moisten with 15 ml / 1 tbsp of the oil. Sauté over a steady heat for 6–8 minutes for medium-rare meat or 12–15 minutes for well done.

Cook's Tip
Do not season cut pieces of meat with salt before cooking. This can cause the meat to dry and toughen. Season before serving.

2 Transfer the lamb to a plate, cover and keep warm. Pour off any excess oil from the pan and heat the sediment until it browns. Add the red wine and stir with a flat wooden spoon to loosen the sediment. Add the mushrooms, stir briefly and then add the chicken stock and simmer for 3–4 minutes.

3 Place the cornflour, mustard and olive paste in a cup and blend with 15 ml / 1 tbsp cold water. Stir into the pan and simmer briefly to thicken. Add the vinegar, stir in the butter and season to taste. Season the lamb with a little salt, spoon the sauce over the top and serve with sautéed potatoes, French beans and carrots.

Black Pepper Beef Steaks with Red Wine and Mushroom Sauce

SERVES 4

4 × 225 g / 8 oz sirloin or rump steaks
15 ml / 1 tbsp black peppercorns, cracked
15 ml / 1 tbsp olive oil
120 ml / 4 fl oz / ½ cup red wine
225 g / 8 oz assorted wild and cultivated mushrooms such as ceps, bay boletus, chanterelles, horn of plenty, saffron milk-caps, blewits, morels, Paris mushrooms, field, oyster, Caesar's and St George's mushrooms or cauliflower fungus, trimmed and sliced
½ garlic clove, crushed
300 ml / ½ pint / 1¼ cups beef stock
15 ml / 1 tbsp cornflour
5 ml / 1 tsp Dijon mustard
10 ml / 2 tsp fish sauce (optional)
5 ml / 1 tsp wine vinegar
75 ml / 5 tbsp crème fraîche

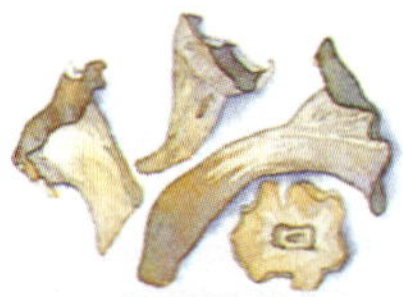

1 Place a large frying pan over a high heat. Season the steaks with cracked pepper and moisten with oil.

Cook's Tip
In terms of both flavour and tenderness, the best cut of steak is taken from the rump end. Rib steaks are also good, but because of their size, they are best suited to serve two.

2 Fry the steaks for 6–8 minutes for medium-rare meat, or 12–15 minutes for well done, turning once. Transfer to a plate and keep warm.

3 Pour off any excess fat, return the pan to the heat and brown the sediment. Add the wine and loosen the sediment with a flat wooden spoon. Add the mushrooms and garlic and soften for 6–8 minutes. Add the stock.

4 Place the cornflour and mustard in a cup and blend with 15 ml / 1 tbsp cold water. Stir into the pan juices and simmer to thicken. Add the fish sauce, if using, the vinegar, and the crème fraîche. Spoon the sauce over the steaks and scatter with parsley.

Beef Stroganoff with a Chanterelle Parsley Cream

This dish is believed to be named after a 19th century Russian diplomat, Count Paul Stroganoff. It was originally made with fillet steak, wild mushrooms and cream, but has suffered many changes. Here is an attempt at the original.

SERVES 4

450 g / 1 lb fillet or rump steak, trimmed and cut into thin strips

salt and freshly ground black pepper

30 ml / 2 tbsp olive oil

45 ml / 3 tbsp brandy

2 shallots, finely chopped

225 g / 8 oz chanterelle mushrooms, trimmed and halved

150 ml / ¼ pint / ⅔ cup beef stock

75 ml / 5 tbsp soured cream

5 ml / 1 tsp Dijon mustard

½ sweet gherkin, chopped

45 ml / 3 tbsp chopped fresh parsley

1 Season the steak with pepper, heat half of the oil in a pan and cook for 2 minutes. Transfer the meat to a plate.

Cook's Tip
If you can't afford fillet steak, buy best rump or sirloin.

2 Place the pan over a moderately high heat and brown the sediment. Stand back from the pan, add the brandy, tilt towards the flame (or ignite with a match if cooking on an electric hob) and burn off the alcohol vapour. Pour these juices over the meat, cover and keep warm.

3 Wipe the pan clean, heat the remaining oil and lightly brown the shallots. Add the mushrooms and fry gently for 3–4 minutes to soften.

4 Add the stock and simmer for a few minutes and then add the soured cream, mustard and gherkin together with the steak and its juices. Simmer briefly, season to taste and stir in the chopped parsley. Serve with buttered noodles dressed with poppy seeds.

Sauté of Pork with Jerusalem Artichokes and Horn of Plenty

The Jerusalem artichoke has an earthy quality not unlike the flavours of the horn of plenty.

SERVES 4

- *45 ml / 3 tbsp vegetable oil*
- *1 medium onion, halved and sliced*
- *1 celery stick, sliced*
- *1 medium carrot, peeled, halved and sliced*
- *675 g / 1½ lb lean pork, loin or thick end, cut into strips*
- *45 ml / 3 tbsp plain flour*
- *500 ml / 18 fl oz / 2¼ cups chicken stock*
- *75 g / 3 oz Jerusalem artichokes, peeled and thickly sliced*
- *115 g / 4 oz horn of plenty or winter chanterelles, trimmed*
- *15 ml / 1 tbsp green olive paste*
- *15 ml / 1 tbsp lemon juice*
- *salt and freshly ground black pepper*

1 Heat the oil in a heavy skillet or frying pan, add the onion, celery and carrot and fry gently for 6–8 minutes to soften.

2 Push the vegetables to one side of the pan, add the pork and seal. Stir in the flour and remove from the heat.

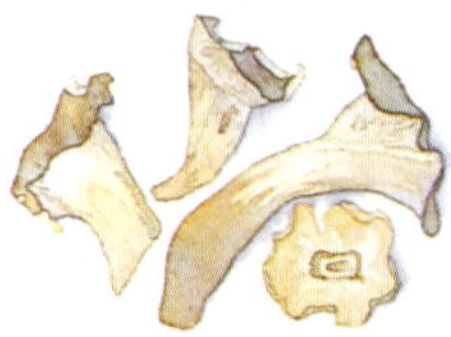

Cook's Tip

Jerusalem artichokes go a long way to provide richness to a dish. If used in excess, however, they sometimes cause flatulence.

3 Add the stock gradually and stir so that the flour is completely absorbed by the stock.

4 Add the artichokes, mushrooms and olive paste and bring to a simmer. Cover with a lid or foil and cook very gently for about 1 hour. Add the lemon juice, adjust the seasoning and serve with a mixture of wild and long grain rice and petits pois.

Pork Sausage Puff with a Seam of Wild Mushrooms

Fresh pork sausages needn't be cooked in their skins. To make the most of them, remove the meat and wrap it in a puff pastry parcel. A thick seam of wild mushrooms gives a seasonal twist.

SERVES 4

- *50 g / 2 oz / 4 tbsp unsalted butter*
- *½ garlic clove, crushed*
- *15 ml / 1 tbsp chopped fresh thyme*
- *450 g / 1 lb assorted wild and cultivated mushrooms such as ceps, bay boletus, chanterelles, horn of plenty, saffron milk-caps, blewits, chicken of the woods, oyster, field, Caesar's and St George's mushrooms, trimmed and sliced*
- *50 g / 2 oz / 1 cup fresh white breadcrumbs*
- *75 ml / 5 tbsp chopped fresh parsley*
- *salt and freshly ground black pepper*
- *350 g / 12 oz puff pastry, thawed if frozen*
- *675 g / 1½ lb best pork sausages*
- *1 egg, beaten with a pinch of salt*

1 Preheat the oven to 180°C / 350°F / Gas 4. Melt the butter in a large non-stick frying pan, add the garlic, thyme and mushrooms and soften gently for 5–6 minutes. When the mushroom juices begin to run, increase the heat to evaporate the juices. When quite dry, stir in the breadcrumbs and chopped parsley and season well.

2 Roll out the pastry on a floured surface to form a 36 × 25 cm / 14 × 10 in rectangle and place on a large baking sheet.

3 Immerse the sausages in a bowl of water, pierce and pull off their skins. Place half of the sausagemeat in a 13 cm / 5 in strip along the centre of the pastry. Cover with mushrooms, then with another layer of sausagemeat.

4 Make a series of 2.5 cm / 1 in slanting cuts in the pastry each side of the filling. Fold the two ends of pastry over the filling, moisten the pastry with beaten egg and then cross the top with alternate strips of pastry from each side. Allow to rest for 40 minutes, brush with a little more egg and bake in the oven for 1 hour.

Cook's Tip

A good pinch of salt added to a beaten egg will break down and improve the finished glaze.

Coriander Lamb Kebabs with an Almond Chanterelle Sauce

The delicate sweetness of lamb combines well with apricot-scented chanterelles, used here to make this especially delicious almond sauce.

SERVES 4

- *8 lamb cutlets, trimmed*
- *25 g / 1 oz / 2 tbsp unsalted butter*
- *225 g / 8 oz chanterelle mushrooms, trimmed*
- *25 g / 1 oz / ¼ cup whole almonds, toasted*
- *50 g / 2 oz white bread, crusts removed*
- *250 ml / 8 fl oz / 1 cup milk*
- *45 ml / 3 tbsp olive oil*
- *2.5 ml / ½ tsp caster sugar*
- *10 ml / 2 tsp lemon juice*
- *salt and cayenne pepper*

For the Marinade

- *45 ml / 3 tbsp olive oil*
- *15 ml / 1 tbsp lemon juice*
- *10 ml / 2 tsp ground coriander*
- *½ garlic clove, crushed*
- *10 ml / 2 tsp clear honey*

1 Mix all marinade ingredients together, pour over the lamb and leave for at least 30 minutes.

2 Fry the chanterelles gently in butter without colouring for 3–4 minutes. Set aside.

3 Place the almonds in a processor and grind finely. Add half of the chanterelles, the bread, milk, oil, sugar and lemon juice, then process.

4 Preheat a moderate grill. Thread the lamb onto four metal skewers, and cook for 6–8 minutes on each side. Season the sauce then spoon over the kebabs. Add the remaining chanterelles and serve with potatoes and a salad.

Cook's Tip

Almond chanterelle sauce makes a delicious dressing for pasta. Serve with a handful of chanterelles cooked in butter.

Beef Wellington made Rich with Mushrooms

There are two ways of preparing beef Wellington: both involve a length of fillet steak wrapped and baked in flaky pastry. Traditionally the beef is spread with a layer of goose liver pâté, but because of its high price, many cooks turn to an equally delicious and infinitely cheaper pâté of woodland mushrooms.

SERVES 4

675 g / 1½ lb fillet steak, tied
freshly ground black pepper
15 ml / 1 tbsp vegetable oil
350 g / 12 oz puff pastry, thawed if frozen
1 egg, beaten, to glaze

For the Parsley Pancakes

50 g / 2 oz / 5 tbsp plain flour
a pinch of salt
150 ml / ¼ pint / ⅔ cup milk
1 egg
30 ml / 2 tbsp chopped fresh parsley

For the Mushroom Pâté

25 g / 1 oz / 2 tbsp unsalted butter
2 shallots or 1 small onion, chopped
450 g / 1 lb assorted wild and cultivated mushrooms such as oyster mushrooms, ceps, bay boletus, orange birch bolete, shaggy ink caps, chanterelles, saffron milk caps, parasol mushrooms, blewits, closed field or St George's mushrooms, trimmed and chopped
50 g / 2 oz / 1 cup fresh white breadcrumbs
75 ml / 8 tbsp double cream
2 egg yolks

1 Preheat the oven to 220°C / 425°F / Gas 7. Season the fillet steak with several twists of black pepper. Heat the oil in a roasting tin, add the steak and quickly sear to brown all sides. Transfer to the oven and roast for 15 minutes for rare, 20 minutes for medium-rare or 25 minutes for well-done meat. Set aside to cool. Reduce the temperature to 190°C / 375°F / Gas 5.

2 To make the pancakes, beat the flour, salt, half the milk, the egg and parsley together until smooth, then stir in the remaining milk. Heat a greased, non-stick pan and pour in enough batter to coat the bottom. When set, turn over and cook the other side briefly until lightly browned. Continue with remaining batter – the recipe makes three or four.

3 To make the mushroom pâté, fry the shallots or onion in butter to soften without colouring. Add the mushrooms and cook until their juices begin to run. Increase the heat and cook briskly so that the juices evaporate. Combine the breadcrumbs with the cream and egg yolks. When the mushrooms are quite dry, add the bread and cream mixture and blend to make a smooth paste. Allow to cool.

Cook's Tip

Beef Wellington can be prepared up to 8 hours in advance but should be kept at room temperature as the meat will not heat through in the cooking times given if it is chilled before cooking begins. Instead of using a meat thermometer, you can insert a metal skewer into the meat. If the skewer is cold the meat is not done, if it is warm the meat is rare and if it is hot it is well-done.

4 Roll out the pastry and cut into a rectangle 36 × 30 cm / 14 × 12 in. Place two pancakes on the pastry and spread with mushroom pâté. Place the beef on top and spread over any remaining pâté. Cover with the remaining pancakes. Cut out four squares from the corners of the pastry. Moisten the pastry edges with egg and then wrap them over the meat.

5 Decorate the top with the reserved pastry trimmings, transfer to a baking sheet and rest in a cool place until ready to cook.

6 Brush evenly with beaten egg. Cook the Wellington for about 40 minutes until golden brown. To ensure that the meat is heated through, test with a meat thermometer. It should read 125–130°F (52–54°C) for rare, 135°C (57°F) for medium-rare and 160°C (71°F) for well-done meat.

Roast Leg of Lamb with a Wild Mushroom Stuffing

When the thigh bone is removed from a leg of lamb a stuffing can be put in its place. This not only makes the joint easier to carve but also gives an excellent flavour to the meat.

SERVES 4

1 × 1.8 kg / 4 lb leg of lamb, boned

salt and freshly ground black pepper

For the Wild Mushroom Stuffing

25 g / 1 oz / 2 tbsp butter, plus extra for gravy

1 shallot or 1 small onion

225 g / 8 oz assorted wild and cultivated mushrooms such as chanterelles, ceps, bay boletus, horn of plenty, blewits, oyster, St George's, field and Caesar's mushrooms, trimmed and chopped

½ garlic clove, crushed

1 sprig thyme, chopped

25 g / 1 oz crustless white bread, diced

2 egg yolks

salt and freshly ground black pepper

For the Wild Mushroom Gravy

50 ml / 3½ tbsp red wine

400 ml / 14 fl oz / 1⅔ cups chicken stock, boiling

5 g / ⅙ oz / 2 tbsp dried ceps, bay boletus or saffron milk-caps, soaked in boiling water for 20 minutes

20 ml / 4 tsp cornflour

5 ml / 1 tsp Dijon mustard

2.5 ml / ½ tsp wine vinegar

knob of butter

watercress, to garnish

1 Preheat the oven to 200°C / 400°F / Gas 6. To make the stuffing, melt the butter in a large non-stick frying pan and gently fry the shallot or onion without colouring. Add the mushrooms, garlic and thyme and stir until the mushrooms juices begin to run; then increase the heat so that they evaporate completely.

2 Transfer the mushrooms to a mixing bowl, add the bread, egg yolks and seasoning and mix well. Allow to cool slightly.

3 Season the inside cavity of the lamb and then press the stuffing into the cavity, using a spoon or your fingers. Tie up the end with fine string and then tie around the joint so that it does not lose its shape.

4 Place the lamb in a roasting tin and roast in the oven for 15 minutes per 450 g / 1 lb for rare meat and 20 minutes per 450 g / 1 lb for medium-rare. A 1.8 kg / 4 lb leg will take 1 hour 20 minutes if cooked medium-rare.

5 Transfer the lamb to a warmed serving plate, cover and keep warm. To make the gravy, spoon off all excess fat from the roasting tin and brown the sediment over a moderate heat. Add the wine and stir with a flat wooden spoon to loosen the sediment. Add the chicken stock, the mushrooms and their soaking liquid.

6 Place the cornflour and mustard in a cup and blend with 15 ml / 1 tbsp water. Stir into the stock and simmer to thicken. Add the vinegar. Season to taste, and stir in the butter. Garnish the lamb with watercress, and serve with roast potatoes, carrots and broccoli.

Cook's Tip

If you buy your meat from a butcher, ask for the thigh bone to be taken out.

Fish & Shellfish

Shellfish Risotto with Fruits of the Forest

The creamy nature of short-grain rice cooked with onions and a simple stock provides the basis for this delicious combination of shellfish and mushrooms.

SERVES 4

45 ml / 3 tbsp olive oil

1 medium onion, chopped

225 g / 8 oz assorted wild and cultivated mushrooms such as ceps, bay boletus, chanterelles, chicken of the woods, saffron milk-caps, horn of plenty, wood blewits, oyster, St George's, Caesar's and truffles, trimmed and sliced

450 g / 1 lb / 2¼ cups short-grain Arborio or Carnaroli rice

1.2 litres / 2 pints / 5 cups chicken or vegetable stock, boiling

150 ml / ¼ pint / ⅔ cup white wine

115 g / 4 oz raw prawns, peeled

225 g / 8 oz live mussels

225 g / 8 oz Venus or carpet shell clams

1 medium squid, cleaned, trimmed and sliced

3 drops truffle oil (optional)

75 ml / 5 tbsp chopped fresh parsley and chervil

celery salt and cayenne pepper

Cook's Tip
Before cooking, scrub the mussels and clams, then tap them with a knife. If any of the shells do not close, discard them. After cooking (see step 3), if any of the shells have not opened discard them too.

1 Heat the oil in a large skillet and fry the onion for 6–8 minutes until soft but not brown.

2 Add the mushrooms and soften until their juices begin to run. Stir in the rice and heat through.

3 Pour in the stock and wine. Add the prawns, mussels, clams and squid, stir and simmer for 15 minutes.

4 Add the truffle oil if using, stir in the herbs, cover and stand for 5–10 minutes. Season to taste with celery salt and a pinch of cayenne pepper and serve with open-textured bread.

Deep Sea Scallops in a Forest of Wild Mushrooms

From the depths of the sea and forest come two flavours that marry perfectly in a smooth creamy sauce.

SERVES 4

350 g / 12 oz puff pastry, thawed if frozen
1 egg, beaten, to glaze
75 g / 3 oz / 6 tbsp unsalted butter
12 scallops, trimmed and thickly sliced
salt and freshly ground black pepper
2 shallots, chopped
½ stick celery, cut into strips
½ medium carrot, peeled and cut into strips
225 g / 8 oz assorted wild mushrooms, such as chanterelles, chicken of the woods, cauliflower fungus, oyster, Caesar's and St George's mushrooms, trimmed and sliced
60 ml / 4 tbsp Noilly Prat or other dry vermouth
150 ml / ¼ pint / ⅔ cup crème fraîche
4 egg yolks
15 ml / 1 tbsp lemon juice
celery salt and cayenne pepper

1 Roll the pastry out on a floured surface, cut into four 13 cm / 5 in circles, and then trim into shell shapes. Brush with a little beaten egg and mark a shell pattern on each with a small knife. Place on a baking sheet, chill and rest for 1 hour. Preheat the oven to 200°C / 400°F / Gas 6.

2 Melt 25 g / 1 oz / 2 tbsp of the butter in a pan, season the scallops and cook for not longer than 30 seconds over a high heat. Transfer to a plate.

3 Bake the pastry shapes for 20–25 minutes until golden and quite dry. Fry the shallots, celery and carrots gently in the remaining butter without colouring. Add the mushrooms and cook over a moderate heat until the juices begin to run. Pour in the vermouth and increase the heat to evaporate the juices.

4 Add the crème fraîche and cooked scallops and bring to a simmer (do not boil). Remove the pan from the heat and blend in the egg yolks. Return the pan to a gentle heat and cook for a moment or two until the sauce has thickened to the consistency of thin cream, remove the pan from the heat. Season and add the lemon juice.

5 Split the pastry shapes open and place on four plates. Spoon in the filling and replace the tops. Serve with potatoes and salad.

Cook's Tip
Take care not to use dark mushrooms in a cream sauce.

Clam, Mushroom and Potato Chowder

SERVES 4

48 medium clams, washed
50 g / 2 oz / 1 tbsp unsalted butter
1 large onion, chopped
1 celery stick, sliced
1 medium carrot, peeled and sliced
225 g / 8 oz assorted wild mushrooms such as chanterelles, saffron milk-caps, chicken of the woods or St George's mushrooms, trimmed and sliced
225 g / 8 oz potatoes, peeled and thickly sliced
1.2 litres / 2 pints / 5 cups light chicken or vegetable stock, boiling
1 sprig thyme
45 ml / 3 tbsp chopped fresh parsley, plus 4 parsley stalks
salt and freshly ground black pepper

1 Place the clams in a large stainless steel pan, put 1 cm / ½ in of water in the bottom, cover and steam over a moderate heat for 6–8 minutes.

2 When open, drain the clams over a bowl, remove the shells and chop. Strain the juices over and set aside.

3 Add the butter, onion, celery and carrot to the pan and soften without colouring. Add the mushrooms and cook for 3–4 minutes until their juices begin to run. Add the potatoes, the clams and their juices, the stock, thyme and parsley stalks. Bring to the boil and simmer for 25 minutes, or until the potatoes begin to fall apart. Season to taste, ladle into soup plates, scatter with parsley and serve.

Cook's Tip
If clams are not available, use the same quantity of mussels.

Snails with Ceps

SERVES 4

350 g / 12 oz puff pastry, thawed if frozen
1 egg, beaten, to glaze
25 g / 1 oz / ½ cup grated Parmesan
50 g / 2 oz / 4 tbsp unsalted butter
2 shallots, finely chopped
50 g / 2 oz fennel, finely chopped
50 g / 2 oz fine green beans, cut in three
115 g / 4 oz fresh ceps, sliced, or 15 g / ½ oz / ¼ cup dried ceps, soaked in warm water for 20 minutes and chopped
1 garlic clove, crushed
75 ml / 5 tbsp dry sherry
150 ml / ¼ pint / ⅔ cup beef stock, boiling
10 ml / 2 tsp cornflour
5 ml / 1 tsp Dijon mustard
2 × 200 g / 7 oz cans snails, drained
2.5 ml / ½ tsp black olive paste
5 ml / 1 tsp balsalmic or wine vinegar
salt and freshly ground black pepper
45 ml / 3 tbsp chopped fresh parsley

1 Roll out the pastry on a floured surface to a 30 cm / 12 in square. Cut out eight 10 cm / 4 in fluted rings, then cut four circles with a 7.5 cm / 3 in plain cutter. Place the four circles on a baking sheet, top each with two pastry rings and brush with beaten egg.

2 Roll out the trimmings in a dusting of Parmesan cheese, cut into 2 cm / ¾ in wide strips and wind around four cream horn moulds. Chill all the pastry shapes for about 1 hour.

3 Preheat the oven to 200°C / 400°F / Gas 6. Melt the butter in a large non-stick frying pan, and gently fry the shallots, fennel and beans until soft but not brown. Add the ceps and garlic and soften for a further 6 minutes. Add the sherry and stock and simmer briefly. Bake the pastry shapes for 25 minutes until crisp.

4 Place the cornflour and the mustard in a cup and blend with 15 ml / 1 tbsp cold water. Stir the cornflour mixture into the pan and simmer to thicken. Add the snails and the olive paste and simmer to heat through, then add the vinegar and season to taste.

5 Spoon the mixture into the pastry shapes and scatter with chopped parsley. Serve with creamed potatoes and Savoy cabbage.

Fillets of Trout with a Spinach and Field Mushroom Sauce

Many people like the idea of trout, but have trouble getting it off the bone. Trout fillets are the answer to this problem and taste delicious with a rich spinach and mushroom sauce.

SERVES 4

4 brown or rainbow trout, filleted and skinned to make 8 fillets

For the Spinach and Mushroom Sauce

75 g / 3 oz / 6 tbsp unsalted butter

1/4 medium onion, chopped

225 g / 8 oz closed field or horse mushrooms, chopped

300 ml / 1/2 pint / 1 1/4 cups chicken stock, boiling

225 g / 8 oz frozen chopped spinach

10 ml / 2 tsp cornflour

150 ml / 1/4 pint / 2/3 cup crème fraîche

salt and freshly ground black pepper

grated nutmeg

1 To make the sauce, melt 50 g / 2 oz / 4 tbsp of the butter in a frying pan and fry the onion until soft. Add the mushrooms and cook until the juices begin to run. Add the stock and the spinach and cook until the spinach has completely thawed.

2 Blend the cornflour with 15 ml / 1 tbsp of cold water and stir into the mushroom mixture. Simmer gently to thicken.

3 Liquidize the sauce until smooth, add the crème fraîche and season to taste with salt and pepper and a pinch of nutmeg. Turn into a serving jug and keep warm.

4 Melt the remaining butter in a large non-stick frying pan. Season the trout and cook for 6 minutes, turning once. Serve with new potatoes and young carrots with the sauce either poured over or served separately.

Cook's Tip

Spinach and mushroom sauce is also good with fillets of cod, haddock and sole.

Puff Pastry Salmon with a Chanterelle Cream Filling

The flavour of farmed salmon is helped by a creamy layer of chanterelle mushrooms.

SERVES 6

2 × 350 g / 12 oz puff pastry, thawed if frozen

1 egg, beaten, to glaze

2 large salmon fillets, about 900 g / 2 lb total weight, skinned and boned

375 ml / 13 fl oz / 1⅝ cups dry white wine

1 small carrot

1 small onion, halved

½ celery stick, chopped

1 sprig thyme

For the Chanterelle Cream

25 g / 1 oz / 2 tbsp unsalted butter

2 shallots, chopped

225 g / 8 oz chanterelles or saffron milk-caps, trimmed and sliced

75 ml / 5 tbsp white wine

150 ml / ¼ pint / ⅔ cup double cream

45 ml / 3 tbsp chopped fresh chervil

30 ml / 2 tbsp chopped fresh chives

For the Hollandaise Sauce

175 g / 6 oz / ¾ cup unsalted butter

2 egg yolks

10 ml / 2 tsp lemon juice

salt and freshly ground black pepper

1 Preheat the oven to 200°C / 400°F / Gas 6. Roll out the pastry on a floured surface to form a rectangle 10 cm / 4 in longer and 5 cm / 2 in wider than the fillets. Trim into a fish shape, decorate with a pastry cutter and glaze with beaten egg. Chill for 1 hour and then bake for 30–35 minutes until well risen and golden. Remove from the oven and split open horizontally. Reduce the oven temperature to 170 °C / 325 °F / Gas 3.

2 To make the chanterelle cream, fry the shallots gently in butter until soft but not coloured. Add the mushrooms and cook until their juices begin to run. Pour in the wine, increase the heat and evaporate the juices. When dry, add the cream and herbs and bring to a simmer. Season well, transfer to a bowl, cover and keep warm.

3 To poach the salmon fillet, place in a fish kettle or roasting tin. Add the wine, carrot, onion, celery, thyme and enough water to cover the fish. Bring to the boil slowly. As soon as the water begins to tremble, remove from the heat, cover and allow the fish to cook in this gentle heat for 30 minutes.

4 To make the sauce, melt the butter, skim the surface of any scum and pour into a jug, leaving behind the milky residue. Place the yolks and 15 ml / 1 tbsp of water in a glass bowl and place over a pan of simmering water. Whisk the yolks until thick and foamy. Remove from the heat and very slowly pour in the butter, whisking all the time. Add the lemon juice and season.

5 Place one salmon fillet on the base of the pastry, spread with the chanterelle cream and cover with the second fillet. Cover with the top of the pastry "fish" and warm through in the oven for about 10–15 minutes. Serve with the sauce.

Wild Mushroom and Cep Cockle Puffs

This dish is as much a soup as it is a fish course. Oyster mushrooms, ceps and cockles combine in a rich herb broth which is covered with pastry. When baked, the broth produces steam and the pastry puffs in a dome.

SERVES 4

350 g / 12 oz puff pastry, thawed, if frozen

1 egg beaten, to glaze

45 ml / 3 tbsp sesame seeds or celery seed

For the Soup

25 g / 1 oz / 2 tbsp unsalted butter

4 spring onions, trimmed and chopped

1 celery stick, sliced

1 small carrot, peeled, halved and sliced

115 g / 4 oz fresh young ceps or bay boletus, sliced

175 g / 6 oz oyster mushrooms

450 ml / 3/4 pint / 1 7/8 cup full-fat milk

275 g / 10 oz shelled fresh cockles, cooked

50 g / 2 oz samphire, trimmed (optional)

115 g / 4 oz cooked potato, diced

4 sprigs thyme

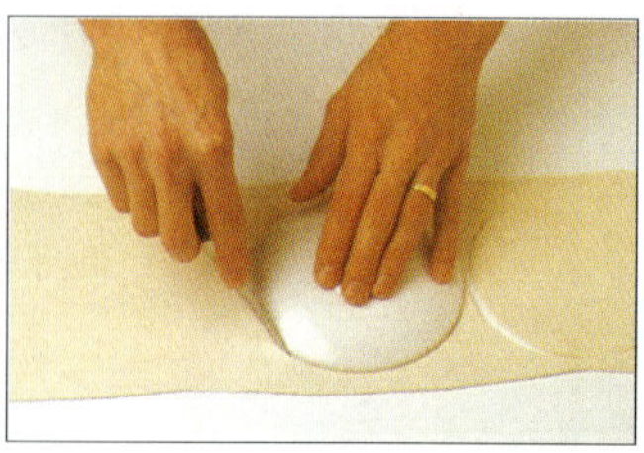

1 Roll out the pastry on a floured surface and cut into four 18 cm / 7 in rounds. Rest in a cool place for 1 hour. Preheat the oven to 190°C / 375°F / Gas 5.

2 Fry the spring onions, celery and carrot in butter for 2–3 minutes. Add the mushrooms and soften until the juices begin to flow. Transfer to a large saucepan.

3 Pour the milk over the mushrooms and bring to a simmer. Add the cockles, samphire and diced potato.

4 Heat through the contents of the saucepan and then ladle into four deep ovenproof soup bowls. Add a sprig of thyme to each.

5 Moisten the edges of the bowls with beaten egg, cover with the pastry rounds and firm the edges to seal. Brush with more beaten egg, sprinkle with sesame seeds and bake in the oven for 35–40 minutes until the pastry top is puffed and golden.

Cook's Tip

If fresh ceps are unavailable use closed button or Paris mushrooms.

Fresh Tuna Shiitake Teriyaki

Teriyaki is a sweet soy marinade usually used to glaze meat. Here Teriyaki enhances fresh tuna steaks served with rich shiitake mushrooms.

SERVES 4

4 × 175 g / 6 oz fresh tuna or yellow tail steaks
salt
150 ml / ¼ pint / ⅔ cup Teriyaki sauce
175 g / 6 oz shiitake mushrooms, sliced
225 g / 8 oz white radish, peeled
2 large carrots, peeled

1 Season the tuna steaks with a sprinkling of salt, then set aside for 20 minutes for it to penetrate. Pour the Teriyaki sauce over the fish and mushrooms and marinate for a further 20–30 minutes or for longer if you have the time.

Cook's Tip
One of the finest Teriyaki sauces is made by Kikkoman and can be found in most large supermarkets.

2 Preheat a moderate grill or barbecue. Remove the tuna from marinade and reserve the marinade. Cook the tuna for 8 minutes, turning once.

3 Transfer the mushrooms and marinade to a stainless steel saucepan and simmer for 3–4 minutes.

4 Slice the radish and carrot thinly, then shred finely with a chopping knife. Arrange in heaps on four serving plates and add the fish, with the mushrooms and sauce poured over. Serve with plain boiled rice.

Turbans of Lemon Sole with a Paris Mushroom Twist

The Paris mushroom *champignon de Paris* or chestnut mushroom is the French equivalent of the English white button mushroom. Its mild woodland flavour goes well with the lemon sole.

SERVES 4

900 g / 2 lb lemon sole, filleted and skinned to yield 450 g / 1 lb of fish
75 ml / 5 tbsp dry white wine
120 ml / 4 fl oz / ½ cup water
50 ml / 3½ tbsp double cream
10 ml / 2 tsp cornflour
10 ml / 2 tsp lemon juice
celery salt and cayenne pepper
For the Mushroom Filling
50 g / 2 oz / 4 tbsp unsalted butter, plus extra for greasing
1 shallot, finely chopped
175 g / 6 oz Paris or oyster mushrooms, finely chopped
15 ml / 1 tbsp chopped fresh thyme
salt and freshly ground black pepper

1 Preheat the oven to 190°C / 375°F / Gas 5 and butter an ovenproof dish. Make the mushroom filling. Melt the butter in a frying pan and fry the shallot until soft.

Cook's Tip
If planning ahead, the fish can be rolled and kept ready to cook for up to 8 hours.

2 Add the mushrooms and thyme and cook until dry. Transfer to a bowl, season and allow to cool.

3 Lay the fish skin side uppermost, season and spread with the filling. Roll up each fillet, then place in the buttered dish.

4 Pour in the wine and water, cover with a piece of buttered greaseproof paper and cook in the oven for 20 minutes.

5 Transfer the fish to a warmed serving platter and strain the cooking juices into a small saucepan. Add the cream and bring to a simmer.

6 Blend the cornflour with 15 ml / 1 tbsp of water, add to the pan, stir and simmer to thicken, then add the lemon juice and season with celery salt and a pinch of cayenne pepper. Pour the sauce around the fish and serve with new potatoes, beans and carrots.

Truffle and Lobster Risotto

To capture the precious qualities of the fresh truffle, partner it with lobster and serve in a silky smooth risotto. Both truffle shavings and truffle oil are added towards the end of cooking to preserve their flavour.

SERVES 4

50 g / 2 oz / 4 tbsp unsalted butter
1 medium onion, chopped
400 g / 14 oz / 2 cups Arborio or Carnaroli rice
1 sprig thyme
1.2 litres / 2 pints / 5 cups chicken stock
150 ml / ¼ pint / ⅔ cup dry white wine
1 freshly cooked lobster
45 ml / 3 tbsp chopped fresh parsley and chervil
3–4 drops truffle oil
2 hard-boiled eggs, sliced
1 fresh black or white truffle

1 Melt the butter in a large shallow pan, add the onion and fry gently until soft without letting it colour. Add the rice and thyme and stir well to coat evenly with fat. Pour in the chicken stock and wine, stir once and cook uncovered for 15 minutes.

2 Twist off the lobster tail, cut the underside with scissors and remove white tail meat. Slice half of the meat then roughly chop the remainder. Break open the claws with a small hammer and remove the flesh, in one piece if possible.

3 Remove the rice from the heat, stir in the chopped lobster meat, herbs and truffle oil. Cover and leave to stand for 5 minutes.

4 Divide among warmed dishes and arrange the lobster and hard-boiled egg slices and shavings of fresh truffle on top. Serve immediately.

Cook's Tip
To make the most of the aromatic truffle scent, keep the tuber in the rice jar for a few days. Alternatively store with the eggs at room temperature.

Creamy Fish and Mushroom Pie

Fish pie is a healthy and hearty dish for a hungry family. To help the fish go further, mushrooms provide both flavour and nourishment.

SERVES 4

225 g / 8 oz assorted wild and cultivated mushrooms such as oyster, button, chanterelle or St George's mushrooms, trimmed and quartered

675 g / 1½ lb cod or haddock fillet, skinned and diced

600 ml / 1 pint / 2½ cups milk, boiling

For the Topping

900 g / 2 lb floury potatoes, peeled and quartered

25 g / 1 oz / 2 tbsp butter

150 ml / ¼ pint / ⅔ cup milk

salt and freshly ground black pepper

grated nutmeg

For the Sauce

50 g / 2 oz / 4 tbsp unsalted butter

1 medium onion, chopped

½ celery stick, chopped

50 g / 2 oz / ½ cup plain flour

10 ml / 2 tsp lemon juice

45 ml / 3 tbsp chopped fresh parsley

1 Preheat the oven to 200 °C / 400°F / Gas 6. Butter an ovenproof dish, scatter the mushrooms in the bottom, add the fish and season with salt and pepper. Pour on the boiling milk, cover and cook in the oven for 20 minutes. Using a slotted spoon, transfer the fish and mushrooms to a 1.5 litre / 2½ pint / 6¼ cup baking dish. Pour the poaching liquid into a jug and set aside.

2 Cover the potatoes with cold water, add a good pinch of salt and boil for 20 minutes. Drain and mash with the butter and milk. Season well.

3 To make the sauce, melt the butter in a saucepan, add the onion and celery and fry until soft but not coloured. Stir in the flour, then remove from the heat.

4 Slowly add the reserved liquid, stirring until absorbed. Return to the heat, stir and simmer to thicken. Add the lemon juice and parsley, season, then add to the baking dish.

5 Top with the mashed potato and return to the oven for 30–40 minutes until golden brown.

Pan-fried Salmon with a Tarragon Mushroom Sauce

Tarragon has a distinctive aniseed flavour that is good with fish, cream and mushrooms. This recipe uses oyster mushrooms to provide both texture and flavour.

SERVES 4

- *50 g / 2 oz / 4 tbsp unsalted butter*
- *salt and cayenne pepper*
- *4 × 175 g / 6 oz salmon steaks*
- *1 shallot, finely chopped*
- *175 g / 6 oz assorted wild and cultivated mushrooms such as oyster mushrooms, saffron milk-caps, bay boletus or cauliflower fungus, trimmed and sliced*
- *200 ml / 7 fl oz / 7/8 cup chicken or vegetable stock*
- *10 ml / 2 tsp cornflour*
- *2.5 ml / 1/2 tsp mustard*
- *50 ml / 3 1/2 tbsp crème fraîche*
- *45 ml / 3 tbsp chopped fresh tarragon*
- *5 ml / 1 tsp white wine vinegar*

1 Melt half of the butter in a large non-stick frying pan, season the salmon and cook over a moderate heat for 8 minutes, turning once. Transfer to a plate, cover and keep warm.

2 Heat the remaining butter in the pan and gently fry the shallot to soften without letting it colour. Add the mushrooms and cook until the juices begin to flow. Add the stock and simmer for 2–3 minutes.

3 Put the cornflour and mustard in a cup and blend with 15 ml / 1 tbsp of water. Stir into the mushroom mixture and bring to a simmer, stirring, to thicken. Add the cream, tarragon, vinegar and salt and cayenne pepper.

4 Spoon the mushrooms over each salmon steak and serve with new potatoes and a green salad.

Cook's Tip

Fresh tarragon will bruise and darken quickly after chopping, so prepare the herb as and when you need it.

Fillets of Sole Bonne Femme

To capture the delicate flavour of flat fish, it is best cooked simply with wine and few good mushrooms.

SERVES 4

115 g / 4 oz / ½ cup unsalted butter

1 shallot, finely chopped

150 g / 5 oz chanterelles, Paris or button mushrooms, trimmed and sliced

900 g / 2 lb lemon sole, skinned and filleted to yield approximately 450 g / 1 lb of fish

salt and cayenne pepper

75 ml / 5 tbsp dry white wine

200 ml / 7 fl oz / ⅞ cup fish or chicken stock

5 ml / 1 tsp lemon juice

900 g / 2 lb potatoes, peeled, boiled and mashed

15 ml / 1 tbsp chopped fresh parsley, to garnish

1 Preheat the oven to 170°C / 325°F / Gas 3. Fry the shallot in 25 g / 1 oz / 2 tbsp of the butter until soft. Turn into an ovenproof earthenware dish and add the mushrooms. Place the fish fillets on top and season lightly.

2 Pour in the wine and stock and cover with buttered greaseproof paper. Cook in the oven for 25 minutes.

3 Transfer to a flameproof serving dish and keep warm. Strain the liquid into a shallow frying pan, reserving the mushrooms and shallot. Boil the sauce rapidly until reduced to a syrupy liquid. Remove from the heat, add the remaining butter cut into small pieces and shake the pan (the sauce must not boil). Add the mushroom mixture, the lemon juice and seasoning.

4 Heat the grill to a moderate temperature. Pipe a border of potatoes around the dish, spoon over the sauce and heat under the grill.

Prawn and Mushroom Kebabs

The flavour of grilled or barbecued prawns combines especially well with chanterelles, chicken of the woods and saffron milk-caps. The mushrooms need to be blanched and then moistened with oil to prevent them from burning over the coals.

SERVES 4

175 g / 6 oz wild mushrooms such as chanterelles, chicken of the woods, saffron milk-caps, or shiitake, trimmed and cut into pieces

about 45 ml / 3 tbsp olive oil

12 large raw prawns

1 fennel bulb, thickly sliced

8 cherry tomatoes

celery salt and cayenne pepper

1 Preheat a moderate grill or barbecue. Bring a saucepan of water to the boil, and blanch the mushrooms for 30 seconds. Transfer to a bowl with a slotted spoon and add a little oil.

Cook's Tip
Raw prawn tails offer the best flavour and can be obtained frozen from oriental supermarkets.

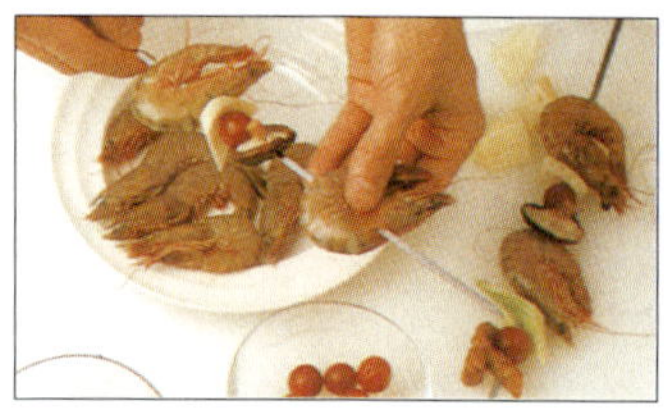

2 Moisten the prawns with a little more oil, then thread onto four metal skewers alternating with the pieces of fennel, tomatoes and mushrooms.

3 Season lightly, then grill for 6–8 minutes turning once. Serve on a bed of long grain and wild rice with a simple green salad.

Rendezvous de Fruits de la Mer et du Bois

The freshest fish and the finest wild mushrooms are combined here in a delicious cream sauce. The spectacular puff pastry case is easier to make than it looks.

SERVES 4

350 g / 12 oz puff pastry, thawed if frozen

1 egg, beaten, to glaze

200 ml / 7 fl oz / ⅞ cup dry white wine

200 ml / 7 fl oz / 1 cup chicken or vegetable stock

350 g / 12 oz assorted wild and cultivated mushrooms such as oyster, chanterelles, shiitake, hedgehog fungus, cauliflower fungus, saffron milk-caps or St George's mushrooms, trimmed and cut into thumb-sized pieces

1 medium squid

115 g / 4 oz monkfish tail, boned and cut into large pieces

12 live mussels, scrubbed

225 g / 8 oz salmon fillet, skinned and cut into bite-sized pieces

12 large raw prawns, peeled

6 scallops, halved

50 g / 2 oz / 4 tbsp unsalted butter

2 shallots, finely chopped

50 g / 2 oz / 4 tbsp plain flour

75 ml / 5 tbsp crème fraîche

10 ml / 2 tsp lemon juice

salt and cayenne pepper

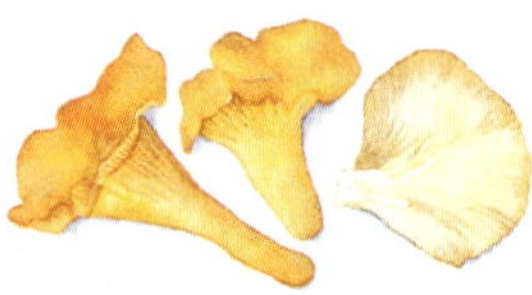

Cook's Tip

Take care when choosing the mushrooms for this dish, dark varieties will send the sauce brown.

1 Roll out the pastry on a floured surface to form a rectangle 30 × 38 cm / 12 × 15 in. Cut out a 23 cm / 9 in circle and place on a baking sheet. Prick all over with a fork and brush the surface with beaten egg. Cut out 20 × 4 cm / 1½ in circles with a fluted pastry cutter. Overlap these shapes around the edge of the large circle, brush again with egg and chill for 1 hour. Preheat the oven to 200°C / 400°F / Gas 6.

2 Bring the wine and stock to a simmer, add the mushrooms and cook gently for 3–4 minutes. Remove with a slotted spoon and set aside in a large bowl.

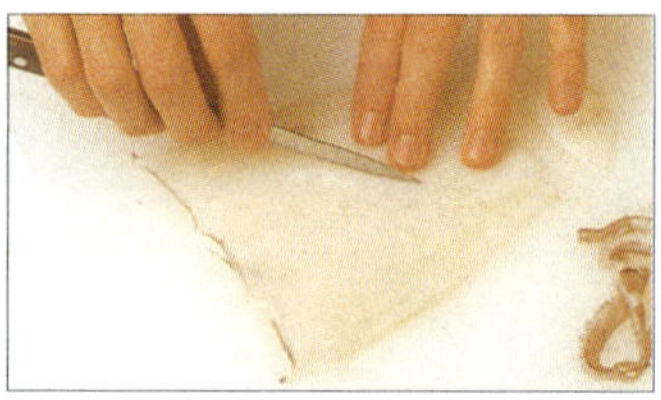

3 To prepare the squid, pull the head and tentacles away from the body, sever the tenticles and chop roughly. Remove the quill from inside the body, pull off the side fins and set aside. Rinse the body piece under water and rub off the fine outer skin. Cut the body piece in half lengthways, open out and score a criss-cross pattern with a sharp knife over the inside surface. Cut the squid into wide strips.

4 Tap the mussels sharply and discard any that do not close.

5 Bring the wine and stock to a simmer and add the squid, monkfish, mussels, salmon, prawns and scallops and cook for 6 minutes. Remove with a slotted spoon and add to the bowl with the mushrooms. Discard any mussels which have not opened. Strain the cooking liquid and make up to 350 ml / 12 fl oz / 1½ cups with water, if necessary. Bake the pastry for 25–30 minutes until golden.

6 Melt the butter in a saucepan, add the shallots and fry gently until soft but not coloured. Stir in the flour and remove from the heat. Gradually add the stock to make a smooth sauce and then return to the heat and simmer to thicken, stirring frequently.

7 Add the crème fraîche and then stir in the mushrooms and fish. Add the lemon juice and season to taste. Spoon the mixture into the pastry case and serve with buttered parsley potatoes and spring vegetables. There will be enough filling for an extra serving.

Vegetarian Dishes

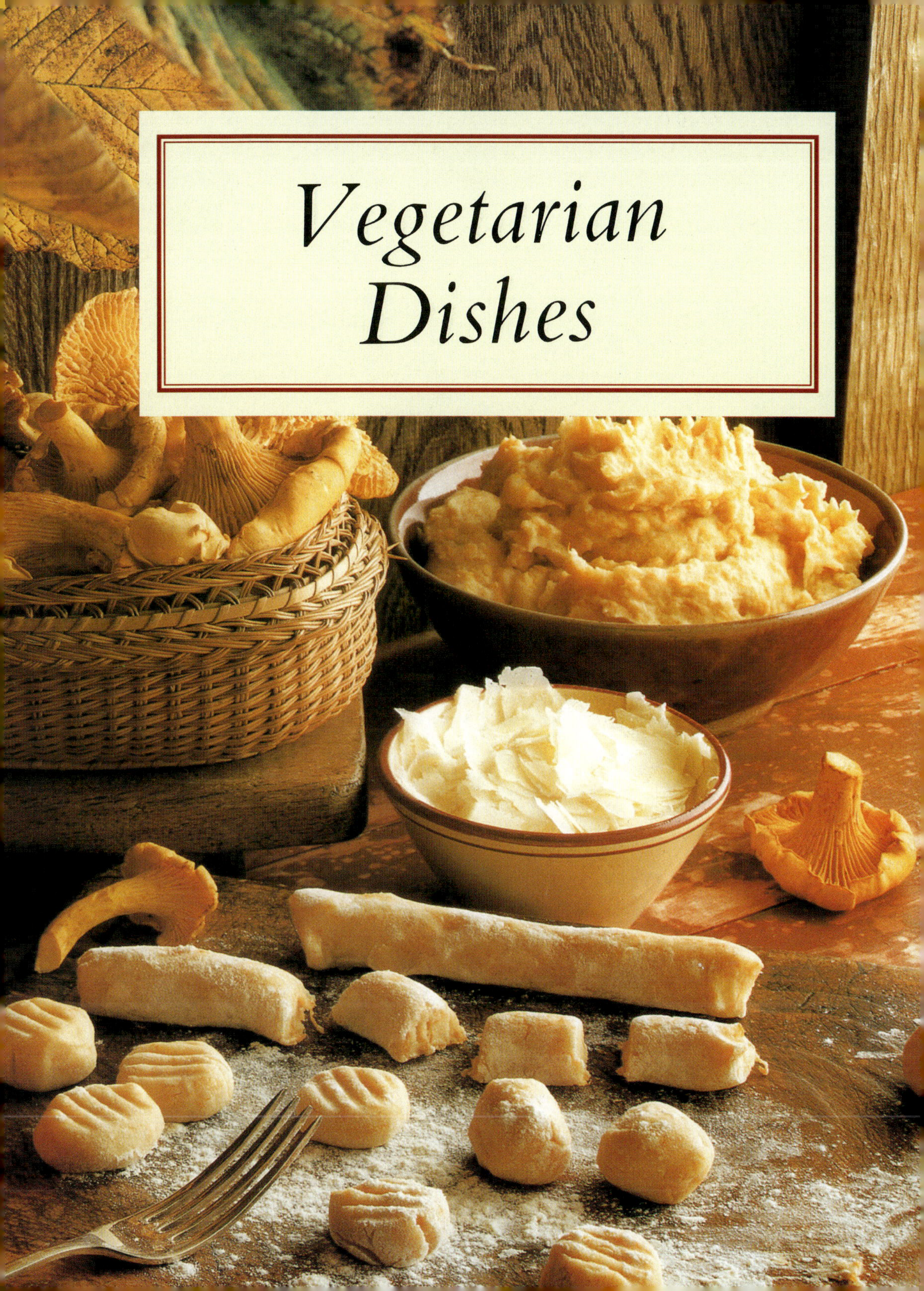

Wild Mushroom Brioche with an Orange Butter Sauce

The finest wild mushrooms deserve the best treatment. Try this butter-rich brioche stuffed full of flavoursome fungi.

SERVES 4

5 ml / 1 tsp active dried yeast

45 ml / 3 tbsp milk, at room temperature

400 g / 14 oz / 3½ cups strong white bread flour

5 ml / 1 tsp salt

15 ml / 1 tbsp caster sugar

3 eggs

finely grated rind of ½ lemon

200 g / 7 oz / ⅞ cup unsalted butter, at room temperature

For the Filling

50 g / 2 oz / 4 tbsp unsalted butter

2 shallots, chopped

350 g / 12 oz assorted wild and cultivated mushrooms, such as ceps, bay boletus, chanterelles, winter chanterelles, saffron milk-caps, oyster mushrooms and horn of plenty, trimmed, sliced and roughly chopped

½ garlic clove, crushed

75 ml / 5 tbsp chopped fresh parsley

salt and freshly ground black pepper

For the Orange Butter Sauce

30 ml / 2 tbsp frozen orange juice concentrate

175 g / 6 oz / ¾ cup unsalted butter, diced

salt and cayenne pepper

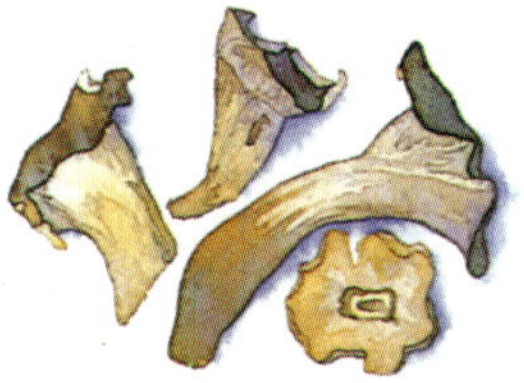

1 Dissolve the yeast in the milk, add 115 g / 4 oz / 1 cup of the flour and mix to form a dough. Fill a bowl with hand-hot water, then place the dough in the water. Leave for 30 minutes to activate the yeast.

2 Place the remaining 275 g / 10 oz / 2½ cups of flour in the bowl of a food processor fitted with the dough blade and add the salt, sugar, eggs, lemon rind and the risen dough and process briefly to mix. Add the butter in small pieces and process until the dough is silky smooth and very slack. Lift the dough out onto a sheet of clear film, wrap and refrigerate for 2 hours until firm. Preheat the oven to 190°C / 375°F / Gas 5.

3 Fry the shallots in the butter without letting them brown. Add the mushrooms and garlic, allow the juices to run and then increase the heat to reduce the moisture. When dry, turn into a bowl, add the parsley and season.

4 Grease and line a 900 g / 2 lb loaf tin with non-stick baking paper. Roll the brioche out on a floured surface to form a rectangle 15 × 30 cm / 6 × 12 in. Spoon the cooked mushrooms over the dough and roll up to make a fat sausage. Drop the dough into the loaf tin, cover with a damp tea towel and leave to rise in a warm humid place for 50 minutes. When the dough has risen above the level of the rim, place in the oven and bake for 40 minutes.

5 To make the sauce, place the orange juice concentrate in a heatproof glass bowl and heat by standing in a saucepan of simmering water. Remove the pan from the heat, and gradually whisk in the butter until creamy. Season to taste, cover and keep warm. When the brioche is cooked, turn it out, slice and serve with orange butter sauce and a simple green salad.

Cook's Tip

Allow plenty of time for this recipe. It helps to make the dough and filling ahead and chill them until needed.

Mushroom Picker's Omelette

Enthusiastic mushroom pickers have been known to carry with them a portable gas stove, an omelette pan and a few eggs, ready to assemble an on-site brunch.

SERVES 1

25 g / 1 oz / 2 tbsp unsalted butter, plus extra for cooking

115 g / 4 oz assorted wild and cultivated mushrooms such as young ceps, bay boletus, chanterelles, saffron milk-caps, closed field mushrooms, oyster mushrooms, hedgehog and St George's mushrooms, trimmed and sliced

3 eggs, at room temperature

salt and freshly ground black pepper

1 Melt the butter in a small omelette pan, add the mushrooms and cook until the juices run. Season, remove from pan and set aside. Wipe the pan.

2 Break the eggs into a bowl, season and beat with a fork. Heat the omelette pan over a high heat, add a knob of butter and let it begin to brown. Pour in the beaten egg and stir briskly with the back of a fork.

Cook's Tip
From start to finish, an omelette should be cooked and on the table in less than a minute. For best results use free range eggs at room temperature.

3 When the eggs are two-thirds scrambled, add the mushrooms and let the omelette finish cooking for 10–15 seconds.

4 Tap the handle of the omelette pan sharply with your fist to loosen the omelette from the pan then fold and turn onto a plate. Serve with warm crusty bread and a simple green salad.

Open Cap Mushrooms Stuffed with Hummus and Herbs

The up-turned cap of the field mushroom provides an ideal resting place for a spoonful of hummus; made here from canned chick-peas.

SERVES 4

12 medium open cap field mushrooms
60 ml / 4 tbsp olive oil
30 ml / 2 tbsp lemon juice

For the Hummus

2 × 400 g / 14 oz can chick-peas, drained
30 ml / 2 tbsp tahini paste
2 garlic cloves, crushed
75 ml / 5 tbsp olive oil
celery salt and cayenne pepper
90 ml / 6 tbsp chopped fresh parsley
30 ml / 2 tbsp mild paprika
stuffed olives, to garnish

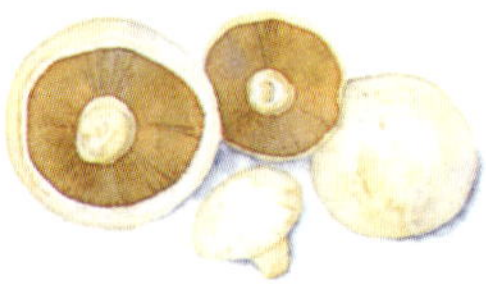

1 Preheat the oven to 190°C / 375°F / Gas 5. Snap off the mushroom stems at the base and save for use in another recipe.

2 Combine the olive oil with 10 ml / 2 tsp lemon juice in a cup and liberally brush over the insides of the mushroom caps. Arrange on a baking sheet and cook in the oven for 25 minutes. Allow to cool.

3 To make the hummus, blend the chick-peas in a food processor until smooth, add the tahini paste, garlic and olive oil. Process well then season with celery salt and cayenne pepper.

4 Spoon the hummus into the mushroom cups, then mould into cone shapes, mask one side with the chopped parsley and dust the other with mild paprika. Serve at room temperature garnished with the olives, with bread and pickled green peppers.

Cook's Tip
Tahini is a thick paste made from sesame seeds. It can be found in Middle Eastern food stores and most large supermarkets.

Creamy Beetroot and Potato Gratin with Wild Mushrooms

Polish communities make the most of robust flavours in their cooking and are often first in the woods when mushrooms appear. This inexpensive dish captures the spirit of their autumn menus.

SERVES 4

30 ml / 2 tbsp vegetable oil
1 medium onion, chopped
45 ml / 3 tbsp plain flour
300 ml / ½ pint / 1¼ cups vegetable stock
675 g / 1½ lb cooked beetroot, peeled and chopped
75 ml / 5 tbsp single cream
30 ml / 2 tbsp creamed horseradish
5 ml / 1 tsp hot mustard
15 ml / 1 tbsp wine vinegar
5 ml / 1 tsp caraway seeds
25 g / 1 oz / 2 tbsp unsalted butter
1 shallot, chopped
225 g / 8 oz assorted wild and cultivated mushrooms such as ceps, bay boletus, chanterelles, chicken of the woods, blewits, fairy ring, parasol, oyster, field, shiitake, St George's and Caesar's mushrooms, trimmed and sliced
45 ml / 3 tbsp chopped fresh parsley

For the Potato Border

900 g / 2 lb floury potatoes, peeled
150 ml / ¼ pint / ⅔ cup milk
15 ml / 1 tbsp chopped fresh dill (optional)
salt and freshly ground black pepper

1 Preheat the oven to 190°C / 375°F / Gas 5. Lightly oil a 23 cm / 9 in round baking dish. Heat the oil in a large saucepan, add the onion and fry until soft without colouring. Stir in the flour, remove from the heat and gradually add the stock, stirring until well blended.

2 Return to the heat, stir and simmer to thicken, then add the beetroot, cream, creamed horseradish, mustard, vinegar and caraway seeds.

3 Bring the potatoes to the boil in salted water and cook for 20 minutes. Drain well and mash with the milk. Add the dill if using and season to taste with salt and pepper.

4 Spoon the potatoes into the prepared dish and make a well in the centre. Spoon the beetroot mixture into the well and set aside.

5 Melt the butter in a large non-stick frying pan and fry the shallot until soft, without browning. Add the mushrooms and cook over a moderate heat until their juices begin to run. Increase the heat and boil off the moisture. When quite dry, season and stir in the chopped parsley. Spread the mushrooms over the beetroot mixture, cover and bake for 30 minutes.

Cook's Tip

If planning ahead, this entire dish can be made in advance and heated through when needed. Allow 50 minutes baking time from room temperature.

Chicken of the Woods Saté with a Spiced Hazelnut Sauce

To capture the texture and flavour of chicken of the woods, marinate them in a rich hazelnut sauce.

SERVES 4

350 g / 12 oz chicken of the woods, trimmed and diced
75 g / 3 oz / ½ cup hazelnuts, toasted
1 shallot, quartered
50 g / 2 oz crustless white bread
30 ml / 2 tbsp hazelnut or olive oil
450 ml / ¾ pint / 1⅞ cup boiling vegetable stock
1.5 ml / ¼ tsp ground cinnamon
5 ml / 1 tsp honey
grated rind and juice of ½ small orange
2.5 ml / ½ tsp celery salt
1.5 ml / ¼ tsp cayenne pepper

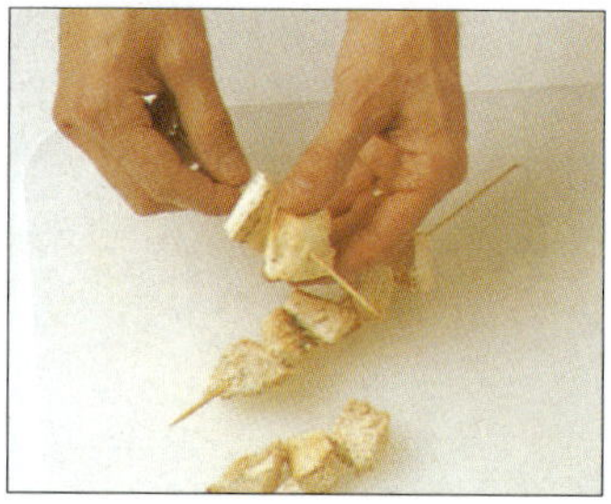

1 Cover the chicken of the woods with boiling water and leave for 2–3 minutes to soften. Thread onto bamboo skewers and set aside.

2 Grind the hazelnuts in a food processor, add the shallot and process until smooth. Add the bread, oil, stock, cinnamon, honey, rind and juice. Blend again then season to taste with celery salt and cayenne pepper.

3 Spoon half of the marinade over the skewered chicken of the woods and set aside at room temperature for 30–40 minutes. Preheat a moderate grill and cook for 8 minutes, turning once.

4 Serve with couscous or rice, green salad and the remaining sauce, warm or at room temperature.

Cook's Tip
Young chicken of the woods is best suited for this recipe. Older fungi tend to dry with age.

Savoy Cabbage Stuffed with Mushroom Barley

The veined texture of savoy cabbage provides good cover for an earthy rich stuffing of barley and wild mushrooms.

SERVES 4

50 g / 2 oz / 4 tbsp unsalted butter

2 medium onions, chopped

1 celery stick, sliced

225 g / 8 oz assorted wild and cultivated mushrooms such as young ceps, bay boletus, closed shaggy ink caps, chicken of the woods, saffron milk-caps, amethyst deceivers, oyster and closed field mushrooms, and blewits, trimmed, sliced and roughly chopped, or 5 g / 1/6 oz / 2 tbsp dried ceps, bay boletus or saffron milk-caps, soaked in warm water for 20 minutes, and 200 g / 7 oz Paris mushrooms, roughly chopped

175 g / 6 oz / 1 1/4 cups pearl barley

1 sprig fresh thyme

750 ml / 1 1/4 pints / 3 2/3 cups water

30 ml / 2 tbsp almond or cashew nut butter

1/2 vegetable stock cube

salt and freshly ground black pepper

1 savoy cabbage

Cook's Tip
A range of nut butters is available in all leading health food stores.

1 Melt the butter in a large heavy saucepan, add the onions and celery and fry for 6–8 minutes until soft. Add the mushrooms and cook until they release their juices, then add the barley, thyme, water and the nut butter. Bring to the boil, cover and simmer for 30 minutes. Add the 1/2 stock cube and simmer for a further 20 minutes. Season to taste.

2 Separate the cabbage leaves and cut away the thick stem. Blanch the leaves in salted boiling water for 3–4 minutes. Drain and refresh under cold running water. Drain again.

3 Lay a 46 cm / 18 in square piece of muslin over a steaming basket. Reconstruct the cabbage by lining the muslin with large cabbage leaves. Spread a layer of mushroom barley over the leaves.

4 Cover with a second layer of leaves and filling. Continue until the centre is full. Draw together opposite corners of the muslin and tie firmly. Place the cabbage in a steaming basket, set in a saucepan containing 2.5 cm / 1 in of simmering water, cover and steam for 30 minutes. To serve, place on a warmed serving plate, untie the muslin and carefully pull it away from underneath the cabbage.

Cook's Tip
If planning ahead, the cabbage can be assembled well in advance before the final cooking. To ensure richness and flavour use a good portion of ceps, chicken of the woods and field mushrooms.

Mushroom Picker's Pâté

A good vegetarian pâté should be as smooth and as rich as one made with fine liver. This recipe compares very favourably to traditional meat ones.

SERVES 4

- *45 ml / 3 tbsp vegetable oil*
- *1 medium onion, chopped*
- *½ celery stick, chopped*
- *350 g / 12 oz assorted wild and cultivated mushrooms such as closed field mushrooms, fairy ring, oyster and shiitake mushrooms, bay boletus and horn of plenty, trimmed and sliced*
- *150 g / 5 oz / ⅔ cup red lentils*
- *500 ml / 18 fl oz / 2¼ cups vegetable stock or water*
- *1 sprig thyme*
- *50 g / 2 oz / 4 tbsp almond or cashew nut butter*
- *1 garlic clove, crushed*
- *25 g / 1 oz bread, crusts removed*
- *75 ml / 5 tbsp milk*
- *15 ml / 1 tbsp lemon juice*
- *4 egg yolks*
- *celery salt and freshly ground black pepper*

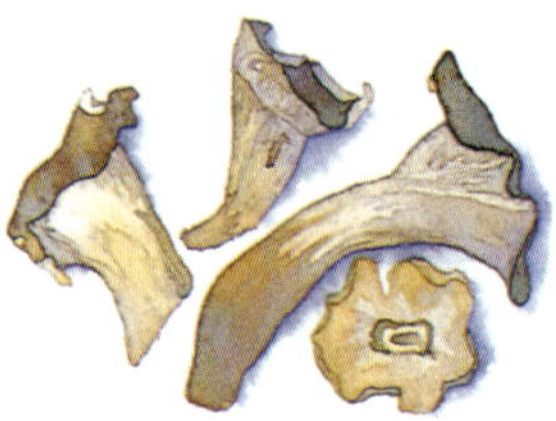

1 Preheat the oven to 180°C / 350°F / Gas 4. Heat the oil in a large saucepan, add the onion and celery and brown lightly. Add the mushrooms and soften for 3–4 minutes. Remove a spoonful of the mushroom pieces and set aside.

2 Add the lentils, stock and thyme, bring to the boil uncovered and simmer for 20 minutes or until the lentils have fallen apart.

3 Place the nut butter, garlic, bread and milk in a food processor and blend until smooth.

4 Add the lemon juice and egg yolks and combine. Add the lentil mixture, blend, then season well. Lastly stir the reserved mushrooms into the mixture.

5 Turn the mixture into a 1.2 litre / 2 pint / 5 cup pâté dish, stand in a roasting tin half filled with boiling water, cover and cook for 50 minutes. Allow to cool before spooning from the dish.

Cook's Tip

If you are using only cultivated mushrooms, an addition of 10 g / ⅓ oz / 3 tbsp of dried ceps, bay boletus, chanterelles and horn of plenty will provide a good wild mushroom flavour. Soak first in warm water for 20 minutes.

Almond or cashew nut butter is available from most good health food shops.

Japanese Mushrooms with Lemon and Walnut Noodles

The flavour of the Japanese enokitaki mushroom is as fine as its appearance. To capture their sweet peppery flavour, they are prepared here in a light broth and served with noodles.

SERVES 4

- *75 g / 3 oz / ⅓ cup somen noodles or vermicelli pasta*
- *1 large carrot, peeled, sliced and shredded*
- *500 ml / 18 fl oz / 2¼ cups dashi, or light vegetable stock*
- *15 g / ½ oz arame or hijiki dried seaweed*
- *50 g / 2 oz enokitaki mushrooms*
- *5 ml / 1 tsp lemon juice*
- *10 ml / 2 tsp walnut oil*
- *1 spring onion, green part only, sliced*

1 Cook the noodles and carrots in salted boiling water for 3–4 minutes. Drain, cool under running water and set aside.

Cook's Tip
The enokitaki mushroom is a cultivated variety and is available from Japanese supermarkets worldwide. Dried seaweed and somen noodles can be found in most health food stores.

2 Bring the dashi or stock to the boil, add the arame or seaweed and simmer for 2 minutes. Add the noodles, mushrooms, lemon juice and oil and briefly reheat.

3 Divide among four Japanese soup bowls, scatter with spring onion slices and serve.

Late Summer Mushrooms and Vegetables in a Hazelnut Dressing

Seasonal flavours merge well with autumn mushrooms to give this vegetable dish distinctive character.

SERVES 4

- *30 ml / 2 tbsp vegetable oil*
- *1 shallot, chopped*
- *1 celery stick, sliced*
- *225 g / 8 oz assorted wild and cultivated mushrooms such as young ceps, bay boletus, chanterelles, amethyst deceivers, horn of plenty, oyster, shiitake, St George's and Caesar's mushrooms, trimmed, sliced or halved if small*
- *salt and freshly ground black pepper*
- *175 g / 6 oz small potatoes, scrubbed or scraped*
- *115 g / 4 oz French beans, trimmed and halved*
- *115 g / 4 oz baby carrots, trimmed and peeled*
- *115 g / 4 oz / 1 cup broad beans*
- *45 ml / 3 tbsp hazelnut oil*
- *15 ml / 1 tbsp groundnut oil*
- *15 ml / 1 tbsp lemon juice*
- *5 ml / 1 tsp chopped fresh thyme*
- *50 g / 2 oz hazelnuts, toasted and chopped*

1 Fry the shallot and celery in vegetable oil until soft but without colouring. Add the mushrooms and cook over a moderate heat until their juices begin to run, then increase the heat to boil off the juices. Season and set aside.

2 In separate pans, boil the potatoes for 20 minutes, beans and carrots for 6 minutes and the broad beans for 3 minutes. Drain and cool under running water, then remove the tough outer skins of the broad beans.

3 Combine the vegetables with the mushrooms, then moisten with hazelnut and groundnut oil. Add the lemon juice and thyme, season and scatter with toasted hazelnuts.

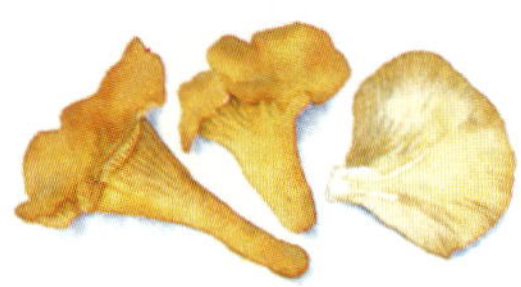

Wild Mushroom Gratin with Beaufort Cheese, New Potatoes, Pickles and Walnuts

This gratin is one of the simplest and most delicious ways of cooking mushrooms. The dish is inspired by the Swiss custom of eating alpine cheeses with new potatoes and small gherkins.

SERVES 4

900 g / 2 lb new potatoes, scrubbed or scraped

50 g / 2 oz / 4 tbsp unsalted butter or 60 ml / 4 tbsp olive oil

350 g / 12 oz assorted wild and cultivated mushrooms such as oyster, shiitake and closed field mushrooms, ceps, bay boletus, chanterelles, winter chanterelles, hedgehog fungus, St George's mushrooms and saffron milk-caps

salt and freshly ground black pepper

175 g / 6 oz Beaufort or Fontina cheese

50 g / 2 oz / ½ cup broken walnuts, toasted

12 medium gherkins and mixed green salad leaves, to serve

1 Place the potatoes in a pan of salted water, bring to the boil and cook for 20 minutes. Drain, add the knob of the butter, cover and keep warm.

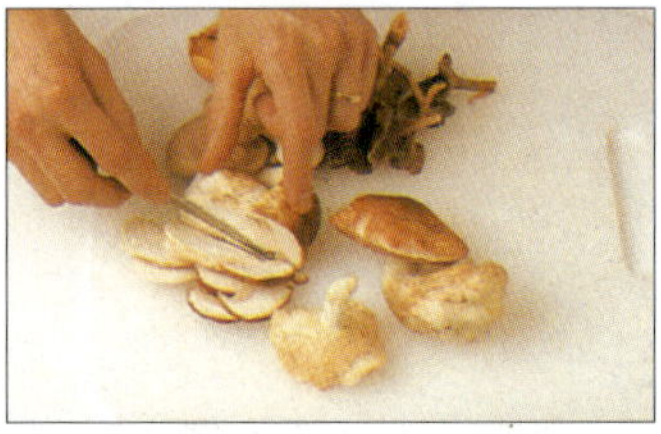

2 Trim the mushrooms and then slice them thinly.

3 Fry the mushrooms in the remaining butter or oil. When the juices appear, increase the heat to evaporate the moisture.

4 Preheat a moderate grill. Slice the cheese thinly, arrange on top of the mushroom slices and grill until bubbly and brown. Scatter with walnuts and serve with buttered new potatoes, gherkins and a green salad.

Cook's Tip
For best results, choose an attractive flameproof dish that can be put under the grill and brought directly to the table.

Hash Brown Chicken of the Woods with Potatoes and Onions

The hash brown dinner can range from a welcome treat to a greasy ruin. This recipe calls for the intriguing *Laetiporus sulphureus*, or chicken of the woods, which looks, tastes and has the texture of chicken.

SERVES 4

900 g / 2 lb potatoes, peeled
50 g / 2 oz / 4 tbsp unsalted butter
2 medium onions, sliced
1 celery stick, sliced
1 small carrot, peeled and cut into short batons
225 g / 8 oz chicken of the woods, trimmed and sliced
45 ml / 3 tbsp medium sherry
45 ml / 3 tbsp chopped fresh parsley
15 ml / 1 tbsp chopped fresh chives
grated rind of ½ lemon
salt and freshly ground black pepper

1 Place the potatoes in a saucepan of salted water, bring to the boil and cook for 20 minutes. Drain, cool and slice thickly.

Cook's Tip
The best hash browns are made from late season floury potatoes that are inclined to fall apart when cooked. This quality helps the mixture to form a more solid mass in the pan.

2 Melt the butter in a large non-stick frying pan, add the onions, celery and carrot and fry until lightly browned.

3 Add the chicken of the woods and the sherry, then simmer to evaporate any moisture.

4 Add the potatoes, herbs, lemon rind and seasoning, toss and fry together until crispy brown. Serve with a salad of frisée and young spinach leaves.

Mushroom Boreg

The Turkish boreg or *börek* is a rich pastry parcel with a savoury filling.

SERVES 4

50 g / 2 oz / 1/3 cup couscous
45 ml / 3 tbsp olive oil
1 medium onion, chopped
225 g / 8 oz assorted wild and cultivated mushrooms such as ceps, bay boletus, chanterelles, winter chanterelles, oyster, field, St George's and Caesar's mushrooms, trimmed and sliced
1 garlic clove, crushed
60 ml / 4 tbsp chopped fresh parsley
5 ml / 1 tsp chopped fresh thyme
1 egg, hard-boiled and peeled
salt and freshly ground black pepper

For the Boreg Pastry

400 g / 14 oz / 3 1/2 cups self-raising flour
5 ml / 1 tsp salt
1 egg, plus extra for glazing
150 ml / 1/4 pint / 2/3 cup natural yogurt
150 ml / 1/4 pint / 2/3 cup olive oil
grated rind of 1/2 lemon

For the Yogurt Sauce

200 ml / 7 fl oz / 7/8 cup natural yogurt
45 ml / 3 tbsp chopped fresh mint
2.5 ml / 1/2 tsp caster sugar
1.5 ml / 1/4 tsp cayenne pepper
1.5 ml / 1/4 tsp celery salt
a little milk or water

1 Preheat the oven to 190°C / 375°F / Gas 5. Just cover the couscous with boiling water and soak for 10 minutes or until the liquid is absorbed. Then soften the onion in oil without letting it colour. Add the mushrooms and garlic and cook until the juices begin to run, then increase the heat to eliminate the juices. Transfer to a bowl, add the parsley, thyme and couscous and stir well. Grate the hard-boiled egg into the mixture, season and combine.

2 To make the pastry, sift the flour and salt into a bowl. Make a well, add the egg, yogurt, olive oil and lemon rind and combine with a knife.

3 Turn out onto a floured surface and roll into a 30 cm / 12 in circle. Pile the mixture into the centre of the pastry, and bring the edges over, to enclose the filling. Turn upside down onto a baking sheet. Press the boreg out flat with your hand, glaze with beaten egg and bake for 25 minutes.

4 To make the sauce, blend the yogurt with the mint, sugar, cayenne pepper and celery salt, adjusting the consistency with milk or water. Serve boreg at room temperature.

Eggy Rice Cakes with Soured Cream and Mushrooms

SERVES 4

1 egg
15 ml / 1 tbsp plain flour
60 ml / 4 tbsp freshly grated Parmesan, Fontina or Pecorino cheese
400 g / 14 oz / 2 cups cooked long grain rice
salt and freshly ground black pepper
50 g / 2 oz / 4 tbsp unsalted butter, plus extra for frying
1 shallot or small onion, chopped
175 g / 6 oz assorted wild and cultivated mushrooms such as ceps, bay boletus, chanterelles, winter chanterelles, horn of plenty, blewits, field and oyster mushrooms, trimmed and sliced
1 sprig thyme
30 ml / 2 tbsp Madeira or sherry
150 ml / 1/4 pint / 2/3 cup soured cream or crème fraîche
paprika for dusting (optional)

1 Beat the egg, flour and cheese together with a fork, then stir in the cooked rice. Mix well and set aside.

2 Fry the shallot or onion in half the butter until soft but not brown. Add the mushrooms and thyme and cook until the juices run. Add the Madeira or sherry. Increase the heat to reduce the juices and concentrate the flavour. Season to taste, transfer to a bowl, cover and keep warm.

3 Fry heaps of the rice mixture in a knob of butter. Cook each one for a minute on each side. When all the rice cakes are cooked, arrange on four warmed plates, top with soured cream or crème fraîche and a spoonful of mushrooms. Dust with paprika and serve with asparagus and baby carrots.

Pumpkin Gnocchi with a Chanterelle Parsley Cream

Gnocchi is an Italian pasta dumpling usually made from potatoes, in this special recipe, pumpkin is added, too. A chanterelle sauce provides both richness and flavour.

SERVES 4

450 g / 1 lb peeled floury potatoes
450 g / 1 lb peeled pumpkin, chopped
2 egg yolks
200 g / 7 oz / 1¾ cups plain flour, plus more if necessary
pinch of ground allspice
1.5 ml / ¼ tsp ground cinnamon
pinch of grated nutmeg
finely grated rind of ½ orange
salt and freshly ground pepper

For the Sauce

30 ml / 2 tbsp olive oil
1 shallot
175 g / 6 oz fresh chanterelles, sliced, or 15 g / ½ oz / ¼ cup dried, soaked for 20 minutes in warm water
10 ml / 2 tsp almond butter
150 ml / ¼ pint / ⅔ cup crème fraîche
a little milk or water
75 ml / 5 tbsp chopped fresh parsley
50 g / 2 oz / ½ cup grated Parmesan cheese

Cook's Tip
If planning ahead, gnocchi can be shaped ready for cooking up to 8 hours in advance. Almond butter is available ready-made from health food shops.

1 Cover the potatoes with cold salted water, bring to the boil and cook for 20 minutes. Drain and set aside. Place the pumpkin in a bowl, cover and microwave on full power for 8 minutes. Alternatively, wrap the pumpkin in foil and bake at 180°C / 350°F / Gas 4 for 30 minutes. Drain well then add to the potato and pass through a vegetable mill into a bowl. Add the egg yolks, flour, spices, orange rind and seasoning and mix well to make a soft dough. Add more flour if the mixture is too loose.

2 Bring a large pan of salted water to the boil, then dredge a work surface with plain flour. Spoon the gnocchi mixture into a piping bag fitted with a 1 cm / ½ in plain nozzle. Pipe onto the floured surface to make a 15 cm / 6 in sausage. Roll in flour and cut into 2.5 cm / 1 in pieces. Repeat the process making more sausage shapes. Mark each lightly with a fork and cook for 3–4 minutes in the boiling water.

3 Meanwhile, make the sauce. Heat the oil in a non-stick frying pan, add the shallot and fry until soft without colouring. Add the chanterelles and cook briefly, then add the almond butter. Stir to melt and stir in the crème fraîche. Simmer briefly and adjust the consistency with milk or water. Add the parsley and season to taste.

4 Lift the gnocchi out of the water with a slotted spoon, turn into bowls and spoon the sauce over the top. Scatter with Parmesan cheese.

Goat's Cheese Kasha with Ceps and Walnuts

Kasha is a Russian staple of cooked grains. Robustly flavoured buckwheat is most common and is often combined with other grains. Couscous is used here and allows the flavour of buckwheat, goat's cheese, dried ceps and toasted walnuts to come through.

SERVES 4

- *175 g / 6 oz / 1 cup couscous*
- *45 ml / 3 tbsp buckwheat*
- *½ oz / 15 g / ¼ cup dried ceps or bay boletus*
- *3 eggs*
- *60 ml / 4 tbsp chopped fresh parsley*
- *10 ml / 2 tsp chopped fresh thyme*
- *60 ml / 4 tbsp olive oil*
- *45 ml / 3 tbsp walnut oil*
- *175 g / 6 oz / 1½ cups crumbly white goat's cheese*
- *50 g / 2 oz / ½ cup broken walnuts, toasted*
- *salt and freshly ground black pepper*
- *salad and rye bread, to serve*

Cook's Tip
The flavour of buckwheat may be too strong for some tastes. In this case replace with couscous. Kasha can also be made from bulgar wheat or millet.

1 Place the couscous, buckwheat and ceps in a bowl, cover with boiling water and leave to soak for 15 minutes. Drain off any excess liquid.

2 Place the mixture in a large non-stick frying pan, add the eggs, season well, then scramble with a flat wooden spoon over a moderate heat.

3 Stir in the parsley, thyme, olive oil, walnut oil, goat's cheese and walnuts. Season to taste with salt and pepper.

4 Transfer to a large serving dish and serve hot with rye bread, salad and Eastern European beer if available.

GLOSSARY

asci The sacs in Ascomycetes in which the sexual spores are formed.

Acomycetes Group of fungi characterized by bearing the sexual spores in a sac (asci).

Basidiomycetes Group of fungi characterized by the presence of spore-bearing cells called basidia.

brackets Shelf-like fruit bodies.

cap The portion of the mushroom bearing the gills and the tubes.

convex A surface that is curved or rounded outwards.

decurrent Running down the stem.

fibrous Composed of fine fibres or threads.

flesh Inner tubes of a fungus.

fruit body Structure on which the spore-producing cells are held.

hymenium Layer of spore-producing cells.

inrolled Curled inwards and down.

marginate With a distinct ridge or gutter-like margin.

milk Sticky fluid released by some fungi when damaged.

network A mesh or pattern of criss-crossed fine ridges.

partial veil The fine web of tissue connecting the cap margin to the stem.

pores The openings of the clustered tubes in Boletes and Polypores.

recurved Curving backwards, i.e. scales with recurved tips.

ring Remains of the partial veil left on the stem.

scales Small to large raised flakes or flaps of tissue, usually on the cap or stem surface.

spore Reproductive cell of typical mushroom.

spore print A thick deposit of spores dropped by a mushroom cap onto paper.

stem The 'stalk' on which a mushroom cap is raised up.

striated With distinct parallel grooves or lines especially at the cap edge.

tubes The downward-pointing clusters of tubes on Boletes and Polypores within which the spores are produced.

universal veil The fine to thick covering of tissue which envelopes some fungi when immature.

volva Example of thick universal veil which remains as a bag at the base of the stem.

OPPOSITE *Horn of plenty*, Craterellus cornucopioides.

LEFT *Saffron milk-caps*, Lactarius deliciosus.

INDEX TO FIELD GUIDE

Numbers in bold indicate the main entry.

Index to Recipes

I N D E X

D

E

F

G

H

J

K

L

T

V

W

Bibliography

ARORA, DAVID, *Mushrooms Demystified* (Berkeley 1986, 2nd ed)

STEVENSON, G., *Field Guide to Fungi* University of Canterbury Publication No. 30, Christchurch, New Zealand (Christchurch 1982)

CARLUCCIO, A., *A Passion for Mushrooms* (London 1989)

CLELAND, J.B., *Toadstools and Mushrooms and other Larger Fungi of South Australia* (Adelaide 1934, reprinted 1976)

DICKENSON, COLIN and LUCAS, JOHN, *The Encyclopedia of Mushrooms* (London 1979)

FINDLAY, W.P.K., *Wayside and Woodland Fungi* (London 1967)

FUHRER, B., *A Field Companion to Australian Fungi* (Victoria 1985)

GARNWEIDNER, E., *Mushrooms of Britain and Europe* (London 1994)

HURST, J. and RUTHERFORD, L., *A Gourmet's Book of Mushrooms and Truffles* (London 1991)

LINCOFF, GARY H., *The Audubon Society Field Guide to North American Mushrooms* (New York 1981)

LINCOFF, GARY H. and PARIONI, GIOVANNI ed., *Simon and Shuster's Guide to Mushrooms* (New York 1981)

KIBBY, G., *An Illustrated Guide to Mushrooms and Other Fungi of Britain and Northern Europe* (London 1982)

MACDONALD, R and WESTERMAN, J., *Fungi of South-eastern Australia* (Victoria 1979)

MILLER, ORSON K., *Mushrooms of North America* (New York 1978)

PHILLIPS, R., *Mushrooms and Other Fungi of Great Britain and Europe* (London 1981)

SHEPHERD, C.J. and TOTTERDELL, C.J., *Mushrooms and Toadstools of Australia* (Sydney 1988)

SMITH, ALEXANDER and WEBER, NANSY, S., *Mushroom Hunter's Field Guide* (Michigan 1980)

WOOD, A., *Australian Mushrooms and Toadstools – How to Identify Them* (Kensington 1980)

Societies

One of the best ways to learn about mushrooms is to go on a foray led by an expert. For details of local groups contact your library. Listed here are some of the main societies you might also like to write to for further information.

UNITED KINGDOM

British Mycological Society
c/o C.A.B. International
Mycological Institute
Ferry Lane
Kew
Surrey TW9 3AF

The Tasty Mushroom Partnership
Poppy Cottage
Station Road
Burnham Market
Norfolk PE31 8HA

AUSTRALIA

Sydney Fungal Studies Group
50 Old Bells Line of Road
Kurrajong
NSW 2758

Australian Society for Microbiology
Unit 23
20 Commercial Road
Melbourne
Victoria 3004

BELOW *Horn of plenty,* Craterellus cornucopioides.

ACKNOWLEDGEMENTS

The publishers and authors would like to thank the following people for their help in the production of this book: Geoffrey Kibby of the International Institute of Entomology, London; Andrew Broderick of the Australian Wild Fungi Research Group, School of Horticulture, University of Western Sydney, Hawkesbury, Bourke Street, Richmond NSW 2753 Australia; Clive Houlder, mushroom hunter and supplier of specialist fungi; L'aquila Products, 40 Caledonian Road, London, for providing the truffles; Valerie Jordan and Avril Henley for their help in typing the manuscript; Mycologue, 35 King Henry's Road, London, for providing the knives; Patricia Michelson, La Fromagerie, 30 Highbury Park, London N5 2AA, specialist food finder; Taste of the Wild, 65 Overstrand Mansions, Prince of Wales Drive, London SW11 4EX, suppliers of wild mushrooms.

Picture credits

t = top, b = bottom, l = left, r = right

Heather Angel page 103br

Timothy J. Baroni 111t, 111b

George Dickson 45t, 45b, 118

Geoffrey Kibby 67tl, 70t, 83, 81tl

George McCarthy 2, 6/7, 15b, 17t, 22/23, 24, 28l, 28r, 29b, 34, 35b, 47b, 59t, 59b, 61t, 63m, 65b, 73t, 77b, 82tr, 82r, 96/97, 98, 106, 107l, 107r, 113b, 246

Gregory Mueller 31b, 61b, 63b, 66/67, 81b, 82l, 93, 115

Oxford Scientific Films (David Thompson) 29t; (G I Bernard) 30, 31t; (Jack Dermid) 105t

BELOW *Winter chanterelle,* Cantharellus infundibuliformis.

Notes

Notes

NOTES

NOTES

NOTES

Notes

Notes

Notes